Borrowed Voices

Borrowed Voices

Writing and Racial Ventriloquism in the Jewish American Imagination

JENNIFER GLASER

RUTGERS UNIVERSITY PRESS
NEW BRUNSWICK, NEW JERSEY, AND LONDON

Library of Congress Cataloging-in-Publication Data
Glaser, Jennifer, 1978–
　Borrowed voices : writing and racial ventriloquism in the Jewish American imagination / Jennifer Glaser.
　　pages cm
　Includes bibliographical references and index.
　ISBN 978–0–8135–7740–1 (hardcover : alk. paper) — ISBN 978–0–8135–7739–5 (pbk. : alk. paper) — ISBN 978–0–8135–7741–8 (e-book (epub)) — ISBN 978–0–8135–7742–5 (e-book (web pdf))
　1. American literature—Jewish authors—History and criticism. 2. American literature—20th century—History and criticism. 3. Jews—United States—Intellectual life. 4. Jews in literature. 5. Identity (Psychology) in literature. 6. Race in literature. 7. Intermarriage in literature. 8. Culture in literature. I. Title.
　PS153.J4G53 2016
　810.9'8924—dc23
　2015024446

A British Cataloging-in-Publication record for this book is available from the British Library.

Copyright © 2016 by Jennifer Glaser

All rights reserved

No part of this book may be reproduced or utilized in any form or by any means, electronic or mechanical, or by any information storage and retrieval system, without written permission from the publisher. Please contact Rutgers University Press, 106 Somerset Street, New Brunswick, NJ 08901. The only exception to this prohibition is "fair use" as defined by U.S. copyright law.

Visit our website: http://rutgerspress.rutgers.edu

Manufactured in the United States of America

For my parents, Risé and Peter Glaser

Contents

Acknowledgments   ix

Introduction   1

1 The Politics and Poetics of Speaking the Other   15
2 The Perils of Loving in America   41
3 What We Talk about When
   We Talk about the Holocaust   62
4 The Jew in the Canon and the Culture Wars   90
5 Race, Indigeneity, and the Topography of Diaspora   109
   Coda   139

Notes   149
Works Cited   163
Index   175

Acknowledgments

Every book is the product of much effort and love. In my case, the effort was collaborative and the love came from every corner of my serendipitous life. I have been lucky enough to be at the receiving end of support from countless institutions and individuals. In no particular order, here are some of those who deserve my gratitude.

At the University of Pennsylvania, I was given the great gift of having known and worked with Amy Kaplan, Beth Wenger, Anne Norton, Liliane Weissberg, JoAnne Dubil, and Max Cavitch. I was also particularly lucky to have met the brilliant, kind, and eminently real Rita Barnard. I am forever in debt to her, both as a colleague and a friend. Thank you also to the program in comparative literature and literary theory, the English department, and the program in Jewish studies for giving me a home in Philadelphia for so many years. I also must acknowledge my wonderful Philly writing group, especially Eliot Ratzman and Terri Geller, who contributed their insights and acumen when this work was in its earliest stage.

In the English department at the University of Cincinnati, as well as in the university's programs in women's, gender, and sexuality studies and Judaic studies, I have been graced with wonderful friends and colleagues, including Lora Arduser, Beth Ash, Chris Bachelder, Don Bogen, Rebbeca Borah, Molly Brayman, Jana Evans Braziel, Julia Carlson, Stan Corkin, Sharon Dean, Mary Beth Debs, John Drury, Russel Durst, Grace Epstein, Ari Finkelstein, Michael Griffith, Jen Habel, Alli Hammond, Tamar Heller, Geri Hinkle-Wesseling, Trish Henley, Lisa Hogeland, Kristen Iversen, Jon Kamholtz, Antoinette Larkin, Nicola Mason, Deb Meem, Lisa Meloncon, Laura Micciche, Christine Mok, Devore Nixon, Furaha Norton, Lee Person, Maria Romagnoli, Kathy Rentz, Alison Rieke, Jim Schiff, Leah Stewart, Philip Tsang, Jay Twomey, and Gary Weissman, just to name a few. I have also been given the gift of intellectual companionship and friendship from my wonderful undergraduate and graduate students, especially Kate Polak, Daniel Dale, Suzanne Warren, Jesseca Cornelson, Catherine O'Shea, Lauren Clark, Jessica Brown, Leah McCormack, Christine Rezk, Dario Sulzman, Brian Trapp, Dan Paul, Bryan Smith, Jamie Poissant, Brenda Peynado, and James Pihakis. Niven Abdel-Hamid has been invaluable to me, not only as a student and an interlocutor but also as a kind and generous child-care provider during my most chaotic days of writing and revising. My working life would be nowhere near as pleasurable—or busy—without these amazing students.

My book would never have been completed without the economic support of the Charles Phelps Taft Research Center, the University Research Council, and the Faculty Development Council at the University of Cincinnati. These research funds, along with my faculty leave, allowed me the time and mental space I needed to write and revise this work. I am also indebted to the Frankel Institute for Advanced Judaic Studies at the University of Michigan, where I finished the book while serving as a faculty fellow under the direction of Deborah Dash Moore and Jonathan Freedman. I can't thank the funders of the institute and the seminar participants enough for their generosity and encouragement during my time in Ann Arbor. I don't miss the winter, but I greatly miss the people.

In addition to these larger avenues of support, I've also received valuable feedback and collegiality as a participant in small summer seminars sponsored by the Posen Foundation and the American Academy for Jewish Research as well as from audiences at the University of California, Los Angeles; the University of Michigan; Pennsylvania State University; the University of Southampton; Miami University of Ohio; and Hebrew Union College in Cincinnati. I would also like to acknowledge the Harry Ransom Center at the University of Texas at Austin for access to its wonderful archive of material related to Bernard Malamud.

In the final stages of this project, I received generous and helpful responses from the blind reviewers of this manuscript. This feedback, along with the editorial encouragement and acumen of the fabulous team at Rutgers University Press, especially Marlie Wasserman, Leslie Mitchner, Katie Keeran, Allyson Fields, Carrie Hudak, and Marilyn Campbell, has been life-changing. Freelance copyeditor Dawn Potter's suggestions helped to polish the book in its final stages.

Part of chapter 4 appeared as "The Jew in the Canon," *PMLA* 123.5 (2008) and is reprinted by permission of the Modern Language Association. A portion of chapter 5 appeared as "An Imaginary Ararat: Jewish Bodies and Jewish Homelands in Ben Katchor's *The Jew of New York*," *MELUS* 3.32 (2007) and is reprinted by permission of Oxford University Press.

I'd also like to thank those whose work, often, although not always, at the crossroads of American and Jewish studies, has inspired me, including Jonathan Freedman, Ranen Omer-Sherman, Anita Norich, Bryan Cheyette, Maeera Shreiber, Sarah Phillips Casteel, Ben Schreier, Emily Miller-Budick, Hana Wirth-Nesher, Laurence Roth, Dean Franco, Michael Kramer, Ethan Goffman, Rachel

Rubinstein, Kirsten Fermaglich, Derek Parker Royal, Rachel Kranson, Priscilla Wald, Naomi Seidman, Jeffrey Shandler, Deborah Dash Moore, Jeffrey Melnick, Lori Harrison-Kahan, Anita Mannur, Eric Sundquist, Matthew Frye Jacobson, Barbara Kirshenblatt Gimblet, Janice Fernheimer, Maya Barzilai, Jonathan Boyarin, Sven-Erik Rose, Daniel Boyarin, Lois Dubin, Lisa Silverman, Daniel Itzkovitz, Joshua Lambert, Kerry Wallach, Riv-Ellen Prell, Shira Kohn, Hasia Diner, and Tatjana Lichtenstein. Some of these people are buddies in real life and others are only my imaginary friends, but all have influenced me and catalyzed my desire to do work at the intersection of two sometimes radically disparate disciplines.

Thank you, too, to the friends, family, and teachers who have nurtured me over the years: Carol and Alvin Weintraub, Sylvia Melikofsky, Thangam Ravindranathan, Nick Dierman, Becky Phillips, Susie Wasserman, Ruth and Joe Plaine, Marilyn and Holly Esterson, Joe Melton, Jane Hennessey, Joey Glaser-Hennessey, the extended Hennessey family, Diane Burrows, Nessa Rapoport, Cynthia Richardson, Mindy Hepner, Elizabeth Gibson, Joy Rochwarger, Jenny Lee, Su Hansen, Kathy Wekselman, Rosalind Morris, Jim Shapiro, Mark Anderson, Carol Jacques, Sam Apple, Ian Rothkerch, David Lobenstine, Anna Haas, Megan Kessler, Caitlin Wood, Martha Schoolman, Alice Finkelstein, Norman Finkelstein, our many lovely Cincinnati neighbors, who are probably the best thing about midwestern living, and my friends in P-Squared, the coolest group of activist women I know. Gratitude goes out also to Sitwell's Coffee House, where so much of this work was completed.

Extra special thanks go to Lauren DeMille, for being my dear friend and soul mate for twenty years and counting; Alison Pase, for being my de facto sister since we were two and four years old respectively; Michael S. Hennessey, for taking care of me and keeping me sane all the years that we've known and loved each other; Risé and Peter Glaser, for being the most irreverent, loving, and truly present people I know; and Cecelia Glaser-Hennessey, for clarifying all that was once murky in my life.

Borrowed Voices

Introduction

If there are no races, then what does it mean to claim that Jews are not a race?
—Steven Kaplan

Revolving Jews: Jewish Racial Ventriloquism and Post-1967 America

"Who is Leonard Zelig?" In Woody Allen's 1983 film *Zelig*, this question is posed via a black-and-white montage of newspaper headlines, newsreels, and psychiatrists' reports. "Who is Leonard Zelig?" The answers to the oft-repeated question are varied. At different moments in the film, Zelig—a frumpy, middle-aged Jewish man played by Allen—is also an Italian mobster, a degenerate pseudo-aristocrat of the Gatsby variety, an African American jazzman, an "Oriental" denizen of a Chinatown opium den, a Scotsman in full tartan plaid, and a Native American out of an old Western film. Very rarely does Zelig claim the identity to which he was born: the son of a Yiddish-speaking Jewish immigrant from the Lower East Side of New York City. The psychiatric experts who study him and keep him contained in Typhoid Mary–like isolation at an unnamed hospital dub Zelig a "human chameleon." Like the lizard, his ability to metamorphose into a variety of different forms functions as a talisman against danger. Like the lizard, he protects himself by camouflaging his identity to better resemble the members of whatever group he is around.

But beyond self-preservation, his rapid-fire transformations call into question the very grounds of identity. Leonard Zelig's life is citational, constituted by and understood only in reference to the words and images of others. This theme is dramatized by "interviews" with Jewish intellectuals, such as Susan Sontag, Irving Howe, and Saul Bellow, who interpret Zelig, explaining him for the audience of Allen's genre-altering mockumentary. Like Leonard Zelig himself, *Zelig* the film operates through a logic of resemblance. As Ella Shohat and Robert Stam argue, *Zelig* is itself a "chameleon," taking on the guise of a variety of different genres, particularly via the archival and pseudo-archival footage that comprises much of its content (176). Allen's formal transgressions bleed into the film's larger message about how identity works in America and the role that Jewishness has played in articulations of identity—particularly racial identity—throughout the twentieth century. Zelig's role in the film is explicitly allegorical; he comes to stand in for all Jews. As Irving Howe declares in his role as a Jewish "expert": "His story reflected a lot of the Jewish experience in America—the great urge to push in and to find one's place, and then to assimilate into the culture. I mean he wanted to assimilate like crazy."[1]

However, Allen's embodiment of racial difference, like the form of *Zelig*, is itself mutable and ambivalent. At times, the film suggests that racial difference, particularly Leonard Zelig's Jewish difference, is fixed. He is repeatedly exhorted to remember who he *really is*; a doctor hypnotizes him, pushing him to bypass his well-crafted defenses and recall his early life, his family's origins on the Yiddish stage, and his childhood experiences with the rabbis who told him the meaning of life in, as he cheekily points out, a Hebrew he couldn't understand. At the same time, Allen's playful insertion of Zelig into a variety of stock footage and his representation of the many sites in which identity was constituted and staged during the period—from the carnival freak show to the jazz club to the Hollywood picture—suggest a more contingent and far less solid, or essentialist, view of the self.

Throughout the film, Zelig's shape-shifting is associated with his Jewishness, but his ability to become another is also belied by the way in which the history of Jewish representation drags after him like a tin-can tail. Traveling to France, he becomes both Dreyfus and an ultraorthodox Jewish rabbi with a black hat and *payes*—transformations that dramatize how the Christian, western gaze sees all Jews as potential Dreyfusards or black hats. (Allen uses that myopic gaze to great effect in *Annie Hall* and elsewhere; what is the famous scene when Grammy Hall sees Alvy Singer as a bearded rabbi—"a real Jew"—but an extended joke about Jewish visibility?)[2] At the same time, Allen takes apart the very idea of Jewishness throughout the film, likening it to passing and depicting it as a type of racial performance that can and will fail.[3] In the few moments when Zelig is not impersonating racial others, he is performing in a kind of "Jewface," an exaggerated performance of Jewish identity that gains its evocative force from the deep archive of Jewish stereotypes.

In some of Zelig's transformations, Allen self-consciously invokes the history of Jewish minstrelsy that critics such as Michael Rogin, Lori Harrison-Kahan, and Rachel Rubinstein see as central to early twentieth-century Jewish self-fashioning.[4] However, for the most part, Zelig/Allen's performance of race is done in the canny, knowing spirit of a late-twentieth-century artist, a sort of postmodern racial performance more akin to that enacted by contemporary satirists Sarah Silverman and Sasha Baron Cohen than that of Al Jolson in *The Jazz Singer*.⁵ Zelig is speaking in the vernacular of the early twentieth century, but with a millennial twist.

While *Zelig*, like much of Woody Allen's nostalgic cinematic output, is set roughly during the Jazz Age, the film itself was produced during a very different moment in American and Jewish American history and aesthetics; and its satirical power comes precisely from its juxtaposition of early and late twentieth-century visual and discursive tropes.⁶ For this reason, *Zelig* is more than a commentary on the age-old anti-Semitic caricature of the Jew as chameleonic figure, dangerously mutable and thus a threat to the stability of conventional identity categories. It is also more than simply a commentary on the Jew as "model minority"—the Jew as supremely assimilable because supremely adaptable to American capitalism.⁷ Certainly, Zelig's ability to change himself to suit his surroundings acknowledges the Jew's purported talent for acculturation and impersonation; the formal transgressions of the film are mirrored in the categorical chameleonism associated with Zelig's Jewishness. However, I argue that it is also something more. *Zelig* the film indexes a particular moment in late twentieth-century Jewish self-fashioning when Jewish writers and intellectuals were drawn to transracial identification in order to speak about their ambivalent position in American politics and aesthetics.⁸

The curious habits of Leonard Zelig, as we shall see, are central to the Jewish American imagination of the past half-century. Though Zelig may be a bit more obsessive than most of his fellow Jews are, his insistence on inhabiting others is merely a more embodied version of what, I believe, is a central tenet in Jewish America. As a result, *Zelig* introduces a number of the preoccupations central to my explorations in this book: that transracial identification and interracial fantasies are central to late twentieth-century Jewish self-fashioning as well as American self-fashioning; that Jewish intellectuals have had a conscious stake in conversations about the politics of difference in the United States; that Jewish writers and artists such as Allen are deeply invested in the politics of appropriation; and that they often speak for others when what they really want to do is talk about themselves.⁹ Most strikingly, the film manifests the ways in which Jews, despite being categorized as "white" in post–World War II America, have never entirely felt comfortable embracing the mantle of undifferentiated whiteness offered to them during the period.¹⁰ In those moments when Jews are deemed to have most clearly melted into the crucible of American whiteness, Jewish writers and artists have embraced what Naomi Seidman identifies as "a Jewish politics of the vicarious"—what I call, in reference to the Jewish writers I explore, Jewish racial ventriloquism (254).¹¹

If we see the Jewish writer as a racial ventriloquist, we gain new insights into two related but competing claims. The first is the idea that, in contrast to their immigrant forebears, postwar Jews unselfconsciously became "white folks," as Karen Brodkin puts it; and the second is that many Jewish American writers and intellectuals have attempted, for varying reasons, to disavow their whiteness (and, with it, their white privilege) during the same period. I am interested in what this collision tells us about larger patterns of racial formation in American culture and aesthetics. Since about 1967, many Jewish American writers have become what Jon Stratton calls "anti-assimilationist," reclaiming an imagined racial otherness so as to speak to their anxieties about the waning of Jewish difference (143). Usually this performance of racial otherness differs from the literal blackface that Allen employs and that Michael Rogin has studied so adeptly and controversially in *Black Face, White Noise*, a history of minstrelsy in the United States that focuses particularly on how Jewish performers such as Al Jolson used blackface to help Jews and other new immigrants cement their sense of whiteness in urban America.[12] My project differs from Rogin's in that, with a few exceptions, it focuses not on literal performance but on more metaphorical forms of ventriloquism, identification, and racial drag. Nonetheless, like Rogin, although perhaps less pessimistically, I am interested in the ethical valences of postwar Jews' acts of identifying across the color line. What does it mean to try to speak for another, as exiled European intellectual Hannah Arendt did when she purported to be in a privileged position "as a Jew" to speak for African Americans during America's desegregation debates?[13] Is this sort of *speaking for* in a political context a racial masquerade that disavows the privileges of whiteness and affirms the exceptional nature of Jewish identity in America? Why does racial ventriloquism occur so often in Jewish American literature and film— for example, in Philip Roth's *The Human Stain*, where his character Coleman Silk, an African American who passes for a Jew speaks in the distinct and distinctly contentious cadences of Roth himself about the canon and culture wars? If speaking for another is often a form of silencing, how do we understand both the Jewish interest in acting as a mouthpiece for other racial and ethnic groups, famously expressed during the civil rights movement, and Jewish writers' and artists' related interest in identifying with or understanding themselves as "Jews" (a vexed identity category if there ever was one) through their relationship to other others? This latter move is perhaps best embodied by Michael Chabon's choice to juxtapose Jewish and Native American identity in *The Yiddish Policemen's Union* in order to comment on the divisive place of Israel in Jewish American culture. Finally, how do Jews' overt performances across racial lines work alongside more nuanced forms of interracial interaction, notably intermarriage and multiracial identity? What do we make of Jewish women writers in America, such as Hettie Jones and Lore Segal, who have posited that marrying "out" of Jewishness into another race has been a necessary precondition of their creative process and finding their own voice?

With such complex identifications in mind, the critic Jon Stratton has offered a brilliant reading of *Zelig* as an ode to both Jewish assimilation in America and its discontents. I believe it is no accident that, although Zelig can seemingly transform into whomever he chooses, the avatars he picks are most often iconic representatives of otherness. As one commentator in the film puts it, his metamorphosis into a variety of racially marked others, coupled with his resolute "Hebrewness" (in one scene, a Father Coughlin-esque radio personality suggests that someone "lynch the Hebe"), makes him a "triple threat" to the Ku Klux Klan. Contrary to the conventional reading of the film, I argue that Zelig does not use his shape shifting to assimilate. While the film culminates in his marriage to the WASP psychiatrist, Eudora Fletcher (played by Mia Farrow), a move that Stratton reads as the ultimate act of assimilation, she is not the only woman whom Zelig marries. In fact, a number of women of various ages and races accuse him of having married and subsequently left them. Moreover, throughout most of the film, both his lovers and his personal transformations provide a distinctly ambiguous message, not just about his ability to assimilate but about his *desire* to do so. In fact, the paradoxical message of the film—a message that abounds, as we'll see, in many works of Jewish American literature over the past half century—is that Zelig identifies most strongly with those who cannot easily assimilate into America's body politic. Yet the more he tries to become someone else, the more Jewish he becomes. Zelig, like many of the writers and artists I will discuss, gets at Jewishness through his relationship to other others.

At the same time, this desire to become another makes Zelig, in the logic of the film, more than an iconic figure of Jewishness: he is also an archetypical American. Like Zelig, the authors and artists we will trace have the capacity to shed light on America's ambivalent relationship to race, ethnicity, gender, class, and other forms of difference. Despite the fact that Zelig traverses the globe, he is fundamentally an American character, bent on reinvention, a funhouse mirror inversion of the radical individualist ideology at the heart of the nation's Horatio Alger myth. In America, you can purportedly be anyone you want to be—but only if you are willing to give up entirely being yourself. Zelig flips that standard story: he embodies many others by adamantly embracing himself.

The transformation of Zelig from object to subject is the film's subtext and, I would argue alongside Jonathan Freedman, part of the subtext of Jewish representation during the course of the twentieth century. This shift from object to subject happens, too, in American literature, where the contemporary Jewish writer has replaced the early twentieth-century representation of Jew as voiceless other. It is not entirely ironic, then, that at the center of the meta-referential *Zelig* is not another film but a novel, Herman Melville's *Moby-Dick*. Leonard Zelig begins his life of chameleonism because of anxiety about his intellectual capital; he is embarrassed that he has never read *Moby-Dick* and tries to pass for someone who would have done so. After this initial mention, the novel returns at key moments in the film to frame Zelig's transformations. This is not entirely surprising. *Moby-Dick*, among many other things, is, like *Zelig*, an important iteration of the American imagination of race and the uncanny multitudes who have been dispossessed by whiteness. It is also, like Zelig, a playful, "chameleonic" text that marries unwieldy forms to unwieldy content in its varied sections (Shohat and Stam 176). In my reading of *Zelig* and of the many texts that comprise *Borrowed Voices*, I am interested in how these formal questions unite with the larger questions of racial difference and identification at play in the work.

The writers I discuss in this book often pair anxieties about form and their place in literary history with a larger ambivalence about ethnic or racial representation. Zelig's anxiety about his relationship to the American literary canon (with *Moby-Dick* as its representative text) and the cultural imprimatur it can supply him is akin to the long-running relationship that a number of Jewish American authors have had to their own position in the canon and the larger structures of the university with which they have long been associated.[14] In contrast to Zelig, however, many of these authors come to worry that they have become too allied with the canon to have a voice in America's burgeoning multiculture. This anxiety, like Zelig's, occasions a series of transformations, impersonations, and identifications, although for an opposite reason. I am interested in historicizing this preoccupation with racial ventriloquism and transracial identification so that it is not merely part and parcel of a larger monolithic notion of the Wandering Jew but both a species of secular Jewish aesthetics and an intervention into the conventional narrative of postwar American literature. Like the discipline of Jewish studies, the field of contemporary American literature is riven by arguments about periodization, canonicity, historiography, and the role that identity could or should play in how we organize and study fiction. *Borrowed Voices* intervenes in these debates by offering an overview of the central, if paradoxical, role that Jewish writers have played in contemporary American fiction and the debates about voice, race, and representation that continue to plague it well into the twenty-first century.

Race and the Jewish "Voice" in American Fiction

To comprehend the importance of the concept of racial ventriloquism for Jewish American authors, we must situate them in the particular social and literary conditions of post–civil rights America. In 1965, at roughly the same time that some African American writers and intellectuals began calling for Black Arts for black artists, *Time* magazine was trumpeting the emergence of the American Jew as a postwar "culture hero" (38). According to the magazine's editorial writers, anti-Semitism was at an all-time low. Upward mobility was *de rigueur* for young Jews. And perhaps most notably, the Jew had become the archetypal postwar American author, looked to as "an expert in estrangement—the perpetual outsider who somehow knows how to keep warm out there" (38). As Morris Dickstein wrote in a retrospective glance at the postwar American Jewish novelist, "this was the brief period when the Jew became the modern Everyman, everyone's favorite victim, *schlemiel* and secular saint" ("The Complex Fate of the Jewish-American Writer"). However, according to *Time*, Jews themselves were more than a little ambivalent about the valorization of Jewish writers and the integration of Jews into every sector of American culture during this period. Many worried, even as they celebrated an "unprecedented freedom of a kind they never knew even in ancient Israel or their golden age in Moslem Spain: freedom to adhere to their faith or abandon it, to emphasize their differences or to become invisible" (38). Would this newfound "freedom" result in the dissolution of a meaningful Jewish identity? Moreover, what did it mean to think of the United States as itself increasingly "Jewish" in some fundamental way? As *Time* put it, "While the U.S. is growing more Jewish, the U.S. Jews may be growing less so" (38).

The results of this shift were manifold. What distinguished postwar Jewish American novelists from their immigrant antecedents was precisely their engagement with these questions of invisibility and difference, "the freedom to adhere to their faith or abandon it," as well as their investment in the privileged role that Jews would inhabit as so-called model minorities in American culture—what we might call the marriage between American and Jewish exceptionalism. Writers from the decades before World War II, such as Anzia Yezierska, Mike Gold, and even Henry Roth, tried to represent the ghettoes in which they grew up so as to write themselves *out* of their narrow confines. In contrast, writers who came to prominence after the atrocities of the war were able to view their antecedents' Jewish immigrant identities from a physical and spiritual remove. According to Dickstein, "the key to the new writers was partly their exposure to the great modernists—Kafka, Mann, Henry James—but also their purchase on Jews not simply as autobiographical figures in a social drama of rebellion and acculturation but as parables of the human condition" (170).

Just as Jewish American authors were reaching the pinnacle of their humanistic, Everyman pull, however, the growth of proto-identity politics and racial nationalisms during the 1960s and 1970s challenged the possibility that any group might be able to speak for or to the universal, much less to speak for others. During this period and its aftermath, what Linda Alcoff calls "the problem of speaking for others" (which I will explore further in chapter 1) troubled Jewish American writers, engaged as they were with questions of identification and representation in the post–civil rights era. Alcoff sketches one of the central tenets of identity politics: that "the problem of speaking for others" is always also "the problem of speaking about others" (9). The line between attempting to represent another and attempting to stand in for, speak for, or appropriate the experience of another is slippery. In her pivotal essay "Can the Subaltern Speak?" Gayatri

Spivak points out that appropriation of this kind is ethically problematic when there is a power imbalance between the speaker and the one being spoken for. Where does this problem leave the author who is seeking to engage in representation without overidentification or wholesale appropriation of the experiences of another? Throughout this book, I argue that to understand "the problem of speaking for others," we must understand that "where one speaks from affects both the meaning and truth of what one says, and thus that one cannot assume an ability to transcend her location" (Alcoff 6–7). I use the idea of racial ventriloquism to explore Jewish American writing precisely because it draws attention to the importance of the "location" of the speaker (what Alcoff defines as her "social location or social identity") as well as the power dynamics often present in the act of speaking for another (7).

According to Stephen Connor, the author of *Dumbstruck: A Cultural History of Ventriloquism*, the defining question in the long history of ventriloquism has been the origin of the voice and its relationship to the body of the speaker. Sometimes this voice is abstracted from its place in the speaking subject and "thrown" into another object or area. Sometimes, as in the case of the writers whom I discuss in this book, it is a literary voice alternately assumed and sloughed off in order to rhetorically assume and slough off the position of the speaker. In the case of Jewish American writers and intellectuals, we must ask how the writer-ventriloquist's own subject position delimits what is at stake in the act of ventriloquism. Why does the impetus to ventriloquize occur when and how it does in both literary and social history? How do Jewish American authors use racialized others to articulate their anxieties about hot-button issues in American life such as Israel, race, postwar acculturation, and the Holocaust? What does this reliance on racialized others say about inter- and intragroup relations, Jewish self-fashioning, and anxieties about what Connor calls the ventriloquial "I" as well as the way in which identity politics put an end to appropriation as a vaunted characteristic of American authorship from the mid-1960s onward?

These questions have particular resonance for many of the authors I explore because, as we will see, the preoccupation with voice was a constitutive feature of Jewish American literature and a growing concern for other American writers during the 1960s and 1970s. In sketching the origin of the category of postwar fiction he calls "high cultural pluralism" (a marriage between modernist formal experimentation and awareness of racial and ethnic difference), Mark McGurl turns to Jewish American fiction, particularly to what he identifies as its investment in literary "voice." To McGurl, Roth's *Portnoy's Complaint*, published to equal amounts of opprobrium and acclaim in 1969, marked the increasing valuation of the writer's authentic voice in postwar fiction. Departing from the novelist's earlier, more restrained, third-person work, it was written in the *shticky* first-person cadences of Alexander Portnoy as he details the origin of his neuroses to his therapist. According to McGurl, "the appearance on the scene of

American fiction of a voice like Portnoy's—miming the emotional, improvisational rhythms of a *spoken* voice, which is also necessarily an *embodied* voice and in this case a distinctly *Jewish-American* voice—in the work of a self-consciously Jamesian craftsman like Roth announces a new turn" (230). Moreover, *Portnoy* "is a symptom of a profoundly (let us dust off the term) *phonocentric* literary historical moment, when the New Critical ideal of narrative impersonality was rotated into a minor position in relation to a dominant ideal of vocal presence" (230).

This idealization of "vocal presence" was coterminous with a growing push for postwar writers to "find [their] voice" (181). While this dictum affected all writers during what McGurl refers to as "the program era," when MFA programs came to dominate the production of fiction in the United States, he believes that it had particular repercussions for self-identified ethnic writers and writers of color.[15] For these writers, "the subjectivism of the imperative to find your voice was an even more conspicuously corporeal one, circling back again and again to the housing of the storytelling imagination not only in a human body, but in a racialized and gendered body with 'bloodlines' or 'roots' in an organic community or culture with its own repository of storytelling tradition" (236).[16] Moreover, "for the ethnically-marked or woman writer especially, it might not be good enough to simply search so as to find one's voice; that voice, it was understood, might have to be 'claimed' in defiance of the silencing forces of social oppression and cultural standardization" (236).[17] Thinking of voice in these immutable terms as "conspicuously corporeal," not to mention "racialized" and "gendered," ushered in debates about what it might mean to attempt to speak in the voice of another—debates that had particular resonance for Jewish writers who had managed to embody both the establishment and the other in American fiction, a racialized literary voice and its lack (236). Pointing to the controversy surrounding William Styron's *The Confessions of Nat Turner* (1967) as illustration, McGurl notes that "'voice' understood this way conceives authorship as a kind of ventriloquism and raises the specter of offensive appropriation, which is an offense against the rule of writing what you know" (234).[18] It is also, as he suggests by using as an example the white Styron's first-person "confession" of the former slave Turner, a definition of authorial voice seemingly designed for conversations about race and representation. Styron, who would later draw criticism for portraying a Holocaust survivor in *Sophie's Choice* (as I discuss in chapter 3) was widely panned by critics for his *Confessions*. As McGurl notes, an entire anthology was devoted to African American writers' responses to Styron's choice to "speak" from the perspective of a former slave. *William Styron's Nat Turner: Ten Black Writers Respond* (1968) accused him of having appropriated the voice and person of another whose experience he, as a southern white man, could never fully comprehend.

As we'll see, for many Jewish American writers of the period, these debates about voice and appropriation were particularly resonant, as was the transition away from the "New Critical ideal of narrative impersonality" and the modernist embrace of personae that McGurl associates with the author-as-ventriloquist (230). Jewish American writers, even more than the other writers McGurl identifies with high cultural pluralism, were caught in a bind because of their dual allegiance to the tenets of white male-identified high modernism and the imperative to express the authentic voice of the author. *Portnoy's Complaint* was notable at the time of its publication because its embrace of a hyperactive, Jewish-identified orality diverged wildly from the tradition of Jewish American writers of the 1940s and 1950s, who had tried to tamp down any markers of ethnicity to better acculturate to the restrained work of their peers.[19]

Faced with the growing imperative to write in their own voices, Jewish writers of the time were unclear about what exactly that voice would or should sound like. Used to professing unfettered access to the interiority of other others, they suddenly faced the limits of the appropriative imagination. Inconveniently, they encountered these limits just as the "textual performance of vocal authenticity," in the form of ethnic and racial particularism, had come to be prized. During the 1960s and 1970s, Jewish writers existed at the crossroads of modernist and postmodernist conceptions of voice, authorship, and authority. They embodied high cultural pluralism because, like the literary alter egos with whom they came to be identified, they moved from representing the authentic, "embodied" voice to colliding with the limits this privileging of corporeality placed on their ability to speak for and about others. Precisely became of this ambivalent positioning, many of the authors I discuss in this book illustrate a missing element in Alcoff's elegant, two-pronged formulation of ventriloquism as relating to the "problem of speaking for others" and the "problem of speaking about others" (18). They show that the desire to speak through the other about the self is deeply interwoven into the complex politics and poetics of "speaking for" and "speaking about." In an era when cultural pluralism was being increasingly replaced by the idealization of racial and ethnic difference in both the public and private spheres, American Jewish authors addressed the question of a hyphenated American Jewish identity through strategic racial identification: speaking the self through the other.

Speaking about Jews and Race

The popular social networking site Reddit recently hosted a conversation centered on the question "Why are Jews treated more like a race than other religions are?" A wide-ranging conversation ensued, comprising almost 2,000 comments and treating subjects as varied as genetics, the history of Jewish last names, the meaning of the term *Semite,* Israel, immigration, anti-Semitism, and Jewish matrilineal descent. Yet confusion about whether to view Jews as a race, a religion, or an ambiguously defined culture extends far beyond this foray into popular culture. The ghost in the machinery of modern Jewish life is the omnipresent question "What is a Jew?" This question has been articulated since the Enlightenment in various forms, such as "What is a Jewish literature?" and "What is a Jewish art?," and it is particularly powerful in the context of twenty-first-century America.[20] For some Jews, their identification is cultural; for others, it is religious. But despite these complications, the most vexed topic of conversation, particularly in the wake of the Holocaust, is whether Jews are to be understood racially and, if not, how to understand the complexity of Jewish identification.

Attempts to situate Jews in relation to other groups in terms of comparative or differential racialization have foundered because of the language of race that such a discussion employs and the accompanying charges of essentialism.[21] The accusation of racial essentialism that rightly follows any discussion of a group belonging to a biologically defined race, along with the largely unimpeachable assertion that Jews in America enjoy the privileges of whiteness, whether they wish to admit it or not, have largely muted any discussion about the importance of race as a category through which many Jews continue to understand themselves. With these paradoxes in mind, we should note that critical ethnic and diasporic studies scholars such as Paul Gilroy, Stuart Hall, Lisa Lowe, and James Clifford have long and deconstructively written about race in literature and culture without suggesting that any group identity is immutable or monolithic. In this book, I have endeavored, like these scholars, to write about race not as biological or fixed but as a nexus of racial processes, which critical race theorists often refer to under the headings of "racialization" and "racial projects" to highlight the role of agency in racial formation.[22] As Michael Omi and Howard Winant point out, "there is a continuous temptation to think of race as an *essence*, as something fixed, concrete and objective. . . . And there is also an opposite temptation: to see it as mere illusion, which an ideal social order would eliminate" (19). Instead, they suggest, race is best defined as "an unstable and 'decentered' complex of social meanings constantly being transformed by political struggle" (19). The process by which these "social meanings" come to be ascribed to a given group is "racialization." "Racial projects," on the other hand, are the ways in which people organize around and through their ideas about race—with radically different results. These projects can be more complicated than they sound. Winant, for instance, reads neoconservatism as a "white racial project" that employs the language of racial "color-blindness" to undermine calls for recognition and redress by people of color.

For the authors and intellectuals I discuss in this volume, race is both project and process. Racial identification and ascription are a tricky and ideologically freighted business in the late twentieth and early twenty-first centuries. Nonetheless, I believe that many of the authors and artists with whom I engage in this book still think of their identities and, at times, their aesthetic projects in racial terms. As Roth laments in "Writing About Jews," Jewish American writers are never entirely free from the politics of representation in a dual sense. Assumed to be representative of all Jews, Jewish American writers alternately reject the responsibilities placed upon them by their "race" and embrace the power inherent in representing Jews and Jewish racial identity as a portal into American culture and literary history. My purpose is not to argue about whether or not Jews have become white in the arena of everyday life but to suggest that Jewish writers and artists have often been deeply concerned about claiming a racialized Jewish difference in the narrative, or symbolic, realm.[23] For instance, we might read this strategic self-othering, distorted relation to the type of strategic essentialism that Gayatri Spivak placed at the center of the subaltern studies group's decolonial discourse, as a type of white privilege because many groups are not able to don and doff their racial identity with such ease. The period since 1967 has witnessed a stream of texts that have simultaneously re-racialized the Jew and challenged the ironclad binaries between Jew and other by insisting upon a transracial identification between Jews and more marginalized racial groups. The literary moments of transracial identification, racial ventriloquism, and interracial fantasy I will explore in this book provide a particular genealogy of Jewish American literature, one in conversation with the larger story of postwar American literature and its growing preoccupation with questions of appropriation, vocal authenticity, and writing and rewriting the canon.

After situating itself in the confused aftermath of World War II, my story will focus on Jewish American literature produced after 1967, a benchmark year in Jewish American self-fashioning and the beginning of a seismic shift in literary and cultural spheres. The Six Day War in Israel, the Newark and Watts race riots, the evolving political landscape of a post–civil rights America grown disenchanted with the mythology of the melting pot—all had vast repercussions within the Jewish American literary imagination. I will investigate works produced in the immediate aftermath of this moment of crisis, such as Bernard Malamud's *The Tenants* and Saul Bellow's *Mr. Sammler's Planet*, both of them racial dystopias composed at the dawn of the 1970s, and follow these trends in Jewish American writing into the culture wars of the 1980s and 1990s, when Jewish American writers contended with their increasingly canonical status alongside the perceived whitening of an identity that just a few decades earlier had been distinctly other. I will end in the contemporary moment, taking stock of the various ways in which writers and artists claim identification with Native Americans in order to critique Israel and seek a ground upon which to build an American Jewish identity in diaspora.

Given the power of such topics for Jewish writers, the narrative I trace can't help but be a political one. Politics figures prominently in the writing of many of the Jewish American writers with whom I engage, regardless of their professed ideological allegiances. I am invested in understanding how the political and literary are intertwined in the preoccupation with race that came to characterize so much Jewish American fiction after World War II. Beginning with works such as Malamud's *The Tenants* (1971), a controversial articulation of the position of the Jewish writer in the purportedly hostile climate of post–"Black Art" America and moving toward the present with Chabon's *The Yiddish Policemen's Union* (2007), a novel that attempts to regain the position of Jew as cultural and political outsider by constructing an imagined diasporic homeland for the American Jew, I tease out some of the strands of American Jewish writers' ambivalent relationship to politics (particularly identity politics) in a world shaped by both the Holocaust and the foundation of the state of Israel. With this in mind, I am interested in literary relations between Jews and African Americans but also, on a more global scale, with the relationship between Jews and a host of other others. I explore the tendency of Jewish American authors to ventriloquize, whether they are appropriating African American characters' voices to speak their own concerns, as Cynthia Ozick does in "A Mercenary," her meditation on the links between the postcolonial and post-Holocaust conditions, or racializing Jews by putting them into Native American bodies, as Ben Katchor does in *The Jew of New York*, his ode to Jewish difference in the nineteenth-century city. Following in the footsteps of Eric Lott in *Love & Theft*, I explore the ways in which these writers appropriate discourses associated with other racial and ethnic groups in order to gain control over the alien others in their midst while speaking of their own increasing alienation. At the same time, I analyze how Jewish aesthetic appropriation often takes the form of a re-appropriation of a Jewish otherness once thought lost. Many of the authors I discuss—from Malamud and Bellow to Segal and Jones—are interested in how Jewish identification with purportedly marginalized racial groups can resuscitate an obsolete, and often politically weighted, Jewish difference. This is not an unproblematic move. As Michael Rogin and Naomi Seidman both note, racial drag is not always a subversive and liberating type of postmodern performance, particularly when the performer possesses more cultural or economic power than do the members of the group he or she is attempting to impersonate. At the same time, as Bryan Cheyette points out, "the anxiety of appropriation" can endanger the sort of metaphorical thinking necessary to make connections among groups, supporting a sense of "disciplinary uniqueness, outside such imaginative connectedness, which results in an inability to embrace the dissimilar" (xiv).

By analyzing the ventriloquial power of Jewish American authors—their intense desire to reclaim otherness by speaking through the mouths of racially other characters—we are able to discern not simply how Jews imaginatively use other others to represent their concerns or deal with their own ambivalence about race and Jewish difference but also how Jews themselves continue to serve as lighting rods for a uniquely American anxiety about questions of identity in the years after the civil rights movement. At the same time, by focusing on how Jewish American authors and intellectuals write their own complex relationship to difference, we can work against the easy tendency to view Jews as merely allegorical, one-dimensional stand-ins for exile, diaspora, and cosmopolitanism on the one hand and an insular, parochial clan mentality on the other. If Jewish American authors are paradigmatic, it is because they are able to be both American and Jewish in ways that problematize the easy theorization of either category. In this book, I analyze how the Jew has long functioned as a figure of otherness in America and how Jews have figured their own otherness, employing to great effect their alternating similarity to and difference from the rest of the American body politic across the past half-century. Often, Jewish American writers and artists have been loath to give up their difference, embarking on a process of reconstituting their negatively valenced otherness in a manner similar to the approach of many gay and lesbian artists, who seek to reclaim queerness as a discourse and an aesthetic.[24] How Jewish American authors negotiate the thorny issue of race in America has profound implications for those seeking to understand the way in which postwar challenges to cultural pluralism have radically redefined America's political and literary landscape and undermined long-held beliefs about Jewish American and American exceptionalism.

CHAPTER 1

The Politics and Poetics of Speaking the Other

SYMPATHY FOR THE CAUSE OF THE NEGROES

In 1959, German-Jewish émigré Hannah Arendt weighed in on the fever-pitch battle over school desegregation in the United States. Her essay, "Reflections on Little Rock," was slated for publication in the journal *Commentary*, but the editors pulled it from the lineup. The controversial piece, which argued that the federal government should not enforce an end to segregation, was eventually published in the noted leftist magazine *Dissent* alongside a series of disclaimers and a carefully worded apology from Arendt herself.[1]

"Reflections" was eloquent but arrogant, drawing the ire and disapproval of Arendt's colleagues on the left and shocking many American readers by advocating for miscegenation as the key to ending the nation's race problem. Most troubling to many critics was not her controversial articulation of the disjuncture between the private and public spheres and the way in which she used this split to legitimize southern efforts to stop the federal government from legislating local education. Nor was it the discomfiting fact that an urbane European intellectual was introducing unheard-of levels of abstraction into the messy realities of school desegregation debates in the United States. It was not even the repercussions associated with a noted Cold War liberal's articulation of segregationist concerns or her unorthodox perspective on miscegenation. Instead, what appalled commentators, from Sidney Hook to Ralph Ellison, was her ease in speaking for the African Americans whose educational and social opportunities were at stake in the desegregation debates.[2] Ralph Ellison later described it as being written with "Olympian authority" (108).[3]

Anticipating criticism, Arendt prefaced the essay with an unusually personal aside, although in general she rarely brandished her Jewishness, even when writing about specifically Jewish subjects: "since what I wrote may shock good people and be misused by bad ones, I should like to make it clear that as a Jew I take

15

my sympathy for the cause of the Negroes as for all oppressed or underprivileged peoples for granted and should appreciate it if the reader did likewise." This address to her readers, a rhetorical means of sloughing off identification with desegregation's foes, prefigures many of the complex contests of discursive identification and disavowal in the post–civil rights era. Yet in her attempt to ward off one identification—that of the *Dissent* writer and magisterial critic with some of desegregation's most violent and red-faced opponents—Arendt enacted another, far more problematic one. For as "Reflections on Little Rock" soon made clear, she took it "for granted" that "as a Jew" she could ventriloquize the concerns of African Americans; after all, she suggested, her "sympathy for the cause of the Negroes" arose from the beleaguered, existential, everyman status of post-Holocaust Jewry (46). For this German-Jewish critic, speaking as a Jew legitimated not only a politics of sympathetic identification but also a politics of representation: both figuratively and literally, *Jew* came to stand in for other oppressed others.[4] It is precisely the Jew's unique purchase on suffering, Arendt suggested, that affords Jewish intellectuals such as herself the right to function as mouthpieces for the concerns of "oppressed or underprivileged peoples," particularly African Americans, without sanction (46).[5]

Writing of Arendt's preface, Andrew Lackritz has noted that "while appeal to our own subject position can generate rhetorical authority, it cannot in itself address another important issue: that the very structure of authority that allows us to identify and empathize inserts us back into the structure of inequality the identification would dismantle" (12). Arendt's status as a Jew, speaking for and of African Americans and their suffering, enabled her to suture her own theoretical speculations about the decline in parental authority in America to the particular pitfalls of the decision of Little Rock parents to involve their children in the desegregation battle—all without acknowledgment of the real distance between her own life and that of the people with whom she identified.[6] It also helped her to articulate a view of Jewish exceptionalism deeply at odds with her insistence that the Holocaust be appraised alongside other forms of state-sponsored racial violence, notably colonialism.[7]

Such sympathetic identification between Jew and African American for rhetorical purposes was not unusual, as Michael Staub points out, and began long before Arendt composed her "Reflections."[8] In the 1930s and 1940s, both Jews and African Americans made analogies between Jewish suffering under fascism and America's internal racial strife, even though the decimation of European Jewry had cast only the faintest shadow on the United States. Nonetheless, Arendt's essay emboldened this historical analogy; her invocation of Jewish ethnic particularity and her identification with the "oppressed and underprivileged" Negro prefigured many later debates about the rights of Jewish writers and intellectuals to speak for or of the other. In the words of Werner Sollors, her trajectory "from universalism to increasing ethnic identification" marked a historical and discursive turning point in Jewish self-representation ("Of Mules and Mares" 177–178). Arendt's embattled presumptuousness in speaking for the other, the way she distinguished between public and private identity, and her embrace of a collective identity structured ironically around individualism shaped the thinking of many mid- and late-twentieth-century Jewish American writers, including Bernard Malamud and Saul Bellow.[9] Many of them imagined writing as the public inscription of an impersonal, lyrical self who was simultaneously free to comment on the decline of universalism and the individual and to invoke Jewishness as floating metaphor for everyman suffering.[10] This literary mindset, which was associated with the then-dominant New Critical approach to literature, fit well with Arendt's arrogance. And in that arrogance we can trace the waning of the culturally pluralist ethos that had defined Jewish American responses to racial and ethnic difference in earlier decades of the century and the rise of a more particularist and presumptive racial discourse.

Arendt's 1959 invocation of her Jewishness as a legitimation of abstract universalist assertions about the lives of African Americans sets the stakes for the far more violent clashes between African American and Jewish writers in the late 1960s and 1970s, when the proto-black separatist movement took issue with how often purportedly liberal Jewish critics and writers "took for granted" their capacity to function as sympathetic spokespeople for the concerns of African Americans (Arendt 46). As Emily Miller Budick, among other critics, has argued, Arendt's ease in "speaking for the negro" was soon superseded by these future disagreements between African American and Jewish American intellectuals.[11] In 1963, Irving Howe published "Black Boys and Native Sons," in part a reprisal of his earlier review of Ralph Ellison's *Invisible Man*. In this celebrated essay, Howe took Ellison to task for rejecting a Richard Wright–style literary realism and, with it, a commitment to representing black experience in America in all the specificity of its horror. In his appraisal, Howe casually slipped into an identification with Ellison (as well as with James Baldwin, whom he also critiqued in this piece) and began to discuss what he would do, were he a black author with the dual imperative to represent and be representative. In his response, the magisterial essay "The World and the Jug," an incensed Ellison argued that, to the leftist white critic, "a Negro" was "not a human being but an abstract embodiment of living hell," easily spoken for and used to represent a host of artistic and political bogeymen (112). Further, Ellison claimed that Howe's audacity in attacking him for failing to be "a good Negro" and "race man" was a result of his uniquely Jewish comfort in "appearing suddenly in blackface" to criticize the black author's commitment to his race (125–126, 111).

These uncomfortable battles between black and Jewish intellectuals were the beginning point in a trajectory of Jewish racial ventriloquism that stretched into the twenty-first century: the tendency of Jewish American writers to appear or dress their characters "in blackface" (or "redface" or "yellowface") as they struggled to negotiate their own identities. During this turbulent era, the racial question in America was coming to resemble nothing so much as the Jewish Question that had vexed enlightened Europeans since the emancipation of their paradigmatic others within. Beginning in the late 1960s, the question of how to accommodate racial difference—which Howe claimed that writers such as Ellison and Baldwin had abandoned in their quest for aesthetic and commercial success—came to test the limits of American liberalism and the heart of enlightened universalism.

In the late 1960s, Ellison became far less representative as a black writer and "race man" as more controversial figures such as LeRoi Jones stepped to the forefront. As a spokesman for the newly minted Black Arts movement, he directly and vociferously engaged in debate with Jewish writers and intellectuals. In 1968, critic Larry Neal proclaimed Black Arts, with Jones at its helm, to be the "aesthetic and spiritual sister of the Black Power concept" (446). In "Black Art," a poetic corollary to Neal's exegesis, Jones painted a picture of what a politicized black art should look like. Employing the repeated refrain "we want poems," he wrote of a world in which the abstractions of the conventional white American poem would be replaced by the daily matter of black existence, the materiality of "teeth or trees or lemons piled / on a step" (lines 2–3). He argued that poems, for black art and black artists, must be a form of combat predicated on an opposition to those who would translate the specificities of black life into the universalizing abstractions of white figurative language.

In "Black Art" and elsewhere, Jones used the Jew as just such an abstraction or allegory. The Jew came to stand for all those who would seek to speak for and about blacks without an authentic knowledge of black interiority. The Jewish landlord and small businessman, whether real or discursive, were particularly monstrous inhabitants of his African American neighborhood: "We want poems / like fists beating niggers out of Jocks / or dagger poems in the slimy bellies / of the owner-jews" (lines 12–15).[12] Even more violently, he invoked the "Liberal / Spokesman for the jews," the greatest foe of the African American writer and intellectual, who "clutch[es] his throat / & puke[s] himself into eternity" when the vengeance of "black art" comes calling (lines 28–30).

In Jones's view, the Jewish liberal had sold the African American man a promise of Americanness that he could never hope to possess.[13] Baldwin echoed Jones's sentiments in his fascinating 1967 essay "Negroes Are Anti-Semitic Because They're Anti-White" (discussed in chapter 3), in which he writes that "very few Americans, and this include[s] very few Jews, have the courage to recognize that the America of which they dream and boast is not the America in which the Negro lives" (742). According to Baldwin, the assimilation long advocated by Jewish proponents of the melting pot ethos was impossible for those whose skin color and uniquely American history of oppression marked them as immutably different. Perhaps invoking Arendt, Baldwin wrote, "One does not wish, in short, to be told by an American Jew that his suffering is as great as the American Negro's suffering. It isn't, and one knows that it isn't from the very tone in which he assures you that it is" (741).

What right did Jewish liberals have to align themselves with African Americans, especially when their own faraway "white" suffering was accorded far more weight than was the prototypically American suffering of African Americans? This question was echoed by a number of Jewish writers and intellectuals who were attempting to negotiate their own complex relationships to America during the era. Although LeRoi Jones and others were portraying Jews as a monolithic entity, intra-group relations had frayed. American Jews were deeply at odds about what might comprise American Jewish identity after the Holocaust and the foundation of Israel. Did Jews possess a distinct ethnic or racial identity in a country in which they had so successfully acculturated? Were they really marginalized and thus able to speak for other marginalized peoples? What would a secular, diasporic Jewish identity look like?

These questions framed the wars over the politics of sympathy, identification, and address that would undergird the works of many Jewish writers and intellectuals from the late 1960s onward. As the once-casual universalism of intellectuals such as Arendt and Howe came to be aligned with ethnically particularist discourses, the specifically Jewish rhetoric of ventriloquism came to the forefront of Jewish American writing. How would humanist fiction writers such as Bernard Malamud respond to this change in the realms of identification and representation? The Newark and Watts race riots, the Six-Day War in Israel, and the Ocean Hill–Brownsville school crisis of 1968 could not help but intrude onto their discursive sphere. As we shall see, the waning of cultural pluralism, with the Jew as its most successful benefactor and representative, and the rise of a politics of racial and ethnic difference would destabilize the American Jewish literary imagination.

A number of Jewish American critics have productively placed postwar Jewish and African American literature into conversation.[14] Although some African American critics, notably Stanley Crouch, have taken an interest in Jewish fiction, they have done so with startlingly less frequency. With this in mind, Daniel Itzkovitz has pointed out that the black-Jewish dialogue is more often than not a black-Jewish monologue that speaks more to Jewish identity and fantasies of interracial congress than to any particular African American interest in Jewishness ("Notes from the Black-Jewish Monologue"). A number of questions about power, agency, and exploitation arise if one probes this "monologue" further. To do so, I use a figure associated with monologism (or, perhaps, a compromised dialogism) to assess the relationship between Jews and African Americans in the discursive or imaginary sphere during this period of racial and ethnic strife: that of "speaking for" or "ventriloquizing" through the other. I am most interested in how Jewish writers, in ways that are both ethical and unethical, have instrumentalized the other to get at the compromised, multifarious nature of late twentieth-century Jewish identity. Jews speak for the other in order to talk about themselves.

Talking Ain't Telling: Voicing *The Tenants*

Bernard Malamud's controversial novel, *The Tenants* (1971), centers on the seductive pull of speaking for the other and its inevitable failure. At first, however, the novel seems little more than another literary meditation on the perils of writer's block. As the novel begins, protagonist Harry Lesser (characterized primarily as "the Writer" or "the Jewish writer") is living as a "tenant" in multiple senses of the word. Levenspiel, Lesser's landlord and every inch the stereotypical Jewish slumlord, has evicted or paid off the rest of the Manhattan building's residents and intends to knock down the existing structure, which has been pockmarked by the history of immigrant residence, to make way for a luxury apartment complex and a series of high-end stores.[15] The city's labyrinthine rent control laws intervene, however, and Levenspiel is unable to legally remove Lesser, his last tenant, from the property he has long inhabited. Along with enduring daily interruptions from Levenspiel, Lesser is perpetually anxious about finding a legal eviction notice in his mailbox.

The precarious nature of Lesser's reclusive physical existence and the single-minded manner in which he defends his right to remain a tenant are exceeded only by the transience of his emotional life and his career. He makes veiled allusions to a failed first marriage, sacrificed because of his devotion to art. He is repeatedly mocked for composing his third novel around the subject of love, a theme about which he admits to having little practical knowledge. His career, too, is in a tailspin. In *The Tenant*'s early pages, Lesser's refusal to leave Levenspiel's building is primarily framed as a middle-aged author's attempt to revive his flailing reputation by finishing his long-delayed third novel. As becomes increasingly clear, he is an anachronism who adheres to the precepts of western literature that he learned in school. (He quotes Dryden in casual conversation.) His literary standards are becoming as obsolete as the building that he stubbornly inhabits.

The contingency of Lesser's condition as a renter, a temporary resident in "the house of fiction," in the words of the critic Steven G. Kellman invoking Henry James, reflects his compulsion to write himself into a permanence of sorts. As Lesser remarks early in the novel, "nine and a half years on one book is long enough to be forgotten. Once in a while a quasi-humorous inquiry, beginning: 'Are you there?,' the last three years ago. I don't know where's there but here I am writing" (9). His unfinished work has a playfully tentative title, *The Promised End*. Taken from a line near the end of Shakespeare's *King Lear*, the title becomes an early and ironic marker of Lesser's tragic fate as a representative of both pure art and Jewishness. For it is clear that his refusal to leave a building earmarked for destruction, coupled with his desire to cling to outmoded artistic ideals, marks him as an object that has long ceased to be valuable in the literary and social economies of 1960s Manhattan.

Not far into the novel, we meet Willie Spearmint, an itinerant black writer who has taken up residence illegally in the apartment next door. As the newcomer enters the condition of tenancy (which Lesser ironically purports to own), Malamud begins to engage with the era's many debates about art, ownership, voice, and race. Willie Spearmint's name and literary aspirations playfully invoke William Shakespeare's, even as he acts as a mouthpiece for the Black Arts movement, particularly its proponents' insistence on the need for black writers to possess their own literary and artistic genealogy.[16] At the same time, he speaks of and to the greatest fears of writers such as Malamud. Not only does his name invoke Shakespeare's, but its emphasis on "spear" recalls racist stereotypes of primitive Africanness. Simultaneously, as I have noted, the title of Lesser's deferred novel is a link to *King Lear*. When Lear cedes land to his daughters, he becomes a tenant of the space he had formerly owned. Likewise, Lesser's relationship to Spearmint makes him reevaluate his ownership of a property that he thought he had possessed. It is notable that, halfway through *The Tenants*, Willie Spearmint becomes Bill Spear—a shift that marks Malamud's/Lesser's increasing racism and Spearmint's canniness in adapting to the literary marketplace's hunger for racial authenticity. For he and his brethren, like many of the Black Arts movement's most notable players, are tired of renting space in the literary pantheon and mimicking the conventions of American high art. They wish to develop a uniquely Black Art and artistic voice and begin to make demands to that effect. At the same time they are pushing to end Jewish writers' assumptions that they have a special purchase on speaking for the African American condition.

Critics have long speculated that LeRoi Jones was the prototype for Spearmint. In his afterword to the 1997 reissue of *The Tenants*, Paul Malamud, Bernard's son, pointed out the links between the two, writing that "some of Jones' work was considered to be violent and anti-semitic, but this was often treated as an 'authentic' and necessary expression of an oppressed people. Willie Spearmint, the black writer in *The Tenants*, exemplifies this kind of personality" (in Davis 466).[17] Although Malamud borrowed much of Spearmint's biography, from his early life in the south to his time in prison, from the writings of Malcolm X, Eldridge Cleaver, and Richard Wright, the character's ideas are more closely related to Jones's.[18] Many of Spearmint's disquisitions on the links between space and art, as well as the inherent differences between black and white artists and black and white art, mirror Jones's meditations on literature and black nationalism composed during the 1960s. The metaphors of tenancy and ownership that Malamud teases out in *The Tenants* were particularly meaningful figures for Jones and other black artists of the era. According to Jones, the specters of slavery and Reconstruction would hang over black artists until they developed a nation and a national *geist* of their own. Much as European Jewish artists did in the nineteenth century, he embraced the Romantic marriage of land/nation with artistic genealogy, and a number of his poems and essays address the intimate link between possession of national consciousness and ownership of art. Moreover, like his avatar Spearmint, Jones was concerned with what he saw as the immutable difference between whites and blacks as well as between white ethnics and blacks. In "the last days of the American empire (including some instructions for black people)," written in 1964, he drew a distinction between African Americans and formerly racialized immigrant others, such as Italians and Jews, akin to the one Baldwin noted in his aforementioned essay on Jews and whiteness. Jones's essay asks:

> Where are the Italian Anarchists? The Sacco-Vanzetti frame put them on the skids, and the Mafia takes up the wild strong ones whose lifeneeds put them outside straightup WASP-AMERICA. The Jewish Radicals, Socialists, Communists, etc., of the '30s, what happened to them? Have they all disappeared into those sullen suburbs hoping Norman Podhoretz and Leslie Fiedler will say something real? The price the immigrants paid to get into America was that they had to become Americans. The black man *cannot* become an American (unless we get a different set of *rules*) because he is black. (221)

As the *Time* editorial suggested, successfully becoming an "American" was exacting its own price from Jews.

Jones's claims about representing black experience and the limits those claims put on Jewish authors were very much on Malamud's mind as he wrote *The Tenants*. Although it is problematic to conflate Malamud the writer with Lesser the writer, the controversy that later swirled around Malamud's composition of the novel dramatized this conflict between Jewish and African American writers. It also revealed the simultaneous worry and arrogance that Malamud brought to his representation of Spearmint in the novel. *The Tenants* is a less-than-merciful tale of violence between African Americans and Jews, misogyny, the politics of literary history, and anxieties about castration (symbolic and real) rendered in a formally experimental mode that departed radically from anything the magical realist Malamud had previously written.

In "To Blacks and Jews: Hab Rachmones," an essay published in *Tikkun* in 1989, James A. McPherson offered an elegant and nuanced account of black-Jewish relations from the perspective of an African American fiction writer with deep ties to Jewish authors and intellectuals. He framed the essay through his relationship to Malamud and *The Tenants*, even going so far as to borrow "hab rachmones" (have mercy) from the character Levenspiel, who utters the phrase repeatedly to his writer-tenants when they refuse to leave his building. But more than *The Tenants*'s somber spirit hangs over McPherson's speculations about identity and antagonism between Jews and African Americans. According to the essay, Malamud sent McPherson a manuscript of the novel in 1971 because he "had some reservations about the book."

> [He] was anxious over how the antagonism between Harry Lesser, a Jewish writer, and Willie Spear, a Black writer, would be read. We communicated about the issue. On the surface, Malamud was worried over whether he had done justice to Willie Spear's Black idiom; but beneath the surface, during our exchange of letters, he was deeply concerned about the tensions that were then developing between Black intellectuals and Jewish intellectuals (15).

At the time, McPherson was "trying very hard to become a writer." While Malamud was already an established star, McPherson had published only a few short stories, one of which, "The Gold Coast," had won the *Atlantic Monthly* Firsts Award in 1965 and brought him to the attention of Malamud and the rest of the literary world. As McPherson explained, after corresponding with Malamud about his concerns about *The Tenants*, "as a favor to Malamud, [he] rewrote certain sections of the novel, distinguished Willie Spear's idiom from Harry Lesser's, and suggested several new scenes" (15). In an interview published thirteen years after the *Tikkun* essay, he retold the story, saying that Malamud had asked him to read the manuscript "because he was concerned about being called a racist." So "I read it and the only objection I had was that the black people sounded Jewish. And so I decided to work on this idiom" (McPherson 2002).

It is unclear if McPherson did rewrite significant portions of *The Tenants*. It is also unclear if he perceived his relationship to Malamud and the novel as particularly troubling. None of his public statements about his work on the novel have been polemical. The *Tikkun* essay, published three years after Malamud's death, was his first public mention of his reviser's role. Nonetheless, it is impossible not to wonder about McPherson's relationship to *The Tenants* when so much of the novel is concerned precisely with issues of racial performance and appropriation, with the valences of authorship and the literary voice, as well as with what it means to "talk black," "talk Jewish," and talk both for oneself and a larger collective.

A number of scholars, including Budick and Eric Sundquist, have mentioned McPherson's assertion. Yet as far as I know, no one, including Malamud's biographer, Philip Davis, has written extensively about the correspondence and how it might affect the way in which we read the novel as both a singular work and a radical departure from Malamud's usual style.[19] Budick rightly points out that McPherson's contention needs more exploration because, if true, it suggests that "to produce a viable, vital text, Malamud literally imports into his writing culturally different, African American, materials." She continues: "For the American Jew, Malamud is suggesting, it may already be too late to return to cultural origins" (19).

After reading the correspondence between the two writers, I have come to understand that McPherson's and Malamud's interaction took place rather late in the book's production process, when the novelist would presumably have been unable to make significant changes in the manuscript. Nonetheless, their correspondence is fascinating and suggests that McPherson influenced the text—particularly the characterization of Willie Spearmint—in significant ways that merit acknowledgment. In his letters, Malamud is particularly anxious about how to write in a convincing idiom that would make the voices of his African American characters, particularly Spearmint, sound authentic and perhaps less Jewish, as McPherson's later interview also suggests. In a lengthy letter, dated June 12, 1971, McPherson makes it clear that he doesn't think Malamud has been successful on either count, although he shares that he, too, struggles with representing African American speech and has had to visit places where others speak in the vernacular to better articulate this speech in his own fiction.[20] He opens this letter by sharing that he doesn't feel he can identify with Spearmint as a black man. In particular, the character's hatred of Jews doesn't ring true because it implies, among other things, that, for African Americans, Jews exist on an entirely different plane from that of other white people—a criticism that echoes both Jones's and Baldwin's arguments about Jewish whiteness. McPherson also criticizes the virulence of Spearmint's self-hatred and distaste for other African Americans, which, he writes, seems far deeper than his dislike for white characters. Rather than a realistic or developed character, Spearmint, in McPherson's view, is something of a fool who speaks to and of white people's anxieties about black men. Moreover, McPherson takes issue with the portrayal of Spearmint's romantic life. As we will see, the character's relationship with Irene, a Jewish woman, and Lesser's competition with him for her attention, is at the center of *The Tenants*. McPherson suggests that the relationship between Irene and Spearmint seems less like a true love affair than another way for the character—and, by extension, Malamud—to speak about Jewishness in the novel.

These criticisms, which support the idea that McPherson saw Willie Spearmint as a mouthpiece for Malamud's worries about blacks and Jews, are complicated by the central topic of the correspondence: how to accurately render black speech. According to McPherson, the voices of the black characters in *The Tenants* often resemble Jewish voices. For instance, when discussing a scene in which Spearmint and Lesser participate in a game of the dozens, he mentions hearing a Jewish cadence in Spearmint's speech and wonders if this was purposeful.[21] He discerns Jewish language and cadences in Spearmint's argument that Lesser can't comprehend anything about black experience as well as in an important conversation about Irene. To McPherson, when Spearmint isn't sounding Jewish, he is sometimes sounding like Frank Alpine, the non-Jewish foil (and convert) in Malamud's earlier novel, *The Assistant*.

By looking more closely at these assertions, we can frame the tensions at the heart of *The Tenants* and comprehend why it is so thematically and formally distinct from Malamud's previous work and why in this situation the author seemed so desperate to speak in the voice of another. Malamud's attempts to articulate African American difference end up sounding like Jewish difference. This conflation of black and Jew is not incidental and suggests that Malamud, like a number of other authors I will discuss in this book, was engaged in a project of strategic reracialization. Rather than accepting the slow fade into whiteness that many critics saw as the Jewish fate in postwar America, he appropriated the otherness of African American experience by putting Jewish concerns into his African American characters' mouths.

The problem of appropriation that haunted Malamud in his correspondence with McPherson resurfaced in his conversations about *The Tenants* as well as in the novel itself. Anticipating criticisms, he directly addressed his portrayal of Spearmint in an interview for the *New York Times:* "If I'm not afraid to invent God in my fiction—or kinds of Jews I've never met—I don't see why I shouldn't invent Willie Spearmint. Willie is singular." Lesser, Malamud's alter ego in *The Tenants*, expresses similar hubris in his relationship to African American identity. He attempts to access Spearmint's psyche in a manner that takes for granted the ability of a Jewish writer to comprehend and portray African American experience, whether "singular" or universal (Malamud, "For Malamud, It's Story"). Throughout *The Tenants*, such battle for "control of discourse" is figured through the conflict between black and white writing, and Lesser's repeated attempts to speak *to* and speak *for* "the black," as he often calls Spearmint (Sundquist 383).

The Tenants opens with two epigraphs that dramatize this conflict as well as the problems attendant to the white Jewish writer who is trying to access African American experience.[22] At the same time, they suggest the relation to the western canon that Lesser, as Malamud's mouthpiece, will adopt throughout the novel. The first epigraph—"Alive and with his eyes open he calls us his murderers"—comes from Antiphon's *Tetralogies* and comments directly on Willie Spearmint's increasingly vociferous accusations against Lesser and other white characters while signaling Malamud/Lesser's clear engagement with the classical tradition that, as I discuss in chapter 4, is common for canonical Jewish American authors. The second epigraph—"I got to make it, I got to find the end"—from the famous Bessie Smith tune "Long Road" has even greater importance in the novel's universe. Even as its black vernacular ventriloquizes Spearmint, the line evokes empathy for Lesser's inability to discover a proper conclusion to his novel *The Promised End* as well as Malamud's own search for an appropriate end to *The Tenants*. (The novel, as we'll see, has multiple, forking endings.) Smith's paradigmatic blues refrain also emphasizes the author's ambivalent relationship to blackness and American black popular culture. By pairing Antiphon and Smith as entryways into the novel, Malamud asks whether white or black art, elite or popular art, offers the appropriate epigraph for the decline of black-Jewish relations in America. The pairing also introduces the difference between orality and literacy, speech and writing, that Malamud uses to draw a contrast between African Americans and Jews.

Mark McGurl writes, "if the figure of the Native American has been made to personify the aesthetic value of silence in U.S. literary history, then the African American has been the patron saint of voice, and first person has been his preferred narrative mode. The case for first person narration as the natural vehicle for this voice comes into focus when one considers the slave narrative" (259–260). If the slave narrative is one archetype of the African American first person, the blues song is another. Both, alongside the contemporary African American autobiographical work of writers such as Baldwin, Wright, Malcolm X, and Cleaver, who were influenced by the form of the slave narrative, become foils for Lesser in *The Tenants*. Yet the Smith epigraph also foreshadows a pivotal early scene of racial antagonism in the novel. Having entered the white writer's apartment for the first time, Spearmint "inspect[s] Lesser's hi-fi, then slowly shuffle[s] through a stack of records, reading aloud titles and artists, mocking some of the names he couldn't pronounce. A Bessie Smith surprise[s] him" (36). Taken aback, he challenges Lesser:

> "What's this girl to you?"
> "She's real, she talks to me."
> "Talking ain't telling."
> Lesser wouldn't argue.
> "Are you an expert of black experience?" Willie slyly asked.
> "I am an expert of writing."
> "I hate all that shit when whites tell you about black." (36)

Spearmint begins by asking "What's this girl to you?" anticipating the racially inflected competition to possess a female erotic object that governs the second half of the novel while foregrounding the difficulty of interpreting or knowing the African American other who dominates the book. His aggressive question about Lesser's relationship to Smith initiates a contest of expertise, one that dramatizes not only the thorny question of "who can speak for the Negro?" but also the related query of "who can hear the Negro?"[23] For as Spearmint sees it, there is a distinction between "talking" and "telling" that the Jewish writer cannot discern (36). Although he hears Smith's words and feels that "she's real, she talks to me," Lesser doesn't possess what Spearmint later calls the proper "feelin chemistry" to receive the "black experience" that her songs transmit (36, 74). By placing this scene around the "hi-fi" and Lesser's record collection, Malamud emphasizes the ventriloquial quality of the white writer's engagement with black experience (36). Lesser depends on the technological transmission of Smith's disembodied voice because, according to Spearmint, he lacks the proper internal equipment to hear the African American woman.[24]

Likewise, Lesser's access to Spearmint's inner life comes through the African American writer's prose but is filtered and amplified through Lesser's own past experiences as a Jewish child in a black neighborhood.[25] Not coincidentally, when Spearmint challenges his capacity to hear Smith's song and what it is "telling" him, Lesser introduces his own favored discourse of authenticity: writing. Asked snidely if he is "an expert of black experience" after his exposure to Smith, Lesser trumpets his expertise in the art of writing, a move that he repeats throughout Malamud's novel and that occasions Spearmint's angry rejoinder that he "hates when whites tell you about black"—that is, absorb black expressions of self into the fabric of an academic disquisition (36).

In *The Tenants*, the conflict between orality and writing—one of the oppositions characteristically used to distinguish between folk and high art—is often transformed into a contest over the ethics of ventriloquism. For instance, midway through the novel, Malamud dramatizes what he imagines as the clash between the immediacy of the spoken word and the artistry of the written: he pits Spearmint, the categorical "black" and categorical black artist, against the Jewish protagonist in a verbal contest in which Lesser tries, and fails, to speak "black." Yet the game, known as the dozens, is one in which he can never hope to triumph. A traditional African American performance of wordplay for wordplay's sake, the game is reputed to have originated in plantation slave quarters and to have reached fruition in the contemporary American hip hop scene.

In the novel, Bill Spear, as he now calls himself, invites the flattered Lesser to a party in Harlem. After recognizing that the bespectacled Jewish writer has transgressed against racial mores by having sex with Mary, one of the African American women at the gathering, Spear asks Lesser to engage in a contest of words:

> "Chum," he said, tapping his stubby finger against Lesser's noisy chest, "we have a game we got we call the dozens. Like the brothers play it no ofay has that gift or the wit, and also since whitey ain't worth but half a black I'm gon play you the half-dozens. Now it's a game of nothin but naked words. I'm gon do mine on you and you do yours on me, and the one who bleeds, or flips, or cries mama, he's the loser and we shit on him. Do you dig?"
>
> "If you gon fuck black you gon face black," said the light-skinned woman....
>
> "If you have to do this, why don't you write it? I thought you were a writer." Lesser's voice was hoarse, his underpants damp.
>
> "Don't tell me what to write, chum," Bill said, raising his head haughtily. "I don't need no bleached-out Charlie to tell *me* what to write." (131)

In this extended scene of racial antagonism, Malamud dramatizes the ventriloquism that recurs throughout his dystopian narrative. Notably, he emphasizes that the contest between Spearmint and Lesser is a dispute over value: how valuable each man is (is Lesser really worth only "half-dozens" because he is white?), how valuable each man is as a writer, and who exactly—the Jewish or the black writer—should get to determine the criteria for evaluating the worth of a work of art (131). At a remove from his comfortably static state in a ramshackle tenement downtown, Lesser is coerced into participating in a Harlem game in which value is determined by another. Outside the realm of "the house of fiction" where he dwells, Lesser is truly the lesser man, "his underpants damp" and his mouth incapable of emitting the "naked words" necessary to make his opponent be the "one who bleeds, or flips, or cries mama" (Kellman 166; Malamud 131).

Throughout the novel, Lesser associates aural/oral violence, such as the dozens, with the violence he fears will come at the hands of the purportedly more embodied African Americans he encounters as well as with his existential anxieties about writing and tenancy. From the vitriolic accusations about "Yids" and "Goldbergs" that start to drip from Spearmint's mouth, to the pleas for mercy that landlord Levenspiel yowls outside the writer's barred door, to the uncanny and agentless utterances of the empty building in which Lesser lives as the last tenant, words and sounds disrupt his barren artist's den. Even the wind echoing through the tenement house becomes frightening. As Malamud writes, "he feared for the house and what was worse sometimes he feared the house. The flat, as Lesser listened, resounded of mournful winds, Aeolus' bag. Why do wailing winds, nothing human, give off human sounds?" (25).[26] As Spearmint increasingly encroaches upon his life, Lesser begins to fear the ways in which even buildings can speak.

This fear of sound increases as Spearmint begins to engage Lesser in verbal war. Lesser recoils from the brutal and scatological associations in his antagonist's assertion that "I'm gon do mine on you and you do yours on me," portents of the increasing ferocity of their battle of words. He responds to the challenge by again invoking the realm over which he possesses a modicum of control: writing. By asking, "If you have to do this, why don't you write it?" Lesser not only attempts to deflect Spearmint and his friends from the issue at hand (Lesser's attempt to "fuck black" by seducing Mary) but also plays at asserting the cultural dominance of writing over speech, the medium of the dozens (131).

Spearmint's angry response—"I don't need no bleached-out Charlie to tell *me* what to write"—is telling on a number of levels. Willie recognizes that Lesser fears the dozens precisely because it is a game, contra writing, in which he cannot hope to speak "black" or speak for blacks. This realization recapitulates Malamud's own fears about his inability to write in a black voice. As Budick relates, one inspiration for Malamud's novel was the nasty falling out between Howe and Ellison over precisely these questions of Jewish blackface. As we saw, these were also the central issues in Malamud's correspondence with McPherson. At the same time, the game marks the moment when Spearmint first clearly becomes a ventriloquist's dummy for the concerns of both Lesser and Malamud by way of Lesser. By calling the Jewish writer a "bleached-out Charlie"—this writer who has spent the early scenes of the novel reaching out to Spearmint as a way of carving out his difference from the rest of white society—Spearmint ventriloquizes Lesser's fear that he has become immutably white, the "ofay" against whom the blacks at the party define themselves (131).[27] As the scene progresses, Lesser becomes, because of his Jewishness and its association with ownership of property and discourse, more monstrous and more responsible for black oppression than are the faceless whites whom the Harlemites purport to hate. The truth is just what he had feared.

Spearmint's refusal to be told how and what to write is yet another allusion to Jones's and the Black Arts movement's radical stand against the conventions of white art and Jewish liberal spokesmanship. Ironically, however, when he refuses to be told what to write, Spearmint, like Lesser, moves from being a "singular" individual to an allegorical figure, the black writer who speaks aloud the myriad fears that haunt Lesser from the first pages of *The Tenants* (Malamud, "For Malamud, It's Story"). He mouths Lesser's fear that there can be no place for a Jewish writer intent on rendering the universal human in an era that embraces racial difference. He articulates the Jewish writer's worries about the waning of the Jew as a figure for universal suffering and thus the Jewish writer as a figure with privileged access to representing humanity's suffering. Most significantly, he makes Lesser wonder what would happen if the world of the dozens were to triumph over the sphere of high art that he espouses throughout *The Tenants*. Would Lesser become as obsolete as the building in which he dwells? Would there be any space in which he could live? How could he compete in a "game of nothin but naked words," a nakedness that is essential to Spearmint's racial and literary project, in contrast to the diffuse, watery cast of Lesser's own agenda (36)?[28] How could Lesser cope with the unadorned expression of the Black Arts movement—where value is measured by the link between art and life, the intimacy of the relationship between writing and lived experience—when he writes in the impersonal argot of universal humanism?

These anxieties fuel many of the characters' battles over the nature of art. When Spearmint shows Lesser the manuscript for his work, *Black Writer*, an autobiographical account of his life thus far, Lesser criticizes the way in which Spearmint's urgent desire to express himself and the particularity of his voice have forced him to compromise the formal aspects of his writing and hence its importance as a work of art. Spearmint grows frustrated and begins to sag under the idea that he will have to revise what he's already written. Lesser tries to comfort him by saying, "I know how you feel, I put myself in your place" (74). Blanching at this sympathetic identification, Spearmint replies:

> No ofay motherfucker can put himself in *my* place. This is a *black* book we talkin about that you don't understand at all. White fiction ain't the same as *black*. It *can't* be. . . . Black ain't white and never can be. It is once and for only black. It ain't universal if that's what you are hintin up to. What I feel you feel different. You can't write about black because you don't have the least idea what we are or how we feel. Our feelin chemistry is different than yours. (74)

Here, Spearmint expresses his belief in the somatic and affective differences between blacks and whites, the fundamental disjuncture between black and white writing and the audiences whom they might address. Lesser responds by asserting that "if the experience is about being human and moves me then you've made it my experience. . . . You can deny universality, Willie, but you can't abolish it" (74, 75).[29]

After engaging in further argument about the relationship of form to the authorial self, Spearmint accepts some of Lesser's suggestions about *Black Writer*, but with an extended caveat:

> What I say about revising some of my ideas don't mean I'm changing how I feel on black writing in comparison to white. Art is O.K. when it helps you to say what you got to, but I don't want to turn into a halfass white writer or an ass-kissing Negro who imitates ofays because he is ashamed or afraid to be black. I write black because I am black and what I got to say means something different to black people than it does to whites, if you dig. We *think* different than you do, Lesser. We *do* and *are*, and we *write* different. If some white prick tears a piece of black skin off your ass every day, when somebody says "Sit down," it's gonna mean two different things to me and you, and that's why black fiction *has got* to be different than white. The words make it different because the experience does. (82)

Spearmint's distinction between white and black art focuses not only on the perils of mimicry for the black author who "imitates ofays because he is ashamed or afraid to be black" but also on the essential differences between black and white experiences. As he says, "we *do* and *are*, and we *write* different," a methodology that places doing black and being black before writing black (82). His insistence on the embodied difference between blacks and whites and the hierarchy of lived experience above writing is discomfiting. Spearmint's belief that an indissoluble link exists between experience and writing pokes holes in Lesser's reverence for the impersonal muse of art while emphasizing, yet again, the impossibility of a white writer's accessing black experience. Strikingly, Spearmint's adoption of the rhetoric of difference undermines the white writer's notion of the universal nature of art and the artist. Yet in seeming contradiction, it also undermines the universality of the Jewish writer as a privileged spokesman for and representative of suffering—the one difference with which Lesser, this paragon of universality, feels comfortable.

When Spearmint and Lesser smoke pot together at a party and engage in a hazy disquisition on art, we immediately understand that the novel's dramatic contest is not so much between two wills as between two ideas of art. In response to Spearmint's assertion that he's "gon win the fuckn Noble Prize . . . a million bucks of cash" for the book he's writing, Lesser admonishes the prize- and money-driven writer to "think of this sacred cathedral we're in, Willie, with lilting bonging iron bell. I mean this flower-massed, rose-clustered, floating island. I guess what I mean is what about art?" (49, 50). When Spearmint responds by denigrating this exalted vision of the appropriate space for art, going so far as to call art a "dirty word," Lesser responds, "Art is the glory and only a shmuck thinks otherwise" (50). Spearmint answers with one of the first lengthy anti-Semitic diatribes of the book, spoken in a stereotypical black vernacular that is one of Malamud's most uncomfortable attempts at racial mimicry.

> Lesser, don't bug me with that Jewword. Don't work your roots on me. I know what you're talking about, don't think I don't. I know you tryin to steal my manhood. I don't go for that circumcise shmuck stuff. The Jews got to keep us bloods stayin weak so you can take everything for yourself. Jewgirls are the best whores and are tryin to cut the bloods down by makin us go get circumcise, and the Jewdoctors do the job because they are afraid if they don't we gon take over the whole goddamn country and wipe you out. . . . None of that crap on me, Lesser, you Jewbastard, we tired of you fuckn us over. (50–51)

Lesser's only response to this provocation emphasizes his belief that racial particularism and high art are mutually exclusive: "If you're an artist you can't be a nigger, Willie" (51).

Throughout *The Tenants*, Lesser cleaves to the possibilities of a universal aesthetic capable of expressing the human condition, but here Spearmint insists that the white writer take account of the way in which his own language is a rebuke to the very universalism he espouses. By admonishing Lesser not to "work your roots" by speaking a "Jewword," he aggressively argues for the tenet that he spouts throughout the novel: the self, with all its markers of racial or ethnic difference, is unavoidably linked to and disseminated by language. The era's complex racial politics of Jewish American identity come to the fore during this scene. Spearmint's hatred of Jews offends Lesser because it conflates Jewishness with whiteness, thus effacing Jewish difference and the long history of Jewish cultural and racial marginality, but also because it dissolves the universal literary and civic ideals that he espouses into a fragmentary discourse of difference and racial separatism. In other words, Spearmint makes Lesser more white, more Jewish, and less liminal. The mere use of the word *shmuck* and its attachment to "art is glory," the sentiment with which Lesser bludgeons the black writer throughout The

Tenants, enrages Spearmint. He asserts that Jews are trying to "keep us bloods stayin weak so [they] can take everything." Spearmint's use of this stereotypical worry—that Jews gain power by exploiting those lower than themselves on America's racial food chain—echoes Jones's assertions about "jew-owners" and "Liberal Spokesmen" in "Black Art" but also acknowledges that Lesser's Jewishness functions as a rhetorical position, one marked in this scene through his use of *shmuck* to degrade Spearmint for his lack of fealty to high art (50).

If Lesser often envisions himself as the "Robinson Crusoe" of his lonely island tenancy, Spearmint possesses and requires no literary prototype for his life as a tenant in the building they share (18). Instead, as becomes increasingly obvious and increasingly contentious, he places his life *before* his art, making confession the precondition for his fiction in a manner that horrifies the elder author. Spearmint's work blurs the line between fiction and autobiography as well as between author and text. In contrast to the indeterminacy of Lesser's deferred novel, *The Promised End*, Spearmint's project, *Black Writer*, flows from his pen because, as Lesser would have it, the novel requires no artistry to compose. Its selling point is its immediacy, the purportedly transparent relationship between the life of the author and the life of the text.

Spearmint's idea of writing collides with Lesser's belief that books should act as veils beneath which their authors might conceal their distinguishing marks. This notion allows Lesser to hide not only from his own painful past but also from the intimacy that a more personal narrative might portend. He has no recourse for addressing the instability of his position in relation to the newly powerful black writing and black writer (*Black Writer*) except to try for the posterity he imagines to be a reward for writing a "masterpiece" rooted in knowledge of the western canon and appropriate for inclusion within its ranks (21). Lesser's conception of writing is clearly a New Critical one, analogous to T. S. Eliot's "impersonal theory" of poetry in his essay "Tradition and the Individual Talent." Like Eliot, who sees submission to the past and to "the mind of Europe" as a precondition for literary production, Lesser embraces the idea that he will find his objective correlative only in "continual surrender of himself" to the higher power of western literary tradition and the universal voice with which it will supply him (Eliot 6). Spearmint, on the other hand, possesses the authority to speak in his own voice—a voice dictated by his life and cobbled together from a history of displacement from south to north and from prison to freedom.

Most of the action in *The Tenants* takes place in a doubly circumscribed space: the space of the empty tenement and the space of literature. That double space is emblematized by the novel within a novel that Lesser is writing, which increasingly becomes conflated with *The Tenants* itself. Often it is difficult to tell if the interaction between Spearmint and Lesser is taking place within Malamud's novel or Lesser's unfinished *The Promised End*. With this proto-postmodern move, *The Tenants* becomes an argument about the space of the novel and whether the black or the Jewish writer possesses more of a right to speak through it.³⁰ Gradually, Spearmint's fears that Lesser will try to speak for him are superseded by Lesser's anxieties about his increasing inability to speak for himself in any meaningful way. Careworn, he watches with envy as Spearmint fuses himself with his fiction-laced memoir, even going so far as to say, "I am art. Willie Spearmint, *black man*. My form is myself" (75). While Spearmint's novel explores the seemingly limitless landscapes of black fiction, Lesser's novel within a novel (and Malamud's with it) dissolves into formlessness and multiple forking paths, which are represented by a number of alternative endings, each marked with the words "The End."

Malamud also comments on this struggle by forcing the bodies of each of these characters to stand in for a literary corpus: the bodies of disparate and mutually exclusive American literary genealogies, black and Jewish. Which voice should dominate the emerging canon of late twentieth-century American literature? What theory and practice of literature should hold sway in the allegorical house of fiction where the men reside? Whose concept of identity and writing should be cherished and disseminated via the novel? To Malamud, the paradigmatically Jewish position clearly ought to hold sway, moving gracefully between "speaking white" and "speaking black" while avoiding altogether the question of what it means to "speak Jewish."³¹

Eventually, Lesser fears that not just his house but his body is haunted, that this sense of possession makes it impossible to speak for himself. In Jewish folklore, the dybbuk is a homunculus, a creature who takes up residence inside a host and speaks through his mouth. Lesser uses this uncanny figure as a model for his relationship with Spearmint, positing the black writer as a parasite in a manner that inverts the conventional anti-Semitic trope of Jew as parasite. Spearmint's colonization of his body, like the spectral inhabitation of the broken-down house, complicates the idea of Jewish ventriloquism. Here, he comes to speak through Lesser and eventually to take over his body. As the novel progresses, Lesser's corporeal desires become increasingly akin to those of the more carnal Spearmint.³² Notably, the desire for sex, which the Jewish writer once thought he had vanquished, returns and transforms into a powerful urge for miscegenation, the intermingling of races, that mirrors Spearmint's own recurring thirst for a "white bitch" (35). As I will discuss in chapter 2, Malamud was not alone in depicting this racialized desire for the other; fantasies of interracial romance became increasingly important for a number of Jewish American writers after *Loving v. Virginia* decriminalized interracial marriage. This theme shapes the second half of *The Tenants*. Beginning with his desire to seduce Spearmint's friend Mary to his arousal at the thought of stealing his antagonist's white Jewish lover, Irene (whom he believes has begun to look and smell black), Lesser is overcome by his longing for interracial sexual congress. By the end of the novel, this urge even comes to dominate the form of the novel itself. One of the alternative endings of *The Tenants/The Promised End* (by this point it is unclear which one we are reading) is an imagined double marriage ceremony joining Lesser and Mary and Irene and Spearmint into perfect unions of black and white.

Such fantasies appear elsewhere in Malamud's oeuvre. Long before he published the controversial paranoid racial fantasy of *The Tenants*, he had written a number of texts addressing what he imagined to be the privileged relationship between enlightened Jewish liberals and disenfranchised blacks. For instance, "Black Is My Favorite Color" (1963) and "The Angel Levine" (1958) explicitly engage with the idea that Jews (and, by extension, Jewish writers) are in a unique position to meld with and speak for the suffering of urban blacks because of their own history of oppression and ghetto life. "Black Is My Favorite Color" tells the story of one of Malamud's prototypical schlemiels and his failed attempts to catch the attention of a black woman. Here, as in *The Tenants*, the author manifests an interest in racial mixing through sexual encounter. "Black Is My Favorite Color" anticipates the frustrating impossibility of true racial exchange depicted in *The Tenants*, notably through its portrayal of the problems attendant to interracial eros but also through its insistence on the importance of affective alliances to the relationships between blacks and Jews.

In *The Tenants*, the desire for and impossibility of true congress with the other become less about black-Jewish relations than about the internecine politics of the American Jewish self. Over the course of the novel, it becomes clear that Lesser's tortured relationship with Willie, and thus with black America, is trumped by only one thing: his tortured relationship with himself. *The Tenants* acts as a mouthpiece for Lesser's and Malamud-via-Lesser's qualms about Jewish identity and intra- rather than intergroup relations. Throughout, as McPherson has averred, Malamud talks Jewish even when he means to talk black. As the book advances, Lesser reaches the limits of his sympathy and skills in representation, not just with Spearmint but also with the paradigmatic Jewish slumlord, Levenspiel, and Spearmint's Jewish girlfriend, Irene. Both become caricatured others against whom Lesser negotiates his ever-waning self.

From the opening pages, Levenspiel pursues Lesser, intruding into the atemporal fictive sphere of his life, knocking on his door with discomfiting reminders of Jewish daughters who are pregnant out of wedlock, the burdens of being a slumlord, and the need to make money to pay his monthly rent. Yet Lesser's own anxieties about Jewish identity begin to be fully expressed in his relationship with the ambiguously white Irene. There is an immediate, seemingly racialized, recognition between the two characters, one that recalls Spearmint's claims about the essential difference between blacks and whites, particularly blacks and Jews. When Irene enters Lesser's apartment for the first time, he is haunted by a sense of having known her before: "Now and then he glanced at Irene sitting by the window, sometimes blankly, as if trying to remember something he had forgotten. Or heard voices?" (43). The voices he hears, Malamud makes clear, increasingly undermine his attempts to efface his own Jewish difference and the particularities of his Brooklyn childhood, so like Irene's own. Like Proust's madeleine, Irene catalyzes the willfully impersonal writer's flight into memory. Descriptions always center on her dyed platinum-blond hair, emblem of Lesser's lust for Spearmint's obscenely white woman and of his increasing interest in seeing her metamorphose back into Iris Belinsky, the intellectual Jewish girl she once was, by allowing her black roots to take over her white hair—a subtle invocation of her indeterminate racial status. An actress, she claims that performing has given her a means of running from her bourgeois Jewish past. Her theatrical pitch, her ability to "speak black," seduces Lesser away from his literary dreams and brings him into increasingly violent conflict with Spearmint.[33]

Though Irene is seductive because she is effectively black, Malamud makes it clear that she is immutably Jewish as well. When Lesser first meets her without Spearmint present, he calls out, "Shalom," the traditional Hebrew greeting (139). She is incensed at this interpellation of herself into Jewishness:

> She wants to know why he had said shalom that day, meeting her outside the museum.
> "I meant don't be a stranger."
> "Be white? Be Jewish."
> "Be close is better."
> . . .
> "Are you in love with me because I'm Willie's Jewish white girl?" (139)

In response, Lesser claims that he is only invoking an intimacy with her, a desire to keep her "close." Although she senses that this desire for intimacy and "love" is inspired by her being "Willie's Jewish white girl," she is clearly powerless to resist the pull of closeness with another Jew (139).[34]

Many critics have downplayed Irene's importance in the novel, given that she takes up less real estate than Spearmint does. However, Malamud's biographer, Philip Davis, suggests that the author wrote *The Tenants* in part to avoid working on what would become the novel *Dubin's Lives*, which narrated the failed love affair between an older man and a younger woman who bear some resemblance to Lesser and Irene. Malamud put off writing that novel because, like Dubin and Lesser, he had conducted a doomed affair with a young woman and feared writing a "confessional" (722). Moreover, the relationship between Irene and Lesser, even more than the one between Lesser and Spearmint, marks the author's ambivalence about the period's Jewish racialization. If Lesser is the "white" Jew in the text, Irene is the "black." Her willed reracialization stands in for the otherness that Lesser has lost. In addition, like the women writers I will discuss in chapter 2, she reflects the connections between women and people of color during the dawning era of identity politics and strategic essentialism, what Gayatri Spivak has called, in regard to a related discourse, "a strategic use of positivist essentialism in a scrupulously visible political interest" ("Deconstructing Historiography" 205).³⁵

Malamud's most famous story, "The Jewbird," also deals with questions of difference and the difficulty of relating to the other (prototypical Malamudian concerns) but does so entirely from the point of view of intragroup relations.³⁶ In it, he first displays his interest in how the relationship between Jews and other others might act as an allegory for relations among Jews themselves as well as how the art of mimicry might play into racial identity formation. "The Jewbird" tells the story of a tenement-dwelling Jewish nuclear family in New York City, the archetypically named Cohens. Outside the Cohens' window wanders a decrepit bird named Schwartz, which means "black" in Yiddish. Often likened to Poe's raven, Schwartz is a character straight out of Jewish vaudeville, performing a caricature of broken-down Jewishness and speaking in the familiar but exaggerated tones of the shtetl. He enters the Cohens' lives in hopes of finding sympathetic Jewish ears that will listen to him whimper about the misdeeds of those whom he calls, using the Yiddish pronunciation, the "anti-semeets." According to Schwartz, the "anti-semeets" are everywhere, pursuing a poor Jewish fowl at every turn (144).

The family is alternately drawn to and repulsed by the Wandering Jew figure's singsong performances of Jewish victimhood. As blithe American Jews who watched Hitler's decimation of European Jewry from afar, they are all too familiar with victimhood and feel all too responsible. In the meantime, this Jewish bird who has washed up onto American shores grows more desperate for care and protection from the imagined ills of the neighborhood's local "anti-semeets." As Schwartz becomes an uncanny reminder of their Jewish past, the family cannot resist pushing him out of their home and back to his wandering. In Malamud's portrayal, the black—or racialized Jewish—bird mocks the Cohens' attempts to assimilate into American culture.

As many critics, most strikingly Robert Alter, have argued, "The Jew-Bird" is a prototypical Malamud story because Jewishness was, for the author, the most mobile of metaphors. From *The Assistant* to *The Magic Barrel*, the Jews in his works allowed him to access a universal trope that exalts the suffering individual and proclaims the possibility that he or she can stand in for all of suffering humanity. Ruth Wisse goes so far as to excise Malamud from her vast work, *The Modern Jewish Canon*, because his interest in the Jew as a suffering and redemptive figure smacks of Christian rather than Jewish symbolism. However, Malamud says much about Jewishness and the Jewish writer in America through both the accusatory Yiddishisms of the uncanny Schwartz, the blackbird, and the dialect-spewing caricature of Willie Spearmint, the black writer.

The use of "black" characters, such as the *schwartze* Jewbird, who can speak to and of Jewishness, is central to Malamud's exploration of the often-vexed connection between Jewish identity and literary voice. As Richard Aczel argues in "Throwing Voices," such ventriloquism is often used in literature to dramatize the complex relationship between voice and the identity of any number of people. Was the increasing importance of blacks in the Jewish imaginary solely about the growth of black radicalism? Or did the black presence indicate a fear that the importance of the Jewish literary artist as a spokesperson for humanity's suffering was on the wane? Why was Malamud so intent on articulating concerns about the waning of both Jewish racial identity and Jewish literary identity through the demise of the black-Jewish alliance? To him, with the decline of the particularity of Jewish identity in America came the decline of a particularly Jewish literary voice in America. There can be little future for the universalist Jewish writer who no longer purports to be able to represent the other.

The Wandering Jew and the Canon

From the Romantic poets' paeans to the Wandering Jew to Richard Wagner's anti-Semitic diatribe about the Jewish lack of *genius loci*, the western literary imagination has long fastened upon the impermanence of the Jew as a metaphor for the ontological instability of modernity.[37] In postwar American literature, however, the Jewish artist has assumed this mantle, exploring the transience at the heart of the diasporic condition with unparalleled fervor. *The Tenants*, composed at the height of debates about the uncertain role for Jews in an America increasingly defined by racial difference, writes the categorical Wandering Jew into a condition of spatial tenancy and existential hand wringing. In Malamud's depiction, Jewish writers and intellectuals in America—here embodied by a writer slumming it in a Manhattan tenement—are standing on quicksand. Particularly, he explores the waning ability of the Jewish artist to speak for other others in an era in which Jewish otherness is contested and the universality of art is increasingly questioned.[38]

The links that Linda Alcoff traces between the problem of speaking for others and the problem of speaking about others (see the introduction) become painfully clear in *The Tenants*. Lesser finds himself increasingly unable to imagine speaking about the other at all, a problem that makes writing an ever-increasing, ever-compelling hell. Formal questions about the nature of representation are inextricably woven into visceral questions about representation and ventriloquism. Most of the conflicts between Spearming and Lesser arise from Spearmint's sense that Lesser is trying to speak for him or enforce his literary standards upon him, while Lesser increasingly comes to feel that his inability to speak for Spearmint manifests an underlying inability to speak for himself.

The disappearance of the empathic imperative in literature is particularly worrisome for Malamud because, as Cynthia Ozick points out in her polemical "Literary Blacks and Jews" (1973), representing "the anguish of the other" is central to his literary project (230, 92). This desire also connects the author to a larger and particularly Jewish preoccupation, she avers: a sympathetic identification with what Arendt would have called the "oppressed and underprivileged" (46). Malamud's early work reveals an idea that is "almost always taken for granted by Jews": "that Jews have always known hard times, and are therefore naturally sympathetic to others who are having, or once had, hard times" (Ozick 93). By contrast, America in the late 1960s was a wake-up call for Jews such as Malamud, whose early work revolved around fantasies of utopian racial sympathy. According to Ozick, "what has surprised some Jews, perhaps many, is that this Jewish assumption—this quiet tenet, to use a firmer word, that wounds recognize wounds—is not only *not* taken for granted by everyone else, especially by blacks, but is given no credibility whatever. Worse, to articulate the assumption is to earn the accusation of impudence" (93).[39] In *The Tenants*, Malamud is at his most impudent and his most impotent.

As Edmund Spevack notes, the conflict between Jewish and African American writers in *The Tenants* inscribed this literary and social history onto black and white writer and prefigured many of the contests over literary value that would take place during the culture wars of the 1980s and 1990s (see chapter 4). Though written long before the heyday of multiculturalism, the novel anticipated its discourse and staged the debates between the movement's adherents and detractors. For Lesser, Spearmint's literary aspirations and his desire to own a piece of literary America arise from a desire to destroy the very canon that Lesser wishes to join and has arguably come to embody in postwar America.

Clearly, Malamud was deeply troubled by the challenges that Black Arts' proponents brought into the literary sphere during the post–civil rights era. His deep engagement in the discourse of universal humanism favored by the era's Jewish intellectuals was contested by the idea of immutable racial difference that Jones and other African American writers disseminated. Moreover, his fictions—from short stories such as "The Last Mohican" and "The Magic Barrel" to novels such as *The Assistant*—manifested a particular preoccupation with representing the self through the other, whether the other was rendered as a character embodying an atavistic, racialized Jewishness or as a racially "primitive" character such as Spearmint. With this fact in mind, Malamud, like many Jewish writers of the time, chafed at the idea that he could no longer write to or for African Americans. Further, like Lesser, he was uncomfortable facing the formal questions about representation introduced by the Black Arts movement. How could the Jewish writer embrace the aesthetic vision propagated by the Black Arts movement, in which the author's autobiography was a primary factor in determining what he could and could not speak about? Just at the moment that Jewish American writers were seeking to distance themselves from the autobiographies of their immigrant forebears, Black Arts proponents were calling for a return to confession as the basis for authentic narrative. In so doing, African American writers were beginning to carve out a uniquely racialized space in the territory of American literature from which to speak to the particularity of their experiences.

The questions of autobiography, agency, and voice in *The Tenants* had a historical corollary in the world that gave birth to it. When asked why he wrote the novel, which critics saw as a divergence from the peaceful, magical realist concoctions of his early career, Malamud listed the following motivations: "Jews and blacks, the period of the troubles in New York City, the teachers strike, the rise of black activism, the mix-up of cause and effect." Those "troubles," about which the author opts to "say a word" in his controversial novel, were the Ocean Hill–Brownsville crisis of 1968 (Stern 61). Only a year after the Newark and Watts race riots had divided middle-class opinion about the place of Black Power rhetoric in the American liberal ethos, the messy machinations of local politics offered New Yorkers an intimate version of the global conflict between black radicalism and the liberal imagination. In 1967, Mayor John Lindsay, in his endless quest to bring enlightenment to the darkest recesses of the outer boroughs, decreed that in Ocean Hill–Brownsville, a predominantly African American neighborhood of Brooklyn, the school board should be representative of the makeup of its community's citizens. After the area heeded Lindsay's call, the school board, in which African Americans were suddenly in the majority, began to fire a number of its unionized Jewish teachers to make the teaching staff at Ocean Hill–Brownsville schools similarly representative of the community's racial composition. The United Federation of Teachers, itself 90 percent white and predominantly Jewish, got involved. There were three citywide teachers' strikes in the fall of 1968, lasting a total of two months and affecting almost a million schoolchildren. Increasingly, the strikes became acrimonious, centering around mutual suspicion and accusations of racism and anti-Semitism. As Jerald Podair puts it, "perhaps more than any other single event in any other city, the Ocean Hill–Brownsville controversy encapsulated the angst and irony of our nation's race relations in the 1960s and 1970s" (206).

The conflict between the mostly African American school board and the mostly Jewish union was divisive for a number of reasons but largely because it divided the city strictly along color lines. It also drew together strange bedfellows among those opposing the African American school board's decision, setting traditional liberals and budding neoconservatives against proponents and practitioners of progressive New Left politics. According to Podair, "the crisis illustrated the historic power and attraction of 'whiteness' in city and national life for marginalized nonblack groups. For decades, New York's Jews had straddled the white and nonwhite worlds of the city, attracted by each. The result was a form of cosmopolitanism that contributed to New York's uniquely open atmosphere in the twentieth century" (209). Jews, for the first time, began to ally themselves with other "white" ethnics who lived in the outer boroughs rather than with the city's black population.

This realignment of ethnic interests reverberated through city politics for decades, dissolving the long-running political alliance between the city's Jews, African Americans, and white Protestants that had held sway since World War II (Podair). The sundering of political alliances over questions of representation—whether the predominantly black residents of Ocean Hill–Brownsville should have jurisdiction over the ethnic composition of their school system—affected writers and artists, particularly those who had relied on the universality of their work and its capacity to represent the triumphs and tragedies of all human beings.[40]

The idea that Ocean Hill–Brownsville made it impossible for Jews to ignore their "whiteness" helps us understand the resentment that seethes throughout Malamud's racial dystopia, which was written at the height of the school tensions. It is clear from the novel that the author was mourning the results of the Ocean Hill–Brownsville conflict and the rhetoric of black separatism from which it was born, primarily because those conflicts created loss among Jewish artists such as himself: loss of the strategic power of liminality, of being the almost-white in an America that alternately celebrated and demonized racial others, a power analogous to the one Arendt claims in her writing about desegregation. To Malamud, who grew up near Ocean Hill–Brownsville and was long ambivalent about his role as representative Jewish writer, the New York City school crisis, coupled with the "rise of black activism" and the Black Arts movement, provoked an uncomfortable realization (Stern 61). The assumption among so many Jewish writers that white liberals could speak for the concerns of African Americans would no longer go unquestioned. If "the raw power of Malamud's stories is based on a simple principle—that every moral impulse has its Nietzschean dark side, its streak of lust or the will to power, just as every self has its anti-self, a double or shadow that exposes its vulnerabilities and limitations," as Morris Dickstein suggests, then the alteration of art demanded by the growth of racial identity-based movements forces a crisis of representation for the Jewish author (172). This urgent, frustrated need to speak the self through the "anti-self" of the other is at the heart of *The Tenants* and at the heart of the era's Jewish American literary enterprise.

CHAPTER 2

The Perils of Loving in America

Jewish American Women Writing Race

Bernard Malamud was not the only Jewish American author (or Jewish American) intent on imagining the self through the other. As he did in his depiction of the Irene-Spearmint-Lesser love triangle (but with radically different stakes), Jewish women authors used romances between Jewish women and men of color as a way of imagining what an interracial Jewish identity and literary voice might look like. Although their works appeared after Malamud's, they often focused on the 1960s and the repercussions of interracial attraction in pre–*Loving v. Virginia* America; and they point to the importance of thinking about and through gender when addressing racial ventriloquism in Jewish American writing.

Throughout the 1960s and beyond, debates about Jewish interfaith and interracial romances left traces on wider conversations about race in America. That resonance is particularly evident in *Loving v. Virginia*, the landmark 1967 Supreme Court case that I mentioned in chapter 1. Mildred Jeter, a woman of African American and Native American heritage, and Richard Loving, a white man, had met in the state of Virginia but traveled to Washington, D.C., in 1958 to marry. Their aim was to evade Virginia's Racial Integrity Act of 1924, which prohibited marriage between people classified as "white" and those classified as "colored." But when the couple returned to their home in Virginia, local officials learned of their illegal marriage and cohabitation, and they were arrested. The Lovings sued the state, and nine years later, the case reached to the Supreme Court.

The brief submitted by the state of Virginia, which argued for maintaining the state's ban on interracial marriage, is a curious document. The lawyers who constructed it spend a number of pages arguing that the legislature rather than the judiciary should concern itself with the rightness of various laws and the scientific and sociological discourses that surround them. Despite this assertion, however, the lawyers proceeded to provide pages of evidence arguing for the continuing viability of anti-miscegenation statutes such as Virginia's, using the very scientific and sociological accounts they were arguing lay outside the purview of the court.[1]

In its decision, the liberal Warren court overturned state laws prohibiting interracial marriage. As a result, *Loving v. Virginia* is seen as a turning-point in civil rights history even as it manifests America's continuing embrace of the black-white binary system to decode the complexities of race. Although the case suggests that, in 1960s America, race was understood solely via the categories of white and non-white, *Loving* is not entirely a black and white matter. Not only did Asian Americans play a part in the case (the Japanese American Citizens' League filed a brief in support of the Lovings), but the work of rabbi and sociologist Albert I. Gordon and his beliefs about Jewish intermarriage also had a central, if largely unexamined, role.

Born in 1903, Gordon graduated from the Jewish Theological Seminary in New York and became a prominent conservative rabbi and proto-pundit, leading congregations in New York, Minneapolis, and eventually Newton, Massachusetts, and acting for a time as the executive director of the United Synagogues of America. He wrote a number of books about Jews in America, focusing on their move to the suburbs, their religious and cultural continuity, and particularly the repercussions of conversion and intermarriage in Jewish life. The relevance of his 1964 study, *Intermarriage—Interfaith, Interracial, Interethnic*, to the state of Virginia's case is startling and has received, to my knowledge, no critical attention. Although Gordon has been discussed in relation to the midcentury school of rabbi-sociologists who spoke for and about the Jewish community (notably in the work of Lila Corwin Berman) and has been mentioned, usually in a footnote, in reference to *Loving v. Virginia*, I have not been able to find any scholarship that focuses on his important role in the case or questions why the lawyers for Virginia made the work of a rabbi and his arguments about Jewishness so fundamental to their case for upholding Virginia's anti-miscegenation statute.

Extended quotations from *Intermarriage* take up multiple pages of the state's brief as well as a ten-page appendix and were a persistent presence in the state's oral arguments before the Court. The lawyers for Virginia contended that Gordon's book was central to their case because it "ha[d] been characterized as the 'definitive book on intermarriage'" (*Loving v. Virginia*, brief 47). Yet even though his work was certainly read and reviewed at the time it was published, I have found little evidence to support this hyperbolic claim. In fact, the book, despite its title, is not deeply concerned with intermarriage in all its incarnations. Instead, Gordon reads "interracial" and "interethnic" unions almost entirely through the lens of his overriding anxiety about the effects of interfaith marriages on the Jewish community—a fact that makes the book's role in *Loving v.*

Virginia all the more interesting and strange. Some reviewers at the time even complained about this focus, noting that while the first chapter of *Intermarriage* is devoted to a broad-ranging survey of college students' attitudes toward intermarriage of all kinds, much of the book is given over to relating Gordon's own rabbinical experiences with and admonitions against interfaith marriage.[2] Moreover, the state's description of the book is belied by many of the quotations the state lawyers chose to use in their case against miscegenation (47). Often, they mirror his own slippery argument, as in the second extended quotation offered in the brief:

> The argument that persons who oppose intermarriage—religious or racial—are per se "prejudiced," may be true of some persons; true, in degree, about others; and yet be completely untrue about still others. The desire to perpetuate one's own religion or to prevent its assimilation is understandable and reasonable. If it were necessary to "prove" that each of us is entitled to life only because we possess some demonstrably unique or special talent or gift of mind or body, our society would be decimated in short order. (48)

Although Gordon begins by admitting that some people who oppose "religious or racial" intermarriage may be prejudiced, he quickly focuses on "the desire to perpetuate one's own religion or to prevent its assimilation" (48). This shift from the racial to the religious (as well as the gradual conflation of the terms) appears throughout the quotations chosen by Virginia's lawyers and throughout the book as a whole. Gordon's use of the term *assimilation* to support his argument that not all critics of intermarriage are "prejudiced" marks his participation in the wider midcentury discourse of ethnicity, immigration, and assimilation that surrounded Jewish identity and suggests how deeply his views about interracial marriage were affected by his understanding of Jewishness in America.[3]

Although Gordon is portrayed throughout the state's case as an objective analyst, his argument is clearly predicated on his role as a rabbi rather than his training as a sociologist (which appears to have not been very strenuous). His anxieties about the problem of Jewish intermarriage during this period are not unique. In 1964, the same year that Gordon published *Intermarriage*, Thomas Morgan eulogized "the vanishing American Jew" in a cover story for *Look* magazine. The article quotes Rabbi Max Schenk's statement that the locus of Jewishness is not religion or culture but the Jewish "home"—a home that was gradually vanishing, thanks to the growing number of interfaith marriages in America. Schenk and Gordon were members of a group of American rabbis who, Lila Corwin Berman argues, "use[d] sociology as a purportedly unbiased vocabulary in which to clothe their prescriptions about how Jews should react to intermarriage" (34). What was exceptional about Gordon was the self-conscious link between religion and race he made in *Intermarriage* and the way in which this argument lent itself to *Loving v. Virginia*. The unusual emphasis suggests something about the changing vocabulary available for understanding Jewish identity during the early 1960s.

For Gordon, religion and race were not distinct, and his ideas in *Intermarriage* built on a sense of Jewishness as both a racial and religious identity that needed to be protected from dissolution, not just because of its importance to Jews but because of its larger importance in upholding a certain idea of America. His work—and its subsequent place in *Loving v. Virginia*—marks the significant role that race, particularly conversations about African American identity and integration in the early civil rights era, played in Jewish self-definition. This anxiety had a corollary in African American anxieties, both fictional and real, as we saw in *The Tenants*, when Spearmint becomes enraged after Lesser sleeps with an African American woman. As we'll see, anxieties about the dissolution of Jewish difference via intermarriage were often linked to worries about the repercussions of Jewish liberalism. Lila Corwin Berman relates that many postwar critics of intermarriage were concerned that Jews' "overwhelming support for integration and involvement in the civil rights movement were just as much to blame for the crisis as were Jews' marital decisions" (48).[4] Rabbis such as Gordon worried that impressionable young Jews saw intermarriage at the ultimate form of integration and therefore a positive development in the liberal search for a more equitable world. The valorization of marrying the other is part of what Paul Berman has identified "as an old and slightly peculiar Jewish custom of rebelling against Jewishness by identifying with the most marginal of all possible groups, so as to rebel and still not assimilate into the mainstream" (12). By highlighting the deleterious effects of interfaith, inter-ethnic, and interracial marriage on society in general and children in particular, *Intermarriage* creates explicit links among Jewish liberalism, faith in integration, rebelliousness, and the "vanishing of the American Jew."

Nonetheless, despite his worry about how Jews' interracial sympathy would affect Jewish racial continuity, Gordon was useful to Virginia's lawyers precisely because he couched his admonitions against intermarriage in the language of culture instead of race. The lawyers recognized that the Virginia code's designation of who was "white" and who was "colored" and its argument about the inherent danger of mixing them were built on a racialist and eugenicist discourse that had become increasingly contentious after World War II. As I discuss in chapter 3, the way in which the Holocaust came to shadow postwar discussions about race in America may have had something to do with the lawyers' choice of a Jewish-inflected text about intermarriage.[5]

Gordon believed that intermarriage was bad for America, not because one group was superior to the other but because intermarriages were less likely to be successful and produce happy children. The lawyers' adoption of this point of view suggests that the state of Virginia was interested in using sociology (purportedly less ideological than scientific racism) as the basis for their defense. Their oral arguments before the Court further emphasize that they were searching for a discourse that would uphold racial separatism but not alienate the justices. As Gordon's role in *Loving* suggests, the ambivalent valences of Jewishness shadowed postwar conversations about race in problematic yet suggestive ways. Jewishness as metaphor and lived experience was being used to try to understand how race would function in a postwar landscape.

By talking about Gordon's role in *Loving*, I don't mean to suggest that the rabbi would have supported the state of Virginia or the lawyers' use of his book. During a particularly telling moment of the oral arguments, a justice asked precisely that question and was told that Virginia's lawyers were not at all certain that Gordon would support their case before the Court, even if his data did. However, an examination of the unexplored role of Jewishness in *Loving v. Virginia* gives us a way of thinking past the monolithic narrative of black-Jewish relations that continues to hold sway in the United States while forcing us to recognize the mutually constitutive nature of postwar discourses of race and ethnicity that we have come to think of as separate. A rabbi was thinking through the intersections between interfaith and interracial marriage at the same time that the state of Virginia was using a Jewish-inflected discourse of intermarriage to uphold an anti-miscegenation law, and this parallel offers a telling statement on the continuing power of Jewishness as metaphor and lived experience in the figuration of difference in America at a time when some believed that Jews were vanishing into an undifferentiated whiteness.

Literary Intermarriage and the Intimacies of Jewish Racialization before and after *Loving*

Rabbi-sociologists such as Gordon were not the only ones interested in how debates about interfaith marriage were related to conversations about race. What is interesting about these other voices is that they were so different from Gordon's, both in tenor and content. The rabbi's preoccupation with interfaith and interracial marriages was mirrored in postwar Jewish American literature, particularly works written by women. In the decades after *Loving*, marriages between Jewish women and racially or ethnically marked others feature in a number of texts—from Lynn Sharon Schwartz's short story "The Melting Pot," which tells the story of a romance between a Jewish woman and an Indian American man; to Erika Jong's salacious *Fear of Flying*, which features Isadora and her long-suffering Asian American husband; to Lore Segal's novel *Her First American*, arguably based on Segal's own relationship with the well-known African American sociologist Horace Cayton, Jr.[6] And then there was Hettie Jones who, like Segal, wrote a work about interracial marriage from the perspective of a Jewish woman in love with an African American man and negotiates her Jewishness alongside her transgression against racial and legal mores. Both Segal's and Jones's books were published after the Court's decision (Segal's in 1985, Jones's in 1990), but both are based on their experiences as Jewish women in a pre–*Loving* America, a landscape defined as much by Rabbi Gordon's anxieties about marriage as it was by laws that sought to legislate those anxieties.

In a pamphlet on the Jewish American novel, first published in 1959 and later adapted into a chapter of his celebrated *Love and Death in the American Novel* (1960), Leslie Fiedler traces the role of exogamy in American fiction, particularly the novel. For instance, in Charles Brockden Brown's 1799 *Arthur Mervyn*, arguably America's first novel, the protagonist encounters otherness not through the figure of the Native American (a common scenario in early American fiction) but through a Jewish woman, Ascha Fielding, who is imagined as seductively foreign yet more capable of assimilation and representation than her male counterpart would be.[7] (Fiedler points out the echoes of Jessica and Shylock from Shakespeare's *The Merchant of Venice*.)[8] Brown's novel, a picaresque meditation on identity set during a yellow fever epidemic in Philadelphia at the end of the eighteenth century, concludes with Mervyn's marriage to Ascha.[9]

What happens when Jewish women writers transform themselves from objects to subjects of representation and become figures of whiteness in relation to other, more racially marked others? Moreover, how does the representational project of Jewish women authors who write about interracial marriage differ from that of authors such as Philip Roth, whose adamantly male work suggests that the pursuit of the *shiksa* (non-Jewish woman) is at the heart of the Jewish American imagination? What happens when narratives are about the pursuit of a racially marked *shaigitz* (non-Jewish man)? And what happens when this encounter doesn't help the Jewish woman shore up her whiteness so much as complicate and contaminate it? How do these writers challenge the canon of Jewish American fiction, and what do they suggest about the possibilities of an interracial or interethnic literary voice?

If we take Fiedler at his word that exogamy is the great theme of modern Jewish American (and American) fiction, we can see that this shift among contemporary Jewish American women writers—from representing interfaith to interracial marriage, despite its relative infrequency in American life—is significant. Werner Sollors argued that marriage is often the space in which anxieties about ethnicity and race are symbolized and worked through in American literature and culture. This contention is doubly true of Jewish women writers, whose representations of interracial marriage often invert or rewrite Jewish American and larger American gender scripts as they cross the color line. This is certainly the case in the work of Hettie Jones and Lore Segal, whose work straddles the divide between memoir and fiction as it takes up the questions of literary voice, racial ventriloquism, and identity in ways that trouble the boundaries that preoccupied Malamud in *The Tenants*.

How Cohen Became Jones

"Meet Hettie Cohen." So begins *How I Became Hettie Jones*, a memoir of the author's transformation from Hettie Cohen, middle-class Jewish girl from Queens, to Hettie Jones, bohemian writer and the wife of LeRoi Jones (later Amiri Baraka), a prominent black Beat poet and codifier of the Black Arts movement who tangled with Malamud, among others (see chapter 1). Not only does the opening declaration locate the memoir in the *Bildung* tradition (*Hettie Jones* is nothing if not a narrative of education), but the sentence also places it in the long tradition of American spiritual autobiography and immigrant narratives stretching from Jonathan Edwards to Mary Antin.[10] Significantly, Jones introduces herself to the reader in the third person before switching (for the most part) into the first person for the rest of the memoir. The book is fundamentally engaged in looking at interracial—or, following Caroline Rody, interethnic—Jewish identity framed in relationship to other racial groups, using the perspective of first-person interiority as well as third-person generality. Thus, the author's tense switching helps create both a deeply personal life narrative and a somewhat distanced sociological account of an era.

Hettie Jones's life and marriage were extraordinary in many ways. She met LeRoi Jones in 1957, when "there weren't a half-dozen steady interracial couples in the Village" and "thirty states still had miscegenation laws" (32). Nonetheless, from the beginning of the memoir, she makes it clear that she also sees herself as a stand-in for a larger postwar movement of women, particularly Jewish ones. Central to her memoir is a double metamorphosis: from disaffected suburban teen to urban bohemian, from middle-class white woman to interracial wife and mother. Alongside these narrative strands she offers an important rereading of the Beat generation from a woman's perspective. As one critic put it, Jones reveals that "women . . . [were] in a marginalized space—they were supporters of Beat, allowed to be a (silent) part of the scene, but because they were women, they also symbolized parts of society to rebel against" (Schlievert 1095).

Jones's tendency to split the self into "she" and "I," "before" and "after," is characteristic of women of the Beat generation. Joyce Johnson, Jack Kerouac's former partner and another prominent woman writer of the era, enacts a similar sort of semantic and ontological slippage in her memoir, *Minor Characters*.[11] Johnson, too, distinguishes between the self writing the memoir (Johnson) and her younger self (which she designates by her maiden name, Glassman).[12] In a key passage, she writes, "I see the girl Joyce Glassman, twenty-two, with her hair hanging down below her shoulders, all in black like Masha in *The Seagull*—black stockings, black skirt, black sweater—but, unlike Masha, she's not in mourning for her life" (261). Both Johnson and Jones changed their names and their identities when they became Beat. Significantly, for both women, these shifts also erased their visible Jewishness. That absence is mirrored in critical accounts of the women and of the period as a whole: few critics have looked at the ways in which the complexities of postwar Jewish racialization affected such women's experiences.

While there has been some interest in Johnson and her work since *Minor Characters*, there has been comparatively little investment in Hettie Jones's memoir. Yet her narrative of pre-*Loving* Jewish–African American marriage marks a significant moment in the ambivalent project of postwar Jewish racialization, a time when transracial identification and the adoption of an interracial voice and form first appeared. It also illustrates the complicated subject positions of Jewish women writers of the period, whose identifications across racial boundaries often allowed them to claim an authentic literary voice during a time when they were encouraged to remain silent. Deborah Thompson reads *How I Became Hettie Jones* as an extended meditation on postwar whiteness and the ultimate failure of antiracist whites in the 1950s and 1960s to "find a name for the way they were white" (Thompson 84; Jones 226). Yet even though Thompson touches on the importance of Jewishness in the memoir's complex racial identifications, she sees whiteness as more important to her subject position—a move that I believe recapitulates the problem of naming that she identifies as being at the heart of the book.

Thompson's argument rests on the commonplace that during the postwar years "there was a vast whitening of Jewish ethnicity" (91).[13] Contrasting the experiences of LeRoi and Hettie Jones, she writes that "while the 'brown' LeRoi, growing up in New Jersey, learns at a very early age the minute distinctions among his 'own race,' the white Jewish Hettie, growing up not too far away in New York, doesn't begin to knowingly experience 'race' as an identity category until her late college years and even then only in the crudest forms of blackface minstrelsy" (87).[14] Later, she contends that Hettie has "no *names* for racial identity . . . and this absence of names makes different racial identities seem mysterious, exotic, sensual, and unspeakably taboo—and makes white identity at once hegemonic and invisible" (88). Yet throughout the memoir, Hettie Jones is clear that, from a very early age, she understood that Jewish difference made whiteness, and the distinctions within that monolithic category, visible. Certainly, as Thompson suggests, Jones's encounter with segregation and racism as a student at Mary Washington College in pre–civil rights Virginia first introduced her to the problems of the classic black-white binary. Nonetheless, the experience of being what she calls an "outsider Jew" first made her aware of the power and stakes of ethnic and racial difference in America (14).

According to Jones, her Jewish visibility at Mary Washington drew her attention to the ways in which whiteness is naturalized as ideology and lived experience. In the memoir, young Hettie Cohen is "shocked right out of [her] self-absorption" (11). Jones writes, "Before I could think of myself I had to look *out*. Jesus seemed to be everywhere. I had to learn to put down my knife when I ate, to pour and hand tea. . . . I felt very much the Yankee Jew from New York. In the dining room with a kind of tense awe, I was asked, 'Are you Puerto Rican?'" Hettie has to "look *out*" in a dual sense—seeing the world around her while seeing herself as the subject of the gaze of others (12).[15] The passage makes it clear that she locates her difference in a variety of arenas, from the racial to the theological, from class to geography. In the rarified precincts of Mary Washington, Hettie is visible because of what she describes throughout *How I Became Hettie Jones* as her "dark" appearance, an aspect that Baraka comments on throughout his own autobiography. She is marked as a "Yankee Jew" because of her struggle to participate in the class- and race-based feminine rituals prized at the college. Moreover, she detects a slippage between the racial and religious identities of her peers at Mary Washington: "the . . . students, all white, were from various southern and western states. And there was I—alone with the *goyim*" (11). To Jones, the fact that the students were "all white" seems not only synonymous with their goyishness but also a reason for her sense of alienation at the school; she frequently describes herself in quasi-racial terms as a "mutation" (11, 13).

Nonetheless, Jones's sense of difference existed long before her time in the south. "There wasn't much for me in Laurelton, [Queens], where we'd come from polyglot Brooklyn; no Negroes, no Hispanics, Italians, only some Anglos and Irish who couldn't afford to move away from the Jews. I went to school with their children but never to their homes. There was a firm inevitability to this; you just didn't mix, exactly the way you didn't serve milk with meat" (8). As she makes clear, the arbitrariness of this law against mixing with the goyim was mirrored in her family's observance of the kosher laws. "The milk/meat rule was all that remained of the kosher laws. My parents spoke Yiddish only to hide things. Even in English they rarely referred to the past. Their families had come from Poland, or was it Russia, they weren't sure. And Brooklyn was nothing to speak of either, as if poverty rendered you undeserving of history" (9). Throughout the memoir, Jones is preoccupied with moving beyond the vague artifacts of Jewish history to articulate the possibilities of a secular Jewish difference rooted in a return to a more racially marked Jewish past.

After graduating from college, Hettie moved from Queens to Lower Manhattan, which Jones identifies as leaving the white suburban aspirations of her parents and returning to the poverty and ethnic Jewishness of her grandparents. "The only hint I ever had of my future was on our every other Sunday trip to Newark, to visit my mother's family, when we'd stop for a sandwich at Katz's on the Lower East Side. . . . I cared less for the food than for the long, mysterious reach of Houston Street, the way it seemed to hold, river to river, some secret old New York that hadn't ceased to exist, not the way you were led to think" (9).

Although Hettie didn't discover this "secret old New York" in the East Village of 1956, she did immediately encounter a more complex racial landscape than she had found in Laurelton or at Mary Washington. In New York, she landed a job at the *Record-Changer*, a journal for collectors who "bought and sold the fragile, tinny history of jazz, all yet to be reissued on unbreakable LPs." The magazine itself was engaged in a kind of racial ventriloquism; for even though most of its featured musicians were African American, "all these collectors and essayists were white" and balked at the idea that jazz was black-identified (21). Jones writes that, for these men, "to call jazz Negro music meant whites couldn't play it and they wanted to; to call it Negro music also put on it what was put on Negroes themselves, and no one wanted *that*" (22).[16]

It is was at the *Record-Changer* that Hettie met LeRoi Jones. In the memoir, she describes herself as she imagines he saw her when they first met: "a small, dark, twenty-two-year-old Jew from Laurelton, Queens with a paperback book in my hand. Kafka's *Amerika*" (2). The book over which Hettie and LeRoi meet is significant: *Amerika* is an unfinished novel by Jewish-Czech writer Franz Kafka, in which he imagines an immigrant's experience in the United States. Not only is the work preoccupied with the Jewish imagination of race, American approaches to ethnicity, and the ethics of ventriloquism and address, but it introduces a protagonist, Karl Rossmann, who at one point describes himself as a "Negro" and dons a sort of blackface when he visits a traveling theater.

The meeting over *Amerika* is auspicious; Hettie Cohen and LeRoi Jones, a budding poet, cultural critic, and later playwright, soon began dating. A year later, in 1958, they married. Like most marriages, theirs was alternately pleasurable and troubled. They had two daughters. In 1964, they divorced. LeRoi Jones famously based his depiction of the white woman antagonist in *The Slave* on his former wife. But to me, what is most interesting about Hettie Jones's narrative of their life together is how important her Jewishness remained. Moreover, it is clear that, for her, as for many Jewish women at the time, her Jewishness was constituted intersectionally—in relation to her gender identity—just as her later experience of race is.[17] Jones writes that, when she married LeRoi Jones, "mostly [she] was haunted by the problem of remaining a Jew, but [she] didn't know how to reinvent a Jewish woman who wasn't a Jewish wife" (37). LeRoi Jones's own autobiography supports the notion that Hettie's struggle to remain Jewish lay at the center of her anxieties about their marriage:

> I read in a diary of hers one night: "I think I'm losing my Jewishness... Grrr, what is that?" That is, a debate about whether there was such a thing as "Jewishness," and if so, was it a quality worth maintaining? The cultural aggression that is the norm of US cultural life creates such paradoxical questions in the minds of its victims. And so the swarm of self-doubts that confused the young Nellie Kohn [his name for Cohen in his autobiography]. (*Autobiography* 145)

Hettie Jones makes it clear throughout her memoir that she is an "outsider" both to mainstream white America and to the variant of postwar Jewish womanhood available to her. She quotes a Jewish former boyfriend: "the Village is okay now, but you'll end up in Mamaroneck with Marjorie Morningstar, wait and see" (26).[18] As she details in the book, she spent much of her life attempting to rewrite the script of postwar Jewish American femininity, primarily by clinging to her complex ideas about Jewish racialization and consciously inhabiting a subject position that sheds light on how whiteness is constructed and maintained as a dominant ideology. "Black/white was still a slippery division to me. In Laurelton the rabbi had said Jews were a different people, but my schoolmate Mulligan's priest assured her I was another race. The South had only served up reinforcement and by 1957 I'd had little counterexperience. It would be two years before Philip Roth's Neil Klugman (in *Goodbye, Columbus*) described himself—with some difficulty—as 'dark'" (34–35). Jones has been deeply invested in identifying across this "slash" between black and white, in part because, as she notes, her daughters (who were adults when she published her memoir) exist in the interstices of these identity positions. One of them, Lisa Jones, writes in her own memoir, *Bulletproof Diva*, that her mother identifies herself as "the Semitic American mother of black children" when asked to describe her race on census forms (32).

Memoir is not a mimetic form but a collage of facts and feelings gathered into the shape of a narrative. In *How I Became Hettie Jones*, Jewishness is a flexible rhetorical strategy as much as a reflection of lived experience—a means for Jones to retrospectively make sense of the subject position she inhabited before, during, and after her marriage to Amiri Baraka. Jewishness is also the name for what she sees as her countercultural or outsider awareness (what made her open to marrying Baraka at a time when it was so unusual to marry outside one's "race") and for what she lost in that marriage. She writes that her marriage to Baraka made her "white" in her own imagination for the first time. "And white I would be, because I knew the Jews—mine at least—would give me up" (52–53). Her description of this abandonment into whiteness resembles, but is also in tension with, the notion of passing as it is used in the context of African American identity (see chapter 4), which is often described as rendering one "lost to one's people."

The narratives of Hettie Jones, Jewish–African American marriage more generally, and Gordon's role in *Loving* offer a necessary corrective to the tale of black-Jewish relations as a story of simple decline, which many scholars in the United States have embraced. As Katya Gibel Azoulay argues, "in the general field of interracial relations, the subtopic of Blacks and Jews has received an inordinate amount of attention. The significant body of literature on the intersection between and comparison of Jews and Blacks in the United States focuses attention on either alliances or conflicts between the two groups. As a result, the dimension of personal relationships that crossed these boundaries has been obscured" (9). Looking at the intersubjective and highly charged relationships that take place in romantic unions and meditating on their representation in the postwar writings of Jewish American women allow us to see how public selves take shape in private and how Jewish difference has been experienced in relationship to others.

In *The Interethnic Imagination*, Caroline Rody explores how Jewish and Asian American identities are developed intersubjectively. To support her contention, she offers an exegesis of Henry Roth's *Call It Sleep* (1934), focusing on the clash between the protagonist David's troubled family dynamic and the heterogeneous immigrant neighborhood he escapes into when the oedipal entanglements of home become too overwhelming. Rody writes that, in this novel and others like it, "the plot moves the questing subject away from family and ethnos toward resolution, specifically through engagement with others marked by ethnic difference" (5). This theoretical rubric is useful when applied to a number of canonical Jewish American texts, from Henry Roth's to Philip Roth's, yet it becomes more complicated when we apply it to the many Jewish women writers who, like Hettie Jones, portray escape from one family (and one race) as the cost of entry into another, less homogeneous one. What do we make of literature, such as *How I Became Hettie Jones*, that focuses on the family as a potential site for otherness? How might we revise Rody's rubric to encompass Jewish women writers, whose rebellion against their family of origin often took place in the private sphere of the home via their choice of romantic partners?

Not-White But Not-Knowing: Interracial Romance after the Holocaust and before *Loving*

Like *How I Became Hettie Jones*, Lore Segal's autobiographical novel *Her First American* is engaged with the radicalism of the home—particularly romantic and sexual intimacy in the domestic sphere—in rewriting our relationship to race. Likewise, it pivots on the importance of naming and its role in indexing the shifting sands of racial designation in pre-*Loving* America. On the last page, protagonist Ilka Weissnix, a Jewish refugee from war-torn Vienna now living in New York City, reflects on the meaning of her last name. While she translates it as "Knownothing," her African American lover, Carter Bayoux, "[says] it mean[s] 'Notwhite,' because I am a Jew" (287). She relates this story at a memorial held by Bayoux's former students after he dies from complications related to alcoholism, and it is as fitting an epitaph for the narrative of the pair's ill-fated romance as it is for Carter himself. Throughout the novel, which is set in 1950s New York City, Ilka is defined by her "know-nothing" status: the naïveté of a new immigrant who exists somewhat outside the racial codes that govern pre-*Loving* America and the not-quite-whiteness that Carter sees in her Jewishness. She is also poised between her estimation of herself and Carter's view of her. As in Jones's memoir, this sense of being defined from without and from within allows Ilka to understand something about the plight of her African American lover and his friends even as it continually reminds her of the limits of her own knowledge. She is, finally, a "know-nothing" because she is unable to ever get inside Carter's head and understand his experience.[19] *Her First American*, like *The Tenants*, is a novel about the boundaries of the empathic imagination for writer and lover alike. Unlike Malamud, however, Segal is not angry about these limits so much as preoccupied, as an immigrant-outsider herself, with the way in which they reveal the essence of the American relationship to race and gender as well as the racial valences—the not-whiteness—of Jewishness in America.[20]

The problem of naming is echoed in Ilka's larger struggle to understand America. Throughout the novel, she relies on the dictionary to interpret the complexities of the world that Carter introduces to her, often with hilarious or poignant results. Carter's New York is indecipherable to Ilka not only because she is a greenhorn but also because of her relative innocence in the ways of the world.[21] Attempting to visit Carter, she is told he is "in the bughouse" (a nod to his alcoholism and mental illness), and her response is to look up the word *bug* in the dictionary (45). She is unable to understand the nuances of colloquial American speech and has difficulty naming and decoding the racial and social actors who surround her. For much of the early part of the novel, she is blissfully unaware of the hierarchies that govern 1950s New York, particularly those pertaining to race. Despite her experience with Nazi-era racial policies in Austria, she has no vocabulary to explain the way in which American racial designation works, nor does she completely understand its power to constrain intimate relationships.

At a restaurant, she asks Carter about the identity of the waitress serving them.

> "Is she a Negro?" Ilka asked Carter. "Puerto Rican," said Carter, thereby giving a name to the category in which Ilka was now able to file the woman in the early-morning subway who had sighed for her mother; the skimpy brown man with the antique smile and no overcoat; the little brown girl who settled her father, mother and fat brother into the subway booth.... Ilka had acquired the word by which to distinguish this group of people from other groups of people, with the concomitant loss of the likelihood that she would henceforward distinguish any member within the group from any other. (142)

Here, Segal manifests the power of naming to erase the nuances of individual identity. Learning the term *Puerto Rican* gives Ilka a "name" for a number of people she sees around her in New York, many of whom she had previously conflated with Carter as a "Negro," but it also strips the beauty and specificity from her perception of these people. Throughout the novel, she straddles the divide between innocence and the cynicism to which "knowing" about race in America consigns her. As Dean Franco argues in his analysis of the novel, *Her First American* vacillates between a critique of race-based thinking and the contention that it is necessary to understand the limits that race, however constructed, imposes in order to respect the limits of the other. Early in the novel, Ilka asks Carter if she is "color-blind." He replies that she is "a foreigner, but we're going to get you naturalized. We'll open up your eyes" (47). The opening of Ilka's eyes, in both good and bad ways, is the subject of *Her First American*.

Ilka faces a similar issue in her ability to see Carter and his color. During much of their early acquaintance, she is unsure if he is black. She recognizes that he embodies an otherness of sorts and that, like her, he is a person apart. Still, she wonders whether he is that species of other she refers to as a "Negro"; and not until she witnesses him receive a sexually inflected insult from a Jewish man does she realize, "with relief," that he is "definitely a Negro" (40). Carter's racial identity confuses her because she is used to the entirely different racial landscape of prewar Europe and because of Carter's own complicated racial and class performance. "When [she] walks on Broadway and sees an old Viennese pair [she] understand[s] even from behind" who they are and where they fit into society, whereas "she did not recognize [Carter's] hair, and that the size of his mouth and his laughter did not go with the urbane way he bent his wrist and crossed his ankles; that the luxurious tweed of his jacket contradicted his flattened nose with its small outgrowth of wild flesh at the bridge, which intimated to the girl disastrous chances, moving accidents his youth had suffered" (17). Ironically, her inability to see Carter's race correctly is what allows her to see him better than most of the people he encounters do. Because her ability to see race is newfound, the architecture of prejudice and the constructed nature of race are apparent to her in ways that the Americans in the novel do not recognize. For Ilka, Carter is the ultimate American (her "first") precisely because he embodies, in the contradictions of his own being, the contradictions at the heart of America's relationship to race.

Ilka's Jewishness and her romantic appraisal of Americanness make her particularly able to see and appreciate Carter's difference. As *Her First American* opens, Ilka descends onto a train platform in "the New World" (9). She has traveled out west to see "America" after living in New York for a few months.[22] The imagery of the train station, synecdoche for the Holocaust she has escaped, is both tragic and hopeful, a new immigrant's idea of the frontier yet a reminder of the Europe she has left behind. The fact that Weissnix is the product of a now-lost culture—specifically, bourgeois interwar Jewish Vienna—is central to Segal's novel. If *How I Became Hettie Jones* is a memoir of *Bildung*, *Her First American* narrates an even more startling education, with a protagonist who crosses great distances both geographically and emotionally.

Born in Vienna and sent away by her parents after Hitler's annexation of Austria, Ilka washes up in the postwar United States to reside with her kindly but absent-minded cousin, Fishgoppel. When the novel begins, Ilka believes she is an orphan, that both of her parents have died in the Holocaust. However, after her Jewishness helps her land a job at the Council for Eretz Yisrael (an early example of the currency of Jewishness in postwar America), she learns that her mother has been living in Israel since the end of the war and arranges for her to come to New York. Alongside the negotiation of her burgeoning relationship with Carter, Ilka spends much of the novel attempting to deal with her mother's traumatized consciousness and the creeping paranoia she brings to America.

Shared trauma allows Carter and Ilka's mother to feel an immediate connection, one that suggests a powerful link between Jewish and African American experiences of oppression. This relationship is later echoed in Carter's connection with another Holocaust survivor, Samovicz, a fellow patient in the mental institution. He begins to study Talmud with Samovicz, and the two agree that the individual suffering they've both experienced is nothing compared to the affective experience of shame that occurs "when a people—a whole race—is systematically humiliated," an experience "tantamount to genocide" (263). Their use of the term *race* is not incidental. It speaks to a larger current in the novel: the search to name the ways in which Jews are identified and raced, even in America. As Eric Sundquist points out, Ilka is infinitely better than Carter is at assimilating to American assumptions and ideals because she is presumed to be white. Yet whiteness does not sit easily with her; like many postwar Jews, she is searching for a language for her own experience of difference. Franco makes a convincing case that, in *Her First American*, Segal "effaces a politics of race that would otherwise require her characters to contend with the differing social histories and contemporary pressures of 'black' and 'Jew' and likewise foregoes a more trenchant ethics of recognition that would have raced characters find meaning in commonly plotted historical experiences of dispossession, disenfranchisement, or social alienation" (113). I argue, however, that the continuities and discontinuities between the experiences of African Americans and of Jews such as Ilka's mother, harmed by European genocide, come up throughout the novel in a nuanced and nonreductive manner that nonetheless still trades in a "politics of race."[23] After all, Segal, too, "races" Ilka and the other Jewish characters in the novel even as she critiques the way in which race can reduce the complexity of various identities to stereotype.

Although the story of Carter and Ilka's romance is affecting as a document of pre-*Loving* interracial intimacy and the perils attendant in mixing white and black during the period, it also, like the case itself, simultaneously upholds and moves beyond the racial binary as it attests to the growing racialization of Jewish identity in postwar America. The place of Jewishness in racial discourses belies the narrative of Jewish whitening put forward by critics such as Thompson, as I discussed in relationship to Hettie Jones. Segal's novel is preoccupied with the growing investment of Jews and African Americans in racialized discourses and the way in which it undermines sympathy between the groups. Carter and Samovicz's relationship is juxtaposed with Carter's response to a comment from Ilka's new boyfriend (who is identical to the all other nice Jewish intellectual men she meets and whom she compares unfavorably to her African American paramour): "the Negro and the Jew have a parallel experience." "Carter said, 'Yes, indeedy: parallels are two lines that run side by side and never meet except in infinity" (263). This image of a chasm between the experiences of African Americans and Jews recurs throughout the novel and frames Segal's depiction of interracial romance in pre-*Loving* America.

Segal is particularly interested in how some American Jews were reclaiming their Jewishness in the aftermath of the Holocaust, a theme germane both to the immediate postwar setting of the novel as well the 1970s and 1980s when she wrote it. Ilka is often an outsider, not just to the general American scene but to American Jews' increasing investment in ethnic Jewishness and Israel. Her cousin, Fishgoppel, begins the novel as a graduate student at Yale who understands her life through the novels of Henry James; she ends the novel keeping kosher, living in Israel, and rabidly proclaiming the unique importance of Jewish identity in the contemporary world. The novel charts the growing politicization of Jewish and African American identity in part through the relationship between Fishgoppel and the African American characters. Early on in *Her First American*, Fishgoppel and Carter (whom Ilka refers to as "my two Americans") are close, Fishgoppel going so far as to signal her approval of him by saying that he has "a Jewish mind" (123, 125). Later, however, the newly radicalized Fishgoppel tangles with Ilka and Carter's friend Ebony over the question of Jewish versus African American supremacy in matters of education and family feeling. Fishgoppel relates that "in Israel, . . . they have hardly any nursing homes," whereas Ebony notes that "the Egyptian language . . . doesn't have the word 'nursing home' because they don't have the concept, nor 'racism' nor 'slavery'" (273). Their debate expands into arguing if the Bible is right about whether or not the Jews were enslaved in Egypt.

This battle echoes one going on inside Ilka, which comes to the fore when she and her mother are invited to a seder. The hosts, Yiddish-speaking American Jews who are very different from the German-identified Weissnixes, insist on speaking to Ilka's mother in Yiddish despite her unfamiliarity with the language. Their narrative of the story of Exodus irks Ilka because it is so clearly being used as a metaphor for modern-day Israel and Jewish exceptionalism.[24] She is angry that the participants so happily celebrate the murder of the Egyptians' firstborn, although it was God who had "hardened their hearts" against the Jews (254). Her growing political consciousness allows her to reread the Exodus story, long prized in both African American and Jewish communities, from the purview of the African subjects in the story and wonder about the violence to the other that a single perspective might breed.

Such questions about how to read and write the story of another are central to *Her First American*, though Segal's approach to the task is different from Malamud's in *The Tenants*. Like Hettie Jones, she is concerned about the seductive pull of speaking for, or even representing, the other. For instance, halfway through the novel, Carter, incapacitated by alcohol, asks Ilka to write a newspaper column for him.[25] Although she demurs, citing her lack of experience in written English, he insists, saying, "I will tell you what to write," and dictating a fiery column in the key of James Baldwin, giving her every comma and semicolon (102). Carter invokes the lifelong rejection and subordination of the "Negro": "I am not alone comma nor are you alone comma nor are we unusual in our hatred of white people period The next time we riot in Detroit." Ilka insists that "one cannot write things like this" about the "hatred of white people" or about the desire to riot in "Detroit comma or burn down Chicago comma or blow up New York" (103). They call their mutual friend Ebony, who supports Carter's view, saying, "It's amazing we got to the fifties of the twentieth century without somebody saying it." Buffeted by his friend's support, Carter moves on to criticizing the president's response to racial unrest. Ilka says, "You cannot write this about the president." "'You cannot,' said Carter. 'I can write it'" (104). This debate is the heart of Segal's novel, both thematically and representationally. Like Malamud, she is wrestling with the question of how to represent the other and, in a different way, how to represent the self.

The conflict over representation echoes the real-life experiences of Segal and Horace Cayton, who had a five-year romance after her arrival in the United States. As Franco has noted, *Her First American* is part of a dialogue that includes both of their autobiographies. He describes Cayton as a "prominent sociologist; coauthor with St. Clair Drake of the significant two-volume study of race and labor in Chicago, *Black Metropolis*; long-time friend of Richard Wright; and for decades a columnist for the *Pittsburgh Courier*," and Cayton himself has narrated his relationship with Segal in his own autobiography (118). Moreover, *Her First American* is not a stand-alone piece in Segal's oeuvre. An earlier autobiographical work, *Other People's Houses* (1964), narrates the story of a young woman who, like Segal, ends up residing in various "other people's houses" in England as a result of the *Kindertransport* and ends with a meeting between this refugee and an African American intellectual. In both books, Carter serves as the female protagonist's portal to adulthood, challenging her intellectually and sexually and introducing her to an engaged life.

From the beginning, Segal and Cayton's real-life romance was defined by their vocation as writers. In an interview, she has explicitly cast *Her First American* as one writer's response to another: in this case, Cayton's autobiography, which narrates their relationship. She notes that "the facts have fallen off the edge of the world, but I surely knew I was going to write a book." Moreover, she is conscious of the divide between representation and reality in her depiction of Cayton and vice versa: "He asked me, do you mind if I use you as the person to whom I explain myself and the black experience? And I said, go ahead. As a result, I appear dumber than I was in reality. I became the questioner, but I said by all means, use me any way you want because I intend to use you. And he was willing and I was willing" (Johnson, "An Interview with Lore Segal"). In contrast to Malamud's relationship with his character Spearmint (or the real-life McPherson, for that matter) or Bellow's to his voiceless black pickpocket in *Mr. Sammler's Planet* (see chapter 3), both Segal and Cayton had voices as writers, and both sought to speak the self through the other in their writing.[26] Likewise, Carter and Ilka's relationship is defined by intimacy and a more equal power distribution—though it, like the combative one between Lesser and Spearmint, is ultimately doomed.

Although Ilka is not defined as a writer in *Her First American*, she inhabits a writerly position that is akin to Hettie Jones's and Lesser's. Carter may be her introduction to America, but she is intent on writing herself into the larger American narrative. Significantly, by the end of the novel, she has taken the world into her own vernacular. After becoming an American citizen, she revisits Carter's earlier attempt to "naturalize" her—to erase her "foreignness" and "color-blindness." She looks up the word *naturalize* in the dictionary and recognizes that she has become a native, though in a compromised way. She is so comfortable that she even challenges the woman who is granting her citizenship and who asks about Ilka's willingness to "take up arms" in a war to support American values (271). Ilka's refusal, which almost prevents her from gaining citizenship, marks a clear departure from her usual accommodating nature and suggests that she is no longer content to remain silent in her life. This establishment of her voice (as well as, perhaps, Segal's own) is at the center of the novel, yet it does not come at the expense of Carter's voice, which echoes in Ilka's head while she works out the variant meaning of her last name in the final pages of *Her First American*. As in *How I Became Hettie Jones* and *The Tenants*, interracial romance in pre-*Loving* America ends badly in Segal's novel but nonetheless provides a model for an interracial subject position and a literary voice.

Jewish Women Rewriting the Melting Pot

Jones and Segal were not alone in their attraction to the theme of interracial romance. Lynne Sharon Schwartz's "The Melting Pot," the title story of her celebrated 1987 collection, describes her protagonist Rita's anxiety about whether to marry her lover, Sanjay, an older Indian-born physician who has recently lost his wife to cancer. As the title suggests, the story rewrites America's melting-pot narrative—and perhaps, also, Israel Zangwill's 1899 melodrama of the same name, which foretells the dissolution of ethnic difference in the crucible of American intermarriage. Schwartz's story is about the ironies of blood, inescapable as narrative, if not biology. Although she is in love with Sanjay, Rita spends most of the story refusing to marry him for what the author portrays as mysterious reasons. Only at the end does she relate her own history to Sanjay. She is half-Jewish and half-Mexican, facts she learned as a teenager when she was taken in by her Jewish grandparents (only because she was "blood," they told her) after her Mexican mother had been jailed for murdering her Jewish father. Raised without knowledge of her violent early life or her lost Mexican family, Rita nonetheless is preoccupied with the idea that such violence is in her blood.

Like *How I Became Hettie Jones* and *Her First American*, "The Melting Pot" is a story about race, daughterhood, and inheritance, an inversion of the common story of male inheritance. It asks, what do daughters inherit from their parents, and what does it mean when they "marry out" in ways that challenge expectations? This focus on the daughter as carrier of a Jewishness that is both essential and susceptible to compromise and conversion has, as we have seen, a long history. The matriline is fundamental to racialized conceptions of Jewishness, and some critics argue it has always been a construction.[27] Thus, although Rita identifies and is identified as Jewish, by this matrilineal definition she is not.

The issue of heredity, not surprisingly, lies at the center of the story. Sanjay is a scientist who studies blood and genetics, yet it is Rita who is preoccupied with the inescapability of inheritance. "'Heredity,' says Sanjay sleepily, 'doesn't work that way. You make too much of it.' He has exchanged the faith in karma for the science of genetics. And he wants to help. He wants her to turn around and live facing front. Odd, since he comes from a country imprisoned in history, while she is the young West Coast lawyer. Sometimes it seems they have changed places" (8). Ironically, while Rita believes so deeply in heredity that she fears her own capacity to commit violence, her status as an orphan and her ethnically indeterminate appearance lend her a certain freedom from the boundaries of racial and ethnic identity. She feels that "she is so malleable an American, she could become anyone with ease." After discovering her mother's identity, she learns Spanish and tries to pass in her old neighborhood, hoping to see a woman who looks like her in search of a lost daughter. She also comes to believe that, just as she substitutes for her lost father in her grandparents' life, she might come to stand in for Sanjay's dead wife, whose photograph she resembles. She imagines that "she might even let her hair grow long and smooth it down with coconut oil, start frying wheat cakes and clarifying butter and stepping delicately down the hills of San Francisco as Sanjay's wife did, holding up her long skirts" (9). Her identity is a collage of other people's expectations and histories.

Rita's grandfather is also deeply invested in a variant of appropriation, particularly the adoption of "arcane rules" about how to live, which he borrows "with the obsessiveness of a Don Juan appropriating new women." He uses these rules to erect boundaries between himself and those he deems to be outsiders. To him, "the family is the pillar of society. The family is the society. And if a member disobeys, strays too far beyond the pillars, he becomes an outcast. At risk in the wide world, the world of the others. 'Them'" (6). In this vision, the other has a dangerous allure, coaxing the Jew to stray from these pillars. That fear is nearly the opposite of the idea of appropriation as expressed by Malamud and so many other male Jewish writers. It is also related, but ultimately in tension with, the idea of assimilation at the heart of Zangwill's turn-of-the-century melodrama, *The Melting-Pot*. For Schwartz and the other Jewish women writers I discussed in this chapter, melding with another undergirds rather than erases difference.

Schwartz's work explores the nature of blood that destabilizes easy categories of identity and identification, ethnicity and race, but it is also a meditation on the seductions of speaking for or becoming another. Just as Gayatri Spivak's "Can the Subaltern Speak?" explores the ethical valences of speaking for subalterns when their own voices are lost to history (discussed in the introduction), Schwartz's "The Melting Pot" examines the messy intersections of speech, silence, gender, class, and race. Although the point of view is third person, the story is told entirely from Rita's perspective. Despite her purported "silences" about her history, her narrative speaks for the women of color who are absent from the text—her mother and Sanjay's wife. In the final pages of the story, after finally having told Sanjay about her origins, Rita rustles through his bedroom and finds his wife's clothing and makeup. She puts on the dead woman's sari, a form of "dressing up" (34). In her school's Purim play she had always played Vashti because of her dark complexion and racial indeterminacy; now she feels, wearing Sanjay's wife's clothing and makeup, like "Queen Esther, at last." Yet when Sanjay sees her, he is horrified and tells her that her performance is "not right" (35). Rita herself acknowledges that "she can't figure out how to get it on right" (34). The fact that her flirtation with passing fails makes her attempt at replacing his wife all the more painful for Sanjay. He tells her, "'You don't have to masquerade for me to love you.' But she cannot believe it. It costs too much" (35).

Schwartz ends "The Melting Pot" on this dark note, but the pervasive theme of racial intermingling and masquerade in works by Jewish women writers offers a more ambiguous message. Both Hettie Jones and Schwartz's Rita are determined to speak the self through the other and seem fascinated by the exciting, challenging, futile ways in which interracial or interethnic alliances put identities at risk. As Victoria Aarons points out, women writers trouble the conventional narrative of Jewish American literature, which tends to trace a linear trajectory from immigrant otherness to assimilation into the national canon. This narrative echoes a larger and equally problematic rendering of Jewish life in America, turning it into a monolithic story of integration and incorporation, one that we often take at face value, given the dominance of male stalwarts such as Bellow, Malamud, and Roth in the canon of Jewish American literature. Aarons argues that "contemporary Jewish women writers continue to be faced with issues of ethnic identity and self-definition, reinforcing the 'immigrant' status that defined earlier Jewish fiction in America." Moreover, "when coupled as oft-perceived products of a literary subculture, Jewish ethnic identity and an emerging 'women's fiction' become finally questions of voice, a voice that is at once a source of richness and tension in the fiction of Jewish-American women"

(380). Jewish women writers manifest a type of vocal appropriation that is, in the end, not "offensive," as William Styron's adoption of Nat Turner's voice was, but productive—a way to speak to and of their own position, as racial and religious outsiders in America (McGurl 234).

Representations of Jewish-Christian interfaith romance and interracial relationships between Jews and others have indexed changing attitudes about Jewishness as an ethno-racial identity. They also mark the ways in which the Holocaust and the concomitant identification of Jews as racial others affected postwar perceptions of Jewish identity. The transformation demonstrates how interfaith romance, a central mechanism for working out Jewish identity in modernity, was transformed into interracial romance in many works of fiction and memoir during the era. If, as Esther Benbassa and Jean-Christophe Attias argue in *The Jew and the Other*, the figure of the Jewish *converso* is the ultimate trope of modernity, Jewish intermarriage, intimately related to conversion in its subtle undermining of fixed identity categories, might be called its postmodern grandchild. It is also, for the writers I have discussed, a means of claiming a voice through acts of racial ventriloquism and intimacy.

CHAPTER 3

What We Talk about When We Talk about the Holocaust

Racializing the Holocaust in 1970s Jewish American Literature

Lore Segal was not alone in pairing the Holocaust and race in America. As the U.N. Educational, Scientific, and Cultural Organization's 1950 declaration on "The Race Question" makes clear, the Holocaust haunted racial discourse in the years after World War II. Nonetheless, recent historiographical debates about just when the Holocaust came to inhabit American consciousness have pitted noted scholars such as Peter Novick and Hasia Diner against one another. Although I won't attempt to answer once and for all this thorny question of origins, I do argue, alongside Novick, that the Holocaust was not widely discussed or represented in the immediate postwar years but became one of the central organizing principles in Jewish American identity during the latter years of the twentieth century, just as Jews in the United States were in search of a narrative to resuscitate their flagging sense of cultural and racial difference.[1] As the era of identity politics emerged during the 1970s, so did a focus on the subjective experience of race, gender, and sexual orientation. At a time when the genuineness of an author's voice was increasingly valued, the Holocaust became a wellspring from which Jewish American writers could draw to establish the authenticity of their literary voices.[2]

Holocaust literature, too, was not especially popular in the initial postwar years. Although Primo Levi and Elie Wiesel originally published their testimonies in 1958, their works were not widely read or appreciated until the late 1960s, when they were translated into English and became source texts in the era's Holocaust revival.[3] While American authors were certainly writing about the Holocaust before the late 1960s, most chose to focus on the Holocaust as a universal figure rather than a uniquely Jewish concern. In fact, many of the earliest American works about the Holocaust, such as John Hersey's *The Wall* (1950), were written by non-Jewish authors who were interested in the ethical and sometimes Christian-inflected implications of genocide.[4]

Many critics have explained the relative postwar silence and the explosion of Holocaust consciousness in the 1970s and 1980s as a traumatic elision and the subsequent return of the repressed.[5] However, Novick contends in *The Holocaust in American Life* that reading this deferred mourning through a psychoanalytically influenced theory of trauma obscures the historical circumstances surrounding the explosion of Holocaust consciousness. According to him, it is no accident that the Holocaust came to take such a prominent position in Jewish American life in the 1970s. Although the term *identity politics* was not coined until the end of the decade (mostly in reference to black intellectuals such as the members of the feminist Combahee River Collective), ideas about identity, voice, and speaking as a member of a collective or class had been circulating for several years. Moreover, in the late 1960s and early 1970s, Jews in America were beginning to see that their identity as distinct group was imperiled. Their sense of impending annihilation was tied to three related trends: the shifting fortunes of Israel in global consciousness, the visibility of black power and white ethnic revival movements, and the rising New Left's challenges to the university system on which so many Jews had premised their successful acculturation into the American middle class. Fears about the future of Jewishness and the authenticity of a Jewish voice (literary or otherwise) that might speak for Jews and ventriloquize for others had particular power for Jewish American writers.

Moreover, the era's rallying cry of "never again" often married the fortunes of Israel to the legacy of the Holocaust. This rhetorical move had particular repercussions for American Jews. Novick argues that "the assertion that American Jewry was in danger was first advanced in the aftermath of the Six Day War, and it continued to be advanced in the years after the Yom Kippur War" (173).[6] These violent ruptures in Israeli history were often paired with America's own social conflagrations. The Six Day War took place in June 1967, only a month before Newark and Detroit went up in flames during a series of race riots and only two months before the decision in *Loving v. Virginia* legalized interracial marriage in the United States (see chapter 2). The Yom Kippur War occurred in October 1973, only months after the occupation of Wounded Knee, the end of the Vietnam War, the breaking of the Watergate scandal, and the Supreme Court's decision in *Roe v. Wade*. During this chaotic social period, according to Novick, "Jews were mobilized by a combination of high anxiety and activist resolve. Rabbi Irving Greenberg, speaking in 1968 of the legacy of the Six Day War, noted that in Diaspora history, 'no home for the Jews has proven to be more than a temporary *succah*'"(173).[7] The fear that America, too, might well be just such a transient dwelling haunted many Jews after the Six Day War. Gradually, they came to see the conflict in Israel as another potential Holocaust, a chance for American Jews to expiate their guilt over having done little to help European Jews during the war, and a harbinger of the waning role for Jews as privileged spokespeople for marginalized ethnic groups in the United States.

Not only American Jews embraced the Holocaust during this period; during the 1970s and 1980s, the Holocaust was, as Hilene Flanzbaum puts it, "Americanized."[8] One of the hallmarks of twentieth-century American exceptionalism is its use of the Holocaust to cement American uniqueness and displace the racially inflected genocides that took place on the nation's own soil: slavery and Native American removal.[9] The exceptionalist discourse hinged on this question: if America, unlike Europe, could serve as a refuge for the world's embattled Jewish "race," how could it be labeled as truly "racist"? James Baldwin pointed to the connection between the Holocaust and the rhetoric of American exceptionalism in a number of his controversial essays about blacks and Jews, especially "Negroes Are Anti-Semitic Because They're Anti-White" (1967), published shortly before the period of keenest Holocaust commemoration. As he seemed to intuit, the Americanization of the Holocaust would serve a distinct purpose in a country reeling from the challenges to white hegemony.

Not incidentally, the era of Holocaust memorialization coincided with America's romance with racial and ethnic reclamation and the authenticity of the motherland, a movement that also worked to privilege the role of the Holocaust and Israel in the American Jewish imagination. Nathan Glazer and Daniel Patrick Moynihan's *Beyond the Melting Pot* (1963) was a harbinger of the 1970s fascination with the history and rituals of white ethnicity. Just as the Irish celebrated their difference via ever-more-extravagant Saint Patrick's Day parades, America's Jewish population came to see the Holocaust as marking, if more ambivalently, both their difference and their connection to a distant land. It is not by accident that Michael Omi and Howard Winant's germinal work on racial formation (discussed in the introduction) begins with a critique of white ethnic revivalism, arguing that it displaces the discourse of race from the center of conversations about inequality and discrimination in America. According to Matthew Frye Jacobson,

> [these ethnic revivals] often took place because contemporary events in the Old World prompted an emotional involvement in the fate of those whom the migrating generation had left behind. Soviet domination (and particularly the fate of Catholicism) in the nations of the eastern bloc, the Troubles in Northern Ireland, the Israeli wars of 1967 and 1973, the Prague Spring of 1968, the workers' movement in Poland—all such developments captured the attention and pulled on the sympathies of overseas ethnic compatriots, whose diasporic cultures invested Old World nationalist causes with a kind of mantric power. (*Roots Too* 467)

Amid the increasing number of ethnic revivals in America, Jews attempted to define their own particular place, often using African American cultural renewal as a blueprint. During the 1970s, popular cultural representations of the Holocaust joined images of Ellis Island as visible markers of what Herbert Gans has called "symbolic ethnicity" for Jews (1).[10] The celebrated NBC miniseries *Holocaust* (1978), starring Meryl Streep, was a significant, if muddled, voice in the decade-long discourse of ethnic revival. Novick points out that NBC saw the miniseries as an answer to ABC's award-winning *Roots*, the television adaptation of Alex Haley's celebrated book. Along with such seemingly innocuous popular representations of the Holocaust, the role of Israel in American politics and culture, the Holocaust rhetoric that swept the American Jewish community after the Six Day War, and, in Novick's words, "the place of Jews in the racial crisis of the sixties" twined into a Jewish identity (173).

Yet as we have seen in Malamud's muddied attempt to speak for the other in *The Tenants*, the attempt to celebrate what is particular about one's own group nearly always carries a cost. Clayborne Carson writes, "For both African Americans and Jews, the 1967 Arab-Israeli war signaled a shift from the universalistic values that had once prevailed in the civil rights movement toward an emphasis on political action based on more narrowly conceived group identities and interests" (192). The Six Day War, fought between Israel and Egypt, Jordan, and Syria, marked a turning point in American Jewish attitudes about Israel. (The rhetoric surrounding the war suggested that Israel was on the point of annihilation.) It also influenced the attitudes of many progressive intellectuals of color, who began to align themselves with international activist movements such as the Palestinians'. These shifts not only strained connections between Jews and politically committed African Americans but also shook the foundation of many Jews' relationship to America. Charles Silberman suggests that "the Six-Day War was a watershed between two eras—one in which American Jews had tried to persuade themselves, as well as Gentiles, that they were just like everybody else, only more so, and a period in which they acknowledged, even celebrated, their distinctiveness" (201). Difference rather than sameness became the word of the day. This emphasis on difference was fundamental to the prominence of the Holocaust in post-1967 Jewish American discourse. For in these next busy and tense years, as Taylor Branch suggests,

> blacks and Jews veered off on parallel courses of militant ethnic separatism, turning inward upon themselves. America's secular Jews bonded themselves to Israel with special fervor after the Six-Day War, for it was through it that many of them re-discovered their Jewishness. They stopped changing their names, stopped trying to blend in with the Gentiles. Similarly, blacks put on their dashikis and strutted their culture. (749)

Calling this embrace of Jewishness a "re-discovery," as Branch does, is appropriate because it involved both a repetition and a return. Jewish identity during this period took the form of recovering an imagined and often racialized prewar difference that many commentators thought had been lost during the postwar Jewish prosperity and whitening.

Importantly for my argument, this move toward Jewish particularity and reracialization had profound repercussions in the literary sphere. Particularly revealing is a certain strain of novels that marry representations of the Holocaust to concerns about the changing role of Jews in America's racial landscape. For a number of prominent postwar Jewish authors, including Malamud, Bellow, and Ozick, questions about how or whether they might speak as members of a discrete Jewish "race" joined an increasing preoccupation with the Holocaust, a theme that they had previously avoided grappling with in their fiction. In a 1987 letter to Ozick, Bellow wrote,

> It's perfectly true that "Jewish Writers in America" (a repulsive category!) missed what should have been for them the central event of their time, the destruction of European Jewry. I can't say how our responsibility can be assessed. We (I speak of Jews now and not merely of writers) should have reckoned more fully, more deeply with it. Nobody in America seriously took this on and only a few Jews elsewhere (like Primo Levi) were able to comprehend it. (438–439)

Yet beginning in the 1970s, both Bellow and Ozick "reckoned" with the destruction of European Jewry as avowedly "Jewish Writers in America." While this shift reflected growing American investment in the Holocaust, its expression in Ozick's and Bellow's work complicates any monolithic portrait of Jewish opinion. Both writers alternately displayed fascination with and ambivalence about the role of the Holocaust and racial identity politics in American life. Their readings of the Holocaust through the complex racial landscape of the American 1960s and 1970s mark their growing conservatism as well as the complexities of larger responses to the Holocaust and Jewish racialization.

The history of the Holocaust in American literature, like the history of race in America, is long and checkered. Of central importance to the genre and its reception were conflicts over the politics of representation and authenticity. Even the earliest American depictions of the Holocaust, such as Hersey's *The Wall*, introduced questions about truth and mimesis. Although *The Wall* was a fictionalized portrait of the Warsaw ghetto uprising, it drew heavily from documentary sources, particularly historian Emmanuel Ringelblum's ghetto archive, which he and others gathered to document the atrocities in Warsaw and preserve the collective memory of Poland's dwindling Jewish community.[11] Although questions about the ethics of fictional representations of the Holocaust existed during this period, the uncontested authority of the voice of the survivor did not become paramount until the 1970s Holocaust boom. Did writers such as Ozick and Bellow have the right to speak for and about the Holocaust? Was such writing an unethical act of appropriation that undermined the authority of the voice of the survivor? Or did it do important work in demystifying and de-essentializing representations of the Holocaust and its instrumentalization as a source of racialized Jewish difference?

It is not incidental that the metaphor of unspeakability has haunted both creative and critical texts about the Holocaust. Many scholars have argued not only that the Holocaust was essentially unrepresentable but also that the memoir or testimonial are the sole forms commensurate to representing the magnitude of the Jewish genocide because they "speak" in the vernacular of (and with the authority attendant to) personal experience. Under the force of this dictum, Anne Frank's diary became the portal for many into the world of the Holocaust; similarly, Wiesel's memoirs of the concentration camp transformed him into a celebrity and spokesman for Jews everywhere.[12] We cannot know if the nearly complete absence of fictional accounts of the Holocaust in the immediate postwar years was due to the psychological complexities of trauma, as many have long assumed, or to anxieties about precisely these questions of authenticity. But Malamud's tortured attempt to honestly portray a black writer (among many other literary examples) demonstrates the high stakes involved in representing identities and identity experiences that are not one's own.

For non-Jewish and Jewish authors, the spike in fictional portrayals of the Holocaust were often married to these larger questions of genre, voice, and address. In 1979, only ten years after Styron was alternately pilloried and congratulated for his decision to write from the perspective of a slave, he published *Sophie's Choice*, a novel about the trials of a Polish Holocaust survivor. His decision to take on these two fundamentally "American" disasters in succession was not coincidental.[13] Although *Sophie's Choice* does flash back to the European setting, Styron was mostly concerned with the Holocaust and the survivor as American symptoms.[14] Moreover, like the character of Nat Turner, the character of Sophie prods the limits of representation and the capacity of the writer to ventriloquize what Malamud called "the anguish of the other." Both Bellow and Ozick manifest a similar preoccupation with their own capacity to speak for others while locating the tragedy of the Holocaust on American soil and in America's distinct racial landscape.

Bellow and Ozick wrote pivotal Holocaust texts during the 1970s that have remained largely absent from canonical accounts of Jewish American Holocaust literature. Bellow's *Mr. Sammler's Planet*, published in 1970, was one of the first Jewish American novels to represent the Holocaust survivor in contemporary America.[15] Likewise, Ozick's 1976 novella "A Mercenary" was her first exploration of the Holocaust as it pertains to both race and Jewish identity in America—a subject she returned to in her more famous novella "The Shawl."[16] Both Bellow's and Ozick's fictions function as sometimes-ironic commentary on the monopoly that memoirs and testimonials hold in Holocaust literature. Ozick's protagonist is a kind of Jerzy Kosinski with a bit of Elie Wiesel thrown in for good measure. Bellow's Artur Sammler gains his moral weight (and sometimes his smugness) from his exposure to the depravity of the war years. The most striking similarity between the fictions, however, is the way in which both join concerns about representing the Holocaust with those about the changing role of race and racial politics in America. The works were published at the height of debates about what role the Holocaust should play in carving out a distinct Jewish identity and in the midst of concurrent efforts by writers of color to express racially distinct literary identities. Thus, the two fictions are fascinating cultural documents about the interpenetration of the Holocaust and Jewish racialization during the 1960s and 1970s. Moreover, both pivot on the question of speaking for that animated Malamud in his correspondence with McPherson and in his depiction of Willie Spearmint in *The Tenants*. Although "A Mercenary" and *Mr. Sammler's Planet* were published before the term or concept of identity politics had entered the vernacular, both are profoundly concerned with questions of identity and voice and the role they play in political and aesthetic representation.

Jews, Blackness, and the Mouthpiece of Identity in 1970s Manhattan

As Cynthia Ozick was establishing herself as one of the most prominent critics, essayists, and public intellectuals of the latter half of the twentieth century, she was also becoming one of the most successful Jewish American fiction writers. Given the tenor of her essays and public statements, she has often been labeled a rightwing intellectual. Yet in a recent reappraisal, Dean Franco points out that her fiction often takes a more nuanced, if no less biting, view of American culture.[17] In particular, her often-neglected early work offers provocative insights into themes of identity, race, and what she elsewhere calls "cultural impersonation" ("Cultural Impersonation" 113).

"A Mercenary" first appeared in the *American Review* and subsequently in her collection *Bloodshed and Three Novellas*. In it Ozick depicts a Cold War landscape shadowed by both the Holocaust and colonialism. Stanislav Lushinski and Morris Ngambe, her central characters, live against a backdrop of past disaster. Lushinski is a child survivor of the Holocaust who goes on to become "politically African," a diplomat and spokesman for a remote African nation that is engaged in remaking itself in the aftermath of colonialism (47). Alongside his role as a translator of African concerns, he is also an unwitting spokesperson for the Jews; and after moving to America, he becomes a celebrity survivor and a professional raconteur. Similarly, Ngambe, Lushinski's second-in-command, is something of an imposter—an African dignitary whose ideas of Africa originate in the Tarzan films he viewed while coming of age in London.

Ozick's dark novella juxtaposes the post-Holocaust and the postcolonial in a manner that allows her to comment on the tenuousness of identity after violence and oppression as well as the instability that historic rupture creates in identity and representation. Yet despite its commitment to the long-distance disasters of the Holocaust and colonialism, "A Mercenary" is firmly situated in America and the questions about identity and voice facing Jewish and African American writers during the 1970s. Although some scenes flash back to Lushinski's European past, the story is told from the perspective of his present, when he is a Holocaust expert who regularly appears on contemporary American television screens. Throughout the novella, Ozick satirizes what she perceives as the pieties of post-1960s identity politics, revealing the emptiness of any identities, black or Jewish, founded on what she perceives as vicarious memories of victimization. Although she clearly feels affection for Lushinski (as she did for Jerzy Kosinski, the author on whom she models him), she uses the character primarily to critique the unimpeachable authority of Holocaust survivors in America and their often-overdetermined role as spokespeople for Jewish and American concerns. At the same time, she uses Ngambe's character to critique the increasing investment in racial essentialism in post-Black Power America and as a figure through which she can meditate, as Bellow does in *Mr. Sammler's Planet*, on urban racial crises.

The ethical valences of speaking for and about others are central to "A Mercenary," as they were to *The Tenants*. Can a Jew be an African? Is it appropriate for Lushinski, "a white man," to speak "for a black country" (17)? Moreover, can this Jewish diplomat, described throughout "A Mercenary" as "an imposter," comprehend what it means to be African any better than a Jewish writer can understand what it means to be black in America? These questions animate the novella and are intimately linked to the question of whether, as a Holocaust survivor, Lushinski inhabits a privileged position that allows him to speak for other Jews. "A Mercenary" opens with a lengthy description of his role as a spokesman: "People joked that he was a mercenary, and would sell his tongue to any nation that bargained for it. In certain offices of the glass rectangle in New York he was known as 'the P.M.'—which meant not so much that they considered him easily as influential as the Prime minister of his country ... but stood, rather, for Paid Mouthpiece." He is able to inhabit a variety of positions because his identity is both fluid and economically defined; he is not simply a mouthpiece but a "Paid Mouthpiece" (15). By dubbing Lushinski "a mercenary," Ozick can ponder on his particular brand of post-Holocaust Jewishness in an idiosyncratic and highly allusive manner.

Yuri Slezkine argues in his wild magnum opus, *The Jewish Century*, that the figure of the "Mercurian" is one of the most productive lenses through which to look at representations of the Jew in modernity and as prototypical modern. Slezkine contends that the Jew has become the most vilified and most representative figure in modern (primarily European) history because of the supple nature of Jewish identities. Like the god Mercury, the Jew was seen as a highly mobile and mediating force (and simultaneously one that stubbornly kept to itself and its own nation), an image that contributed to the vision, so prevalent in the twentieth century, of the Jew as both cosmopolitan and clannish.[18] Slezkine's theorization of Jew-as-Mercurian, although specious at moments, is a means to explain twentieth-century anti-Semitism—as a negative response to modernity—while also articulating a link between Jews and others, such as Roma, who were persecuted both inside and outside of Europe.

Ozick's assertion that Lushinski is both "a mercenary" and a "Paid Mouthpiece" is significant for another reason. The fact that he is employed as a representative or instrument of others allows her to construct "A Mercenary" as a dual meditation on questions of speaking for and representation. Lushinski is in the position of speaking for a nation in which he has no roots. As Ozick writes, even calling this "small wart" of a nation "his country" is ridiculous. Lushinski muses about the politics of calling the African nation his own when "altogether he had lived in it, not counting certain lengthy official and confidential visits, for something over fourteen consecutive months, at the age of nineteen—that was twenty-seven years ago—en route to America" (15). His deputy, Morris Ngambe also becomes a representative man. The putatively more African member of the Ngambe-Lushinski diplomatic team, he possesses an Africanness nearly as compromised as Lushinski's, and the relationship between the two is complicated. Ngambe tells stories of Africa based on what he's seen in the imperial fantasy films he has watched while living and learning among the next generation of colonists. In turn, "some of Ngambe's tales Lushinski passed off as his own observations of what he always referred to on television as 'bush life'" (20). Lushinski doesn't bother himself with the ethical problems attendant to stealing these stories. To him, Ngambe's Africanness is characterized by its mediated nature. When Lushinski appropriates Africa from Ngambe, he feels that he is taking only the counterfeit Africa of Tarzan. Nonetheless, Ngambe's purportedly authentic, racialized Africanness, however compromised by his class and educational status, becomes an object of increasing value as developing-world politics join 1970s American-style racial essentialism.

Ozick complicates this picture by suggesting that Lushinski, too, is in some fundamental way black. On a talk show, he regales the audience with stories of his days as a child refugee in the forest, switching between narrative modes to emphasize both the unreliability of his own role as storyteller and the way in which the historical realities of race in Nazi-era Europe interrupted the fairy-tale lives that many wealthy Jews lived before the war. He begins his story with the distant and formulaic "once upon a time, long ago in a snowy region of the world called Poland, there lived a man and his wife in the city of Warsaw" (25). This couple had a child, who, like his parents, was wealthy, beautiful, and loved. Lushinski sounds the first discordant note in this idyll when he relates that the child, ostensibly Lushinski himself, possessed "one defect . . . that grieved his parents." In contrast to his "pink" and "ruddy" mother and father, "the boy, it seemed, was a gypsy" (26). Lushinski's fairy tale becomes grimmer when it embraces this description of racialized otherness.

> The parents looked on in fear as they saw that the boy's hair was black with a slippery will of its own, like a gypsy's, his eyes were brilliant but disappointingly black, like gypsy eyes, and even the skin of his clever small hands had a dusky glow, like gypsy skin. His mother grew angry when the servants called him by a degrading nickname—Ziggi, short for *Zigeuner*, the German word for gypsy. But when she forbade it, she did not let it slip that it was the darkness she reviled, she pretended it was only the German word itself. (26)

Here, Ozick makes another link between the post-Holocaust and the postcolonial and between Jewishness and blackness in America, this time by marking Lushinski as "dark" like a "gypsy" or an African. It is this darkness, which he and his parents carefully refuse to mark as Jewish, despite the obvious connotations, that casts him into the forest.

The boy's family pays a Polish farmer to hide him from the Nazis, but on seeing his dark, "gypsy" appearance, the farmer's wife fears for her family's safety and pushes him out to fend for himself. Now Lushinski's narrative becomes an increasingly violent tale about his own attempts to survive in the woods as a boy on the run from the Nazis. But precisely when he moves to this story of pain and degradation, his mode of narration changes to the ironic and mischievous, undercutting the sincerity of his account. Suddenly, "Lushinski is only a storyteller" of a tale of slapstick violence. The television audience, as if on cue, responds with laughter to the diplomat's account of violence and starvation in the woods. To them, "all this was comedy: Marx Brothers, Keystone cops, the audience is elated by its own disbelief" (29). Like Ngambe's Tarzan stories, all of Lushinski's tales of the past are mediated by an ironic distance.

Ozick's depiction of race and ethnic identity in "A Mercenary" is complex and often paradoxical. Despite her discomfort with the essentialist identity claims that Lushinski and Ngambe advance for political gain, she is deeply dismayed by certain acts of ethnic "impersonation," especially of the literary kind—a discomfort that suggests she believes in racial authenticity and the problem of speaking for others herself. In the section of her 1983 essay collection *Art and Ardor* titled "Cultural Impersonation," she evaluates John Updike's ventriloquial performance in *Bech: A Book*, his 1970 novel featuring Henry Bech, a Frankensteinian Jewish writer figure he has cobbled together, according to Ozick, from "Mailer, Bellow, Singer, Malamud, Fuchs, Salinger, the two Roths." Her critique of Updike is germane to her work in "A Mercenary," especially because they were written at about the same time.[19] Ozick's vitriolic review of *Bech* hinges on the accusation that Updike's attempts to speak for and as a Jew function as a reverse *marranism*, a donning of otherness for the sake of "passing"—in this case as a Jew, rather than a Christian, as the real-life *marranos* did. She is not surprised by this marranism because "it is already well-known that John Updike is a crypto-Christian, a reverse Marrano celebrating the body of Jesus while hidden inside a bathing suit." This type of Jewish drag can only end badly, she declares. "The original Marranos, in Spain, were probably the first group in history to attempt large-scale passing. As everyone knows (except possibly Bech), they ended at the stake. So much for Jews posing. What then of Christian posing as Jew? What would he have had to take on, much less shuck off?" (115).

What makes Updike's "impersonation" ineffective, according to Ozick, is precisely how little is at stake for the writer in the masquerade. "Bech-as-Jew has no existence, is not there, because he has not been imagined. Bech-as-Jew is a switch on a library computer. Bech-as-Jew is an Appropriate Reference Machine, cranked on whenever Updike reminds himself that he is obligated to produce a sociological symptom: crank, gnash, and out flies an inverted sentence. Not from Bech's impeccably acculturated lips, but out of the vulgar mouth ('Mother, don't be vulgar,' Bech says in boyhood) of a tough Jewish mother lifted, still in her original wrap, straight out of *A Mother's Kisses*" (115). Ozick's critique of Updike and his appropriation, like McPherson's critique of Malamud, centers on the perils of "cultural impersonation" and the difficulties inherent in trying to richly imagine the other. It is also linked to Ozick's larger critique of the Jewish authors whom Updike is trying to channel in his depiction of Bech. How can Bech be anything other than "an Appropriate Reference Machine" when he ventriloquizes in the worst, most reductive way, using a kind of bankrupt secular Jewishness that Ozick aligns with writers such as Roth and Mailer?

As always, her criticism is multi-edged. In her view, those Jewish writers are themselves impersonators, who put on and take off a series of "sociological symptoms" that have little to do with Jewishness as Ozick defines it. Bech is thus an impersonation of an always already-vapid impersonation of the Jewish writer figure whom Ozick identifies as symptomatic of late twentieth-century America. Just as Lushinski is taken to task for being "politically African" in "A Mercenary," the Jewish writers whom Updike imitates in his portrayal of Bech are politically Jewish: their identification with Jewishness is more about public spectacle than about private belief (47). Throughout the novella, Lushinski makes it clear that he is more comfortable being politically African than being politically Jewish. His lover Louisa accuses him of "hat[ing] being part of the Jews" (40). She notices that "always he was cold to Jews. He never went among them. In the Assembly he turned his back on the ambassador from Israel; she was in the reserved seats, she saw it herself, heard the gallery gasp" (41). Louisa suggests that he becomes

African precisely to avoid being Jewish—an assertion that echoes Ozick's critique in "Cultural Impersonation" and elsewhere.

To Ozick, identity politics have a literary and a cultural history, as both her critical prose and her fiction make clear. In an interview with Tom Teicholz for the *Paris Review*, she explained that she has long been fascinated with the figure of the imposter and its utility for the fiction writer. When asked why she based so many of her early characters on real people, usually well-known writers or intellectuals such as Singer, Malamud, and Kosinski, she replied, "Even when one invents, invents absolutely, one is blamed for stealing real people." The link between "stealing" and invention is connected to her larger preoccupation with "the idea of 'usurpation'" that she explores in her short stories "Usurpation (Other People's Stories)" and the controversial "Envy; or, Yiddish in America."[20] "When I was a small child I remember upsetting my father; I had recently learned, from a fairy tale, the word *impostor* and I made him prove he wasn't an impostor by demanding that he open the pharmacy safe, which had a combination lock. Since only my real father, the pharmacist, knew the combination, his opening it would prove he was my father." According to Ozick, a fascination with imposture and with determining what, if anything, is real is part of the fiction writer's lot.

Ozick combines her preoccupation with the ethics and limits of Jewish literary and cultural appropriation with a more general interest in the writer as impersonator. In her essays "Who Owns Anne Frank?" and "The Rights of History and the Rights of Imagination," published in *Quarrel and Quandary* (2000), she focuses on how literary and critical imposture work in a Jewish context, particularly in debates around questions of Holocaust ownership and appropriation, as in the case of Anne Frank. The act of Jewish literary impersonation has particular relevance in the universe of "A Mercenary" because the character Lushinski is clearly based on Ozick's friend Kosinski, author of the infamous "autobiographical" Holocaust novel *The Painted Bird* (1965). The hallucinogenic story of a dark-complected (implicitly Jewish) child sent to wander in an unnamed Eastern European forest and endure unspeakable violence during the Second World War, the novel was supposedly based on Kosinski's own early years in Poland. Yet there is little evidence that he underwent such struggles, and he has even been accused of plagiarizing much of *The Painted Bird* and his other writings on the Holocaust.

Despite (or because of) his growing disrepute, Ozick has remained fascinated with Kosinski, in large part because he seems to tease his audience with the counterfeit nature of his own performance of identity. In "A Mercenary," this fascination with the counterfeit finds form in Lushinski's and Ngambe's relationship to history and each other. The two often "compare boyhoods"; for instance, Ngambe tells Lushinski that his "grandfather was the brother of a chief; his father had gone into trade, aided by the colonial governor himself. The history and politics of all this was murky; nevertheless Ngambe's father became rich. He owned a kind of assembly-line consisting of many huts." Ngambe goes on to relate the conflict between his mother, his father's "favorite wife" and a keeper of the "old faith," and the missionary-educated Christians in his village, a conflict Ozick foregrounds as prototypically colonial (18). He relates that his mother was eventually murdered by a man who claimed that her faith in plural deities made her "primitive," an insult to the new Christian Africa (19). The Africa that Ozick imagines here is not the continent of historical record; she playfully suggests that, like Ngambe, her vision of Africa is not free from the influence of Tarzan films. Instead, she uses it to draw thought-provoking and productive parallels between colonial and Holocaust-era struggles among Christians and their racial or ethnic others.

The conversations between Lushinski and Ngambe—between the Holocaust and the colonial spheres—provide the raw material for Lushinski's successful diplomacy. Ironically, perhaps, surviving the Holocaust has made him a good colonizer, yet in these "comparisons of boyhood" he also learns how to be an effective translator, albeit one who always loses something of the often second- or third-hand meaning he is attempting to transfer. Ozick's image of Lushinski as "Paid Mouthpiece" is important because it introduces translation as one of the tropes essential to her innovative articulation of identity at the crossroads of the post-Holocaust and the postcolonial: "A white man, he spoke for a black country" (17). He translates the concerns of the African nation not only for a white television audience but also for the audience he garners with the American secretary of state. In one scene, he teaches Ngambe how to "speak the language" of the secretary to get relief for their famine-stricken country (23). Lushinski recognizes that the secretary cares little about the famine but is terrified of the possibility of tribal war, which would threaten American business interests in the nation, so he shows Ngambe how to "start a war" to garner the aid they desire (30).

The trope of speaking for or translating the concerns of the other emerges in another way in the novella. Writing of Lushinski's knowledge of the African nation's language, she explains, "He spoke it not like a native—though he was master of that tangled clot of extraordinary inflections scraped on the palate, the nasal whistles, beetle-clicks—but like a preacher." Because "the language ha[s] no written literature," he has been forced to glean its basic tenets from a Bible translated by early missionaries into an approximation of the local argot (16).[21] "It was out of this Bible, curiously like a moralizing hunting manual, the young Lushinski received his lessons in syntax. . . . he studied alone, and afterward (he was still only approaching twenty) translated much of Jonah, which the exhausted missionaries had left unfinished." He soon realizes that "the story of the big fish seemed simple-minded in that rich deep tongue, which had fifty-four words describing the various parts and positions of a single rear fin. . . . it was an observant, measuring, meticulous language" (17). Cast into the role of translator at a young age, Lushinski feels the incommensurability of the oral and the written. By transferring the rich language of the African nation into the universalizing language of the missionaries' Bible, he perceives that much value and meaning have been lost.

A perceived conflict between the oral and the written is a common, if often problematic, trope for understanding both the postcolonial situation and black and white writing, and it is a powerful one for Lushinski throughout "A Mercenary." Like Lesser in *The Tenants*, Lushinski finds that speaking for others increasingly limits his ability to speak for himself. "Sometimes he wished he could write out of imagination: he fancied a small memoir, as crowded with desires as with black leafy woods, or else sharp and deathly as a blizzard; and at the same time very brief and chaste, though full of horror. But he was too intelligent to be a writer." Lushinski chooses instead to become a "Paid Mouthpiece" who gains authority as a survivor who is performing his past (20). Yet his authority is undermined at every turn because Lushinski, like Kosinski, is not a reliable narrator of his own story. As Amy Hungerford points out, the discourse of the Holocaust in American culture often conflates speaker and text in a manner that privileges the purportedly unmediated voice of the survivor and places the burden of personification on the text itself.

Eventually, Lushinski begins to shirk his diplomatic activities, often asking Ngambe to act as his surrogate and becoming, instead of "a Pole" and "a diplomat," a personality and "a dervish of travel" (44). At this point in the novella, the reader begins to increasingly see the diplomat through his assistant's eyes. As the nation shifts from the colonial era into an age in which "the proletariat" and "dialectical materialism" are the prime minister's watchwords, Ngambe reflects on the fluidity of his own identity (45). He charts his own uncomfortable metamorphosis while witnessing the increasingly manic shifts in Lushinski's self. As Ngambe watches, the diplomat asks a tailor to measure him for the generic costume of an officer. He wears the uniform as he travels around the country; and with the aid of these plumes and medals that connote service to no nation in particular, he receives V.I.P service in hotels and restaurants.

Lushinski's travels as a soldier from an unknown land disturb Ngambe and lead him to "brood about impersonation." He begins to think that "it was no joke . . . that he sought out Tarzan movies: Africa in the mind of the West. It could have been his thesis, but it was not. He was too inward for such a generality; it was his own mind he meant to observe. Was he no better than that lout Tarzan, investing himself with a chatter not his own? How long could the ingested, the invented, foreignness endure? . . . He felt himself to be self-duped, an impersonator" (46). Ngambe's speculation that he might be "no better than that lout Tarzan" because he has invested "himself with a chatter not his own" has resonance in postcolonial criticism. Homi Bhahba, for instance, places the imperative to mimic the colonizer at the center of his theories of the postcolonial psyche. It also ties together Ngambe and Lushinski as African and Jew. As I will discuss in chapter 5, charges of being imitative—of speaking in a "chatter not [one's] own"—have been leveled against Jewish artists, with claims that they cannot possess a true aesthetic voice because they do not have a nation.

Ngambe recalls an incident from his past, when, after watching a particular Tarzan matinee, he saw another film appear on the screen. This film depicted the story of a criminal who impersonated a jailed general so aptly that he began to take on the general's heroic qualities. When the faux general was captured in war, the criminal refused to reveal his true identity and died in place of the general he had impersonated. In this way, the counterfeit general "atone[d] for his past life, a voluntary sacrifice." Ngambe realizes that "the ferocious natives encountered by Tarzan are in the same moral situation as the false General. . . . they accommodate, they adapt to what is expected. Asked to howl like men who inhabit no culture, they howl. . . . If you jump into someone else's skin, doesn't it begin to fit you?" His conundrum is the inversion of the one posed by Paul Joseph Goebbels, which Ozick reprints in her epigraph: "Today we are all expressionists—men who want to make the world outside themselves take the form of their life within themselves" (13). For unlike Goebbels, who saw the way in which the outside world could be constructed around one's interior world, Ngambe sees the dangerous repercussions of the exterior's rule over the psyche; he worries about what it means to "adapt to what is expected" (47).

Soon "the problem of sincerity engrosse[s] him," and this increasing engagement with questions of sincerity heralds Lushinski's end. Faced with the diplomat's claim that "sincerity is only a maneuver like any other," Ngambe recognizes, with some glee, that Lushinski's days as a spokesman are numbered (47). As the African nation, firmly in the postcolonial era, comes to increasingly prize an image of precolonial authenticity, how can he survive as the country's "Paid Mouthpiece"? Lushinski is stripped of his diplomatic role, which he had begun to don as carelessly as the officer's uniform, and sent back to "his country" (15). There, only days before he is murdered by political insurgents, he receives a letter from Ngambe relating a parable about identity. Ngambe tells the story of a Japanese terrorist in Jerusalem who was arrested after setting off a bomb that killed twenty-nine people. Once intent upon killing as many Jews as possible, the terrorist tried to circumcise himself as soon as he went to prison. Ngambe muses, "It may be at length that every man becomes what he wishes to victimize. It may be that every man needs to impersonate what he first must kill." Lushinski realizes that Morris Ngambe "had called him a transmuted, a transfigured, African. A man in love with his cell. A traitor. Perfidious. A fake. Morris had called him a Jew" (51).

The ending of Ozick's story suggests that there is no way to evade the particularity of Jewish identity or the victimization to which it consigns one.

Nonetheless, her project remains unique. Although Lushinski is the ostensible mercenary of the title, he and Ngambe are clearly a paired set. Their identities become deeply intertwined in a manner that offers insight into the black-Jewish dyad so commonly discussed in the 1970s. In his brilliant *Multidirectional Memory*, Michael Rothberg contends that opening up the Holocaust to comparison with other world historical disasters, such as colonialism, allows us to escape the ossified discourse of black-Jewish relations and transcend the kind of competitive memorialization to which Holocaust exceptionalism has given rise. While there is no doubt that Ozick's work engages in this sort of multidirectional comparison, it contributes more directly to what Daniel Itzkhovitz has called the "black-Jewish monologue" than to a genuine dialogue between blacks and Jews, colonialism and the Holocaust. To paraphrase Nathan Englander paraphrasing Raymond Carver: what Ozick talks about when she talks about the Holocaust is the role of Jews in the American political and racial landscape of the 1970s.[22]

Near the end of "A Mercenary," we learn that Ngambe, like Lushinski and the Japanese terrorist, has, against his better judgment, become a Jew. The novella ends with the men's roles inverted: Lushinski is back in Africa, an "African," even if a doomed one. Ngambe finds himself alone in an increasingly uncivilized, jungle-like New York City akin to the one Bellow describes in *Mr. Sammler's Planet*.

> Morris [Ngambe] in New York: Morris in a city of Jews. He walked. He crossed a bridge. He walked. He was attentive to their houses, their neighborhoods. Their religious schools. Their synagogues. Their multitudinous societies. Announcements of debates, ice cream, speeches, rallies, delicatessens, violins, falafel, books. Ah, the avalanche of their books! Where their streets ended, the streets of the blacks began. Mdulgo-kt'dulgo in exile among the kidnapped—cargo-Africans, victims with African faces, lost to language and faith; imposters sunk in barbarism, primitives, impersonators. Emptied-out creatures, with their hidden knives, their swift silver guns, their poisoned red eyes, Christianized, made not new but neuter, fabricated: oh, only restore them to their inmost selves, to the serenity of orthodoxy, redemption of the true gods who speak in them without voice! (49–50)

Ngambe critiques African Americans, whom he calls "cargo-Africans," based on his imported ideas about truth and impersonation. In contrast to the Africans he has known, the black people in America are "imposters sunk in barbarism, primitives, impersonators." By applying such language, he places himself in the position of the colonizer rather than the colonized. His increasing identification with the Jews and "their city" causes him to compare their intellectual precociousness and civility to what he perceives as African American barbarism, a move taken directly, as we will see, from Sammler's approach to the changing racial landscape of Manhattan. Ozick pinballs from Ngambe's meditation on African American inauthenticity (which is the root of black criminality, à la Bellow) to his final "severing" with and usurpation of Lushinski. Learning to impersonate Lushinski the Jew, Ngambe can now replace him. Ozick leaves the reader with the pessimistic sense that this awareness of imposture and how it works allows Ngambe to kill Lushinski symbolically and perform an authentic blackness valuable in America's changing political landscape. In her hands, Ngambe becomes blacker as he becomes more Jewish. He also becomes, like Malamud's Willie Spearmint, a vehicle through which the Jewish writer can speak to and about the waning role of Jewish difference in American culture.

Race, the Holocaust, and the Politics of Extinction

"A Mercenary" builds on many of the ideas about speaking, race, and subjectivity first advanced in Bellow's *Mr. Sammler's Planet* (1970). Since the 1940s, Bellow, along with a number of other postwar Jewish writers, had been criticized for ignoring the role of the Holocaust in Jewish life. All that changed, however, in 1967, after Israel's Six Day War, when he began fervently engaging with the topic. The most notable results of that engagement were the novel *Mr. Sammler's Planet* and the travelogue *To Jerusalem and Back* (1976). Like Malamud's *The Tenants* (1971), which departed from that writer's usual universalism, these works diverged from Bellow's previous oeuvre in a number of ways, notably in their explicit identification with Jewish particularity and concerns.[23] Both the novel and the travelogue sutured narratives of Holocaust remembrance and an imperiled Israel with concerns about the role of Jews in an America that was increasingly preoccupied by race. Both books revealed anxieties about the potential of a second Holocaust in Israel and fears that Jews in America would soon become obsolete.

Mr. Sammler's Planet joins meditations about the subjectivity of Holocaust survivor Artur Sammler with speculations about the visibility of race in America and the special Jewish burden of bearing witness to violence and the increasing barbarism of polyracial New York. Like Ozick's, Bellow's concerns are ostensibly transnational and transhistorical; but he, too, ends up saying more about Jews and race in 1960s New York City than about the trauma of the Holocaust and the way in which it marked the terminus of European Enlightenment thought. At the beginning of the novel, the intellectual Sammler seems to be content with the voyeuristic pleasures of observation. Eventually, though, he recognizes his unique role as witness to the century's most brutal genocide and the decline of America as a paradise of cultural pluralism.[24]

In Yiddish, the word *sammler* means "collector," and in keeping with that reference the character Sammler gathers and narrates the fragmentary experiences of other people's lives, functioning as a detached commentator on what he sees as the decline of civilization in 1960s Manhattan.[25] The spectatorial nature of his life—his thrill in seeing and collecting sensory data from a remove—emerges in the first pages of Bellow's novel. Sammler has been forced to live with a widowed niece-by-marriage, and his view is circumscribed by the open window of a shabby Upper West Side apartment in which he never feels at home. With ethnographic exactitude, he stares out the window and catalogues the Manhattanites he sees, and soon his anthropological insights fasten on questions of race and the shifting racial map of his beloved borough.[26] Taking this fascination to the streets, Sammler marvels at "what one sees on Broadway while bound for the bus. All human types reproduced, the barbarian, the redskin, or Fiji, the dandy, the buffalo hunter, the desperado, the queer, the sexual fantasist, the squaw; bluestocking, princess, poet, painter, prospector, troubadour, guerilla, Ché Guevara, the new Thomas à Becket" (120). He constructs a politically charged taxonomy that encompasses not only racial but also political and psychological types—the leftist "Ché Guevara" and the mad "Thomas à Becket"—who are creating anarchy in the city. Sammler's lists are important because, as Eric Sundquist notes in his analysis of the novel, they are part of Bellow's larger project of charting panethnic New York and, by extension, panethnic America. Sundquist writes that "by calling our attention to the polyglot culture of the United States—by means of the Hispanic women Sammler's survivor friend Walter Bruch makes the object of his lascivious desire, for example, or the Indian, Govinda Lal, with whom Sammler carries on a cerebral dialogue about H. G. Wells—Bellow escapes the white/black, Jewish/black binary even as he is insistently drawn back to it" (362).

Throughout the novel, Sammler plays the role of watcher. Riding the city bus, for example, he witnesses a pickpocket reach into a woman's purse without her knowledge. He soon becomes obsessed with the details of the crime and the criminal—a young black man dressed in luxurious finery. The thief's dandified appearance absorbs Sammler's attention; he seems to see the thief as both a stand-in for the excesses and degeneracy of 1960s America and an erotic object. He describes the minutiae of the criminal's appearance: "the dark glasses, the original design by Christian Dior, a powerful throat banded by a tab collar and a cherry silk necktie spouting out. Under the African nose, a cropped mustache.... [Sammler] believed he could smell French perfume from the breast of the camel's-hair coat." In contrast to his niece Angela, who has fallen for the "romance of the outlaw ... [and has] sent money to defense funds for black murderers and rapists," Sammler believes that "he [doesn't] give a damn for the glamour, the style, the art of criminals" (7). It is easy to see in Sammler's disdain something of Bellow's own distrust of the cult of the literary/cinematic outlaw then in vogue among American intellectuals, revealed in the popularity of Beat writing, films such as the 1967 *Bonnie and Clyde*, and the dashing French author Jean Gênet. In Sammler's eyes, the criminals have taken over not only all of Manhattan but all of aesthetics.

Although Sammler's encounters with the thief organize Bellow's narrative, they are just one instance of his preoccupation with the city's increasing racial hybridity—a metaphor for all that is primitive in the jungle of New York City. Sammler is convinced that race is spurring the city's degeneration, a belief he soon marries to his role as a Holocaust survivor. He is living, he believes, in the twentieth century's second period of Weimaresque social degeneracy, nearly as dangerous as World War II in the perilous position in which it places Jews. It is incumbent on him to bear witness, even if his form of witness does not permit him to see the irony of attaching the labels of degeneracy and decadence (once pinned to Jews) to other others.

The city itself is a metaphor for decay. Pay phones dangle from their cords, barring Sammler's access to the representatives of law and order. Although he contacts the police after witnessing the pickpocket's crime, he knows they will do nothing. Later in the novel, the city's lawlessness becomes even more apparent: the same criminal attacks an old man—an analogue for Sammler—and plays with his necktie. This teasing not only undermines the propriety of the suited man but also emphasizes the castration anxiety that has become central to Sammler's relationship with the idea of the black man.

Sammler's sex-laden fear of the powerful other is central to the racial landscape of the novel. The imagined relationship between the elderly Sammler and the sexually potent black pickpocket echoes Norman Podhoretz's 1963 analysis of Jewish–African American race relations in "My Negro Problem—and Ours." That infamous essay takes the form of a disingenuous apology from a disgruntled liberal who wants to engage in an honest appraisal of his own, and "our," racism. Although Podhoretz's piece was controversial for a number of reasons (notably the way in which it positioned his Jewish readers as fellow possessors of a "Negro problem"), its depiction of masculinity and gender politics is most striking. Throughout the essay, he unselfconsciously marks the ways in which his childhood as a Jewish sissy, unable to compete against neighborhood African American children in athletics or playground battles, was the prehistory of his present Negro problem. Beginning with a Baldwin quotation that asks black and white citizens to look on each other as "lovers" in order to enact a new hybrid racial consciousness, the essay goes on to contrast the Jew and the Negro as opposite poles of sexual and gender identity, as Sammler also does throughout Bellow's novel. According to Podhoretz, "the Negroes were tougher than we were, more ruthless, and on the whole they were better athletes" (93). Like Sammler, he uses the image of a downtrodden New York City and its populace to relate his pessimism about race relations in America.

Podhoretz argues that his early childhood experiences were telling, though he acknowledges hearing about African Americans who have been crippled by "exploitation and economic forces" (93). The essay recalls that when a group of African American children asked Podhoretz and his friends to leave a park, they "refuse[d], proudly and indignantly, with superb masculine fervor." Challenged to a fight, the Jewish children soon "retreat[ed], half-whimpering," "their first experience of cowardice." But how, Podhoretz wonders, could the Jewish children triumph when "there are people in the world who do not seem to be afraid of anything, who act as though they have nothing to lose" (94)? The recognition of his physical impotence before the imagined wildness of "the Negro" has constructed his future relationship to African American people, whom Podhoretz admits to not only hating but also envying: "just as in childhood [he] envied Negroes for the superior masculinity, so [he] env[ies] them today for what seems to [him] their superior physical grace and beauty. They are on the kinds of terms with their own body that [he] should like to be on with [his], and for that precious quality they seem blessed" (99).[27]

Clearly, Podhoretz ascribes both a more authentic masculinity and a stereotypical carnality to African Americans. Likewise, Sammler often hates and envies black men for their perceived physical superiority and masculinity, a politics of envy, desire, and usurpation that echoes the relationship between Lushinski and Ngambe in "The Mercenary" and Lesser and Spearmint in *The Tenants*. The psychosexual politics of *Mr. Sammler's Planet* reach their hysterical zenith in what has become the novel's most controversial scene. As he watches the black pickpocket rob the suited old man, Mr. Sammler is "seen seeing," and he soon becomes the thief's prey (37).[28] The pickpocket follows Sammler home and confronts him in the hallway of his apartment building, where Bellow combines animal and sexual imagery to depict the attack. "[The thief] no more spoke than a puma would." Holding Sammler against the wall, he "opened his fly and [took] out his penis." His genitals, like the man himself, are described as bestial, "with great oval testicles, a large tan-and-purple uncircumcised thing—a tube, a snake; metallic hairs bristled at the thick base and the tip curled beyond the supporting, demonstrating hand, suggesting the fleshly mobility of the elephant's trunk, though the skin was somewhat iridescent rather than thick or rough." The thief holds Sammler's gaze downward on his penis for a few moments and then abruptly leaves, "concluding the session, the lesson, the warning, the encounter, the transmission" (39).

Sammler's figurative rapist preys on the primacy of the visual by forcing the old man to look at his penis and acknowledge its semiotic power. Bellow explicitly emphasizes the phallus's potency as a visual statement: "Quod erat demonstrandum" (39). Sammler might recognize the fact that, in Podhoretz's words, "power is on [his] side, the police are working for [him] and not for them" (99).

Yet this phallic encounter demonstrates that the black man will always maintain a power over the Jewish man, particularly in the jungle of the city. Before forcing Sammler to look at his penis and acknowledge its power, the thief removes the old man's glasses, blurring his victim's vision and making him unable to observe the scene with his usual detachment. The witness becomes impotent. For Sammler, the thief's aggression represents a larger reality: "from the black side, strong currents were sweeping over everyone," and everywhere "the reprobates [were] converted into children of joy, the sexual ways of the seraglio and of the Congo bush adopted by the emancipated masses of New York, Amsterdam, London" (25).[29]

The pickpocket's sexuality, like the overwhelming carnality of various others in *Mr. Sammler's Planet* (including women and Native Americans), forms only one aspect of his dangerousness. His criminality is also central to Sammler's world, as are the ways in which it legitimates Bellow's own move from liberalism to wary neoconservatism, a trajectory common to many Jewish intellectuals of the period. Neocon Ben Wattenberg once joked that a neoconservative is "a liberal who has been mugged by reality" (Unger).[30] This gibe identifies the mugger as reality. Nonetheless, it is clear that he links it to a more concrete image of criminality: the dangerous African American man, whose unchecked masculinity and demands for recognition have disabused the era's sheepish liberals of their utopian fantasies. Race and the distortions of racism brought on by what Howard Winant calls the "white racial politics" of the post–civil rights era are the subterranean catalyst for the neoconservative project (3). As Winant points out, "neoconservative discourse seeks to *preserve* white advantages through the denial of racial difference" (7). Both Podhoretz's essay and Allan Bloom's *The Closing of the American Mind*, a revolt against the encroachment of identity politics into the university (to which Bellow wrote the introduction), embrace the neoconservative rhetoric of color-blindness and exhibit complex negotiations with Jewish identity. Likewise, *Mr. Sammler's Planet* marks some of the ways in which the category of race has guided the New Right in the United States. Near the end of the novel, for instance, the pickpocket reappears to threaten a Columbia University student, Lionel Feffer. This character, who shares the first name and maligned intellectualism of Lionel Trilling, may be Bellow's allusion to the father of those midcentury Jewish intellectuals most undermined by the New Left's vociferous racial politics and challenges to liberalism.

It is no accident that the pickpocket is nameless and mute. Like the jungle beasts with which he is identified, he is seen and not heard. His muteness is important to both the racial universe of the novel and the larger politics of speech and representation at play in American literature of the era. Clearly, Bellow is not worried about speaking for, or ventriloquizing, an African American pickpocket who doesn't even merit a name. As I will discuss, the fact that he cannot and does not speak also links him to the racialized others who appear throughout the writer's contemporaneous work, notably the silent Palestinians in *To Jerusalem and Back*.

The novel's scene of silent homoerotic violence must be situated in the lengthy history of Bellow's representations of race. Like Malamud, he is primarily known for his preoccupations with the role of the intellectual in the twentieth century. Yet throughout his career, he was also deeply engaged with questions of race, especially with black-white relations. Bellow studied with the famous anthropologist Melville Herskovitz at Northwestern University, shortly before Herskovitz wrote *The Myth of the Negro Past*, often seen as the foundation of African American studies. Bellow was profoundly influenced by his professor's work on race as well as the work of an earlier anthropologist, Franz Boas, whose study of the Inuit tribes inspired his senior thesis on what he saw as a fascinating yet primitive Eskimo tribe.

Early in his career, he had strong sympathies with contemporaneous African American writers, particularly Ralph Ellison, who was a close friend and whose *Invisible Man* was a clear influence on Bellow's own work.[31] His first novel, *The Very Dark Trees* (1941), which he destroyed when he couldn't find a publisher, tells the story of a white southerner who is hit by lightning and transformed into a black man.[32] He set *Henderson the Rain King* (1959) in Africa, using it to satirize the colonialist fantasies of writers such as Hemingway. His story "Looking for Mr. Green" (1951), set in the Depression, manifests a belief in the possibility of profound interracial sympathy, as do Malamud's early short stories "The Angel Levine" and "Black Is My Favorite Color." The story's protagonist, George Grebe, scorns a racist Italian grocer and experiences a moment of poignant identification with an elderly black aid recipient and war veteran. Yet like Malamud, Bellow's belief in the possibility of interracial harmony was rattled by the 1960s Black Power movement. *Mr. Sammler's Planet* may be his effort to chart the decline of his own (and "our") midcentury Jewish liberalism. By 1988, when James Atlas did a profile of Allan Bloom and the canon wars, he recorded Bloom's friend Bellow as asking, "Who is the Tolstoy of the Zulus? The Proust of the Papuans? I'd be glad to read him" ("Chicago's Grumpy Guru"). This statement, which Bellow later disputed in an angry rejoinder, disturbed even Bellow's longtime supporter, Alfred Kazin, who saw him as "moving right" in a worrisome way ("Jews" 62).[33]

For the most part, however, critics have avoided labeling Bellow a racist. For instance, in his reading of the encounter between Sammler and his attacker, Ethan Goffman acknowledges that the thief is "a compact, dramatic version of a recurring Euro-American mythologization: blackness as the primitive, the carnal, the return of the repressed." Yet he argues that the Jewishness of *Mr. Sammler's Planet*, instead of buttressing the racist caricature of the black pickpocket, gradually subverts the vision of race embodied by Bellow's early depiction of the thief. According to Goffman, Sammler's Holocaust history, emblematic of the long trajectory of Jewish marginalization, proposes a "muted" identification between black and Jew while "revealing the arbitrariness of racialist distinctions" (706). This reading, like that of many other critics, privileges one strand of Jewish identity over another and effaces the historical particularity of the novel's preoccupation with the black man. At the time Bellow was writing *Mr. Sammler's Planet*, the implications of the Holocaust had moved far from the universalist aspirations that Goffman perceives in the novel. In the first two decades of his career, Bellow had exalted universal humanism and Enlightenment values— starting with *Dangling Man* (1944) and lasting through at least *Herzog* (1964). In *Mr. Sammler's Planet*, we witness a distinct shift in his sympathies. Sammler is not contrasted with the black thief as a civilized white man (one of the ethnically vague intellectuals who populate Bellow's early work) but as a Holocaust survivor, defined by the specialness that his particularly Jewish suffering has given him. "Like many people who had seen the world collapse once, Mr. Sammler entertained the possibility it might collapse twice" (26). The nameless black man becomes a harbinger of this second period of world chaos and the end of America's role as a refuge for the Jews.

In *Mr. Sammler's Planet*, Bellow's representation of the Holocaust as an archetypically Jewish and American tragedy emerges strikingly in his depiction of Israel. Eisen, the novel's primary Israeli character, is married to Sammler's mentally ill daughter, Shula. Throughout, Eisen is a beastly character, nearly on par with the black criminal. Not only does he beat Shula, but (nearly as damning in Sammler's eyes) he lacks his father-in-law's cultivated air and intellectual acumen. Like the black thief, Eisen is one of Sammler's shadow selves, and Sammler's distaste for him only compounds the depth of their connection. On Sammler's last run-in with the black thief, the pickpocket is attacking Feffer, who has been attempting to photograph his crimes. Realizing that he and the flabby Feffer are physically outmatched, he calls on his son-in-law, whose madness and strong laborer's arms are able to subdue the black man. Sammler's distaste for Eisen is complicated by his realization that only this uncultivated Israeli can compete in the newly tribal ethos of American society. As both Sundquist and Emily Miller Budick have noted, Israel and the figure of the Israeli Jew "[have] introduced a crucial triangulating term into the stalemated domestic argument between Jews and blacks" (Sundquist 363). Sammler's brutal Israeli son-in-law is the only one who can defeat the pickpocket at his own violent game.

Budick suggests that Eisen is "antagonist and double" for the black pickpocket and Mr. Sammler himself. For this reason, she sees *Mr. Sammler's Planet* as being "as much, perhaps even more, about the relationship between American Jews and Israelis as it is about American Jews and blacks. And the central black character functions for Bellow not only (or at least not directly) as a way of constructing American Jewish identity, but of portraying the Israeli identity that American Jews must also resist" (154). Although I, too, read Eisen and Israeli identity as central to the novel, I don't see that identity as something that the American Jews in the novel resist. Rather, Israel, like the Holocaust more generally, was growing to inhabit a central place in the American Jewish imaginary as a means of concretizing Jewish difference. Notably, Eisen is not the most significant reference to Israel in *Mr. Sammler's Planet*. Throughout the novel, Bellow explicitly links the Six Day War and the Holocaust, a common feature of Israeli political rhetoric during the era. Yet many readings neglect the strange narrative woven into the second half, when the septuagenarian is suddenly transformed into a war correspondent assigned to report on Israel during the Six Day War.

If Sammler spends the first portion of Bellow's novel as an abject witness to the decline of America and the American city, by the end he becomes a far more committed social actor. Gradually, his tendencies to ruminate on his days in wartorn Poland and to find voyeuristic pleasure in watching the world around him are superseded by an urgent need to travel to Israel to bear witness to the possible annihilation of the Jews. Bellow describes Mr. Sammler's decision, made on the eve of the war, as troops amass at the Israeli border: "No Zionist, Mr. Sammler, and for many years little interested in Jewish affairs. Yet, from the start of the crisis, he could not sit in New York reading the world press. If only because for the second time in twenty-five years the same people were threatened by extermination: the so-called powers letting things drift toward disaster; men armed for massacre. And he refused to stay in Manhattan watching television" (116).

Few critics have noted that the Israeli plotline in *Mr. Sammler's Planet* is echoed in the travelogue Bellow published six years later. Although Bellow's 1975 trip to Israel with his then wife was the ostensible basis of *To Jerusalem and Back* (1976), the account is clearly shadowed by his earlier experiences as a *Newsday* correspondent during the Six Day War, a job often excised from his official curriculum vitae. Bellow visited Jerusalem and filed four dispatches for the paper directly after the June war but generally downplayed the event's impact on his worldview. However, as his biographer James Atlas points out, Bellow's first visit to Israel had an enormous influence on the shift in his political and aesthetic sympathies after the late 1960s: "he didn't pretend to be objective, and he was openly hostile to the superpowers who had abandoned Israel to its fate. As for the Arabs, their zealous national pride could spawn only more destruction" (370–371). In Bellow's eyes, the camps set up for refugee Arabs did little more than give them a place to loiter and practice "politics" (370).

Clearly, the writer's first trip to Israel was paramount in his construction of the world of Artur Sammler. Like the aging Bellow, Sammler is an unlikely traveler to wartime Israel but nonetheless becomes a correspondent for a *Newsday*-like publication. Working as a journalist, he draws what he perceives to be an immutable connection between his experiences during the Holocaust and his role as witness to the dangers of the Six Day War. Budick suggests that Bellow's visit to Israel also had a profound effect on his depiction of the black pickpocket:

"in thinking about Zionism, especially in relation to Israel's Arab citizens, and the Palestinian population put into its control by the 1967 war, Bellow, as an American Jewish writer, would take an oddly familiar path on his way to resolving his conflicts as an American. He would think through his own situation as an American Jew by thinking through the situation of American blacks" (150). While I agree with Budick, I think the connection is even more apparent in his preoccupation with how blacks were imperiling American Jews' identity. As in *The Tenants*, the radical sympathy between American Jews and blacks evident in Bellow's early work is largely missing from *Mr. Sammler's Planet*.

In *To Jerusalem and Back*, Israel functions as both Old and New World—a vision of an authentic Jewish past as well as a potential Jewish future. Moreover, it reminds the author of an idea of Jewish difference that he had long abandoned in his quest to become a disinterested, liberal intellectual. Throughout the travelogue, he worries about the way in which Israel invades his consciousness and prevents his return to the realm of the universal. After going back to his home in Chicago, he reads Homer in an attempt to flee his memories of death and political uncertainty in Israel. But the poet's universal humanism provides no consolation; Bellow is "not able to make room for Homer beside [his] preoccupation with Israel" (189). An effort to read *Lawrence of Arabia* also fails because it reminds him of the Palestinian problem. As the title of the travelogue suggests, Bellow's return to the United States is shadowed by his return to Jerusalem. What he has carried back from Israel disturbs the comfort of his position as a man who has always claimed that his Americanness defines him more than his Jewishness does. The form of the book—sixty-two short essays that meditate on the possibility of return—itself represents this doubleness. Christine Bird argues that Bellow's "solution to the problem of the return journey . . . is to concentrate on himself for the first 48 sections as an American traveling in Israel and, for the next 14 sections, as a Jew traveling through America. He is an American Jew throughout, but his emphasis is on the 'American' at the beginning, 'Jewish' at the end" (51).

This move from American Jew to Jewish American is foreshadowed in the first scene of *To Jerusalem and Back*, when Bellow is traveling with his non-Jewish wife Alexandra and a large group of Hasidim who are "flying to Israel to attend the circumcision of the firstborn son of their spiritual leader, the Belzer Rabbi." The Hasidim signal their difference from the secular Bellow in their sartorial choices: "God instructed Moses to speak to the children of Israel and to 'bid them that they make them fringes in the borders of their garments' [and] they are still wearing them some four thousand years later." They also cleave to various markers of Jewish otherness, including the reason for their visit—the ultimate symbol of Jewish difference. In contrast to Bellow and his wife (a college professor with a temporary teaching fellowship in Israel), the Hasidim "are far too restless to wait in line [to board the plane] but rush in and out, gesticulating, exclaiming," in what he portrays as a stereotypically Jewish fashion (1).

The Hasidic man sitting next to the couple asks Bellow in Yiddish if he will switch seats with his wife so that the Hasid won't have to sit next to her and risk violating the Halakhic proscription that prohibits a man from sitting next to a woman who may be menstruating and thus unclean. At first, the man seems as repulsed by Bellow as he was by his wife; he is uncomfortable with a Jew who has not carried kosher food onto the plane and whose wife "has not had a Jewish upbringing" and speaks "not a word" of Yiddish. He soon "tr[ies] to save" Bellow, offering to pay him fifteen dollars a week for the rest of his life if he "will eat nothing but kosher food" (3). The writer is uncomfortable with the Hasidic man and his insular conception of Jewish identity, but he is also aware of the man's uncanniness, in the sense of being both uncomfortably alien in his religious behaviors and exotic attire yet also a familiar figure from Bellow's childhood among Orthodox Jews in Canada and the United States. "There is nothing foreign in these hats, sidelocks, and fringes. It is my childhood revisited. At the age of six, I myself wore a tallith katan, or scapular, under my shirt, only mine was a scrap of green calico print, whereas theirs is white linen" (1). From this awkward encounter, the travelogue unfolds into an exploration of the uncanny return of Jewishness into the life of a secular American Jew. Long intent on his role as a writer of canonical humanistic fiction, Bellow suddenly finds himself embroiled in public affairs and the question of how Israel can survive both its enemies and the ethical violations of its own practices. The book offers no clear statement about Israel's right to might, but it does close with certainty about the nation's inescapable effect on Jewish American consciousness. By the end of *To Jerusalem and Back*, Bellow has transformed from "an American traveling in Israel" to "a Jew traveling through America," a change that heralds a dawning political consciousness (Bird 51).

The book's publication, on the heels of *Mr. Sammler's Planet*, marked the beginning of Bellow's career as a neoconservative. Although *To Jerusalem and Back* is a fairly even-handed depiction of Israeli politics during the late 1960s and early 1970s, reviewers recognized that it was advocating for a larger American role in the entire Middle East. Like many proponents of American-Israeli friendship, Bellow explicitly linked American support of Israel to the necessity of maintaining a democratic presence in the unfriendly Arab world. Further, because Bellow's own travels to Israel during the Six Day War probably served as a primary text for both *Mr. Sammler's Planet* and *To Jerusalem and Back*, I see an analogy between his representations of blacks in the novel and Palestinians in the travelogue. Both are characterized by silence; neither the black thief nor the rowdy Palestinian children who play outside Bellow's hotel room ever get to talk. It is clear, however, especially in *To Jerusalem and Back*, that Bellow does have sympathy for these marginalized ethnic others. In the midst of his travel narrative, he often stops to puzzle over the ethics of the Israeli occupation of parts of Palestine. Still, as Edward Said has pointed out in *The Question of Palestine*, even though Bellow's book is purportedly about the crisis between Israel and the Arab world, he allows no Palestinians or other Arab nationals to speak for themselves. Instead, they are always translated through the many experts whom Bellow meets in his journey, people who gladly interpret "the Muslim Question" for him and his readers. According to Said, this mediation of the Palestinian experience is part of a larger silencing project:

> Zionism always undertakes to speak for Palestine and the Palestinians; this has always meant a blocking operation, by which the Palestinian cannot be heard from (or represent himself) directly on the world stage. Just as the expert Orientalist believed that only he could speak (paternally as it were) for the natives and primitive societies that he had studied—his *presence* denoting their *absence*—so too the Zionists spoke to the world on behalf of the Palestinians. (39)

In *Mr. Sammler's Planet*, the black thief remains similarly mute and nameless, a native whom Bellow interprets for his readership as well as a screen onto which he projects his ruminations about Jewish American identity. What the black thief comes to mark is the confused response of American Jews to identity politics in the 1960s. Sammler often comments on the poverty of American Jews' connection to Jewish identity and their hunger to identify with European Jewry and the Holocaust to fix a sense of self. Brought from Europe under the auspices of his wealthy nephew, Elya Gruner, Sammler is expected to supply his American Jewish family with authentic anecdotes of prewar life, particularly those that pertain to religion. When asked about their ancestors' synagogue participation in prewar Poland, he disappoints his nephew by saying, "Ah, the synagogue. Well, you see, Elya, I didn't have much to do with the synagogue. We were almost free-thinkers. Especially my mother. She had a Polish education. She gave me an emancipated name: Artur." He "regret[s] that he [is] so poor at family reminiscences. Contemporary contacts being somewhat unsatisfactory, he would have gladly helped Gruner to build up the past" (68). Sammler recognizes that, for his younger Jewish relatives, his job is to collect and disseminate memory. In search of a portal into Jewish identification, they look to the Holocaust survivor for a narrative of Jewishness.

Such questions of identity abound in *Mr. Sammler's Planet*. Sammler's daughter, who was hidden from the Nazis in a Polish convent during the war, is driven mad by her dual commitments to the Polish Catholicism in which she was raised and the essential Jewishness she believes she possesses. Her names embody this doubleness: sometimes she refers to herself by her Hebrew name, Shula; sometimes by her Polish name, Slawa. Like Rosa, the Holocaust survivor protagonist of Cynthia Ozick's "The Shawl," Shula is a scavenger, obsessed with collecting the detritus of other's lives to symbolize or supplement the losses of her own. Throughout the novel, Sammler wonders how he can moor his daughter in the Jewish identity she needs to feel secure. In part, he travels to Israel to give his extended family a proxy expedition into Jewishness.[34]

Bellow's novel is structured as just such an expedition, a search for an appropriate geography for Jewish identity in an age of anarchy and increasing moral relativism. The novel's original title was *The Future of the Moon*, and the moon still plays a central metaphorical role in the final published version. Sammler is fascinated by the theories of the moon introduced by H. G. Wells, whom he met during his Zelig-like prewar life. As Shula goes mad, she steals a scientist's manuscript about the moon. New York City is described as a desolate lunar landscape, and Sammler is preoccupied by the "loonies" who surround him, creatures seemingly driven mad by time and the constellation of the planets. Gradually, however, we learn that the moon preoccupies Sammler primarily because of its blankness. It is a world without the palimpsest of history, a world where the Jew can carve out an identity untouched by the conflicts of the past. He soon realizes that this dream of a perfect planet cannot be reality. It is not the moon but America, Israel, and prewar Poland that form the central geographical spaces of *Mr. Sammler's Planet*. By illuminating the nexus of the Holocaust, the Six Day War, and America's shifting racial landscape after 1967, Bellow constructs a dystopian planet for Sammler and an irreplaceable artifact of the era in which he was writing.

CHAPTER 4

The Jew in the Canon and the Culture Wars

READING RACE AND LITERARY HISTORY

Intimately tied to the issues of Jewish difference and racial ventriloquism that Ozick and Bellow address in their Holocaust fiction is the question of where Jewish writers fit into the American literary canon during the late twentieth century. Long before the rise of multiculturalism and the culture wars of the 1980s and 1990s, critics were asking, What is Jewish literature? In a controversial 2001 essay on the link between race and Jewish literary history, Michael Kramer argues that the persistence of the question "rests firmly upon and is thoroughly enmeshed in the thorny political question 'who is a Jew?'" ("Race, Literary History, and the 'Jewish' Question" 289). According to him, this preoccupation with creating a literary taxonomy—a specifically Jewish canon—correlates with the persistent search for a Jewish racial identity; and he believes the question became especially significant during the late twentieth century, when Jewishness itself seemed ever more intangible. Moreover, he argues, this desire to codify literature along racial or national lines is not new. Since at least the nineteenth century, the generally German-Jewish practitioners of the *Wissenschaft des Judentums* (the school of thought that translates roughly as "the science of Judaism") have sought to classify and understand their "national" literary tradition. "Jewish literature and its study are necessarily and inextricably bound up with the rupture in Jewish history marked by Enlightenment and Emancipation—by the breakdown of rabbinic authority, the de-politicizing of Jewish corporate status, and the consequent renegotiations of Jewish personal and collective identity" (288).

"The rupture in Jewish history" that took place in the eighteenth and nineteenth centuries re-presented "the external 'Jewish Question' as an internal 'Jewish' Question" because it caused Jews' private and public lives to collide in previously unimaginable ways (288).[1] Under the influence of Enlightenment philosophy and its central concepts of subjectivity and natural rights, many rulers of the era offered Jews greater participation in civic life, but Jews did so at a cost. In order to embrace the secular European nation-state, they were obliged to give up the spiritual nation-state of their Jewish identity.[2] Given the influence of Enlightenment values and legal emancipation on traditional Jewish structures of cultural and literary authority, we cannot be surprised that the vast shifts that heralded eighteenth- and nineteenth-century modernity left Jews searching for ways to determine the boundaries of their identity. As peoples across Europe and North America struggled to define their own nations and their own racial meanings, the ever-landless Jews sought to participate in the high-stakes game of nation building in any way they could.

The history of modern Jewish literature and its classification during the Enlightenment prefigure contemporary debates about the place of Jewish literature in America. Now as then, anxieties about the existence of Jewish literature as a category arise at moments when the bedrock of Jewish identity is most contested. They also bring up the question of whether Jews are a race and whether racial characterizations can ever be entirely avoided in the construction or dismantling of canons. Kramer controversially argues that, "to be considered a Jewish writer, in my view, one need not use a 'Jewish' language, or exhibit certain 'Jewish' literary characteristics, or address certain 'Jewish' subjects, or even know how to ask the 'Jewish' question. One need only be a writer of Jewish extraction, a member of the Jewish race." To preempt criticism of this racial definition of Jewish writing, he continues, "Considering the way the category of race has been wielded in the recent culture wars, let me make clear at the same time that by offering a racial definition of Jewish literature, I do not mean that we must see all Jewish writing only 'through the prism of race,' as if the goal of Jewish literary study could or should be reduced to a sorting of out of victims and victimizers." In his view, some agreed-upon idea of race need not be the "end of all" Jewish literary historiography, but it does need to be its precondition (290). Kramer pointedly invokes "the culture wars" in his wary advocacy for a racial definition of Jewish literature. The Jewish writer was elevated to culture hero in the immediate postwar era, becoming a living metaphor for the alienation of the age. In contrast, the post-multicultural era witnessed the rise of an entirely different politics of Jewish literary identity in America. For Jewish writers and intellectuals such as Kramer, the Jewish identification with classic Enlightenment values has made the politics of difference that are so central to multiculturalism's challenge to universalism (and the university) particularly hard to embrace.[3] According to David Biale, Michael Galchinsky, and Susannah Heschel, "many Jews believe that the replacement of the Enlightenment ideal of universalism with a politics of difference and a fragmented 'multiculture' would constitute a threat to Jewish achievement. At the same time, they recognize the dangers of a homogeneous 'monoculture' for Jewish particularity" (7).

Before attending to the tensions of recent Jewish literature, let's explore that earlier moment of taxonomy. During the proto-multicultural moment of the *Wissenschaft des Judentums*, scholars and nation-states began to question whether the universality of Enlightenment philosophy would be able to encompass those archetypical others within: the Jews. While they were committed to the civic ideals of Rousseau or the revolutionary praxis of the French Revolution, rulers also wondered whether the modern nation-state, however enlightened, would be able to absorb a group whose members clung stubbornly to their particularity and separateness from the national body politic. Arguably, Jews were the first minorities to pose an intractable problem for the modern European nation-state, which sought to emancipate so as to absorb. For even though Jews embraced some of the rights that their newly enlightened rulers offered them, they also insisted on maintaining the semi-sovereign status they had won during the Middle Ages and continued to adhere stubbornly to cultural and religious practices (from circumcision and endogamy to the speaking of Yiddish and Hebrew) that advertised their difference from their host society.[4]

As a scholarly and literary movement, the *Wissenschaft des Judentums* arose, like much in Jewish culture, from a mixture of pride and anxiety. Proponents were influenced by the wider ideals of European Enlightenment even as they wished to construct their own Jewish-identified high cultural movement that could rival the German one in which they had been educated. The *Wissenschaft* was radical for many both inside and outside the Jewish community because it suggested an equality of value between Jewish and secular national traditions and thus suggested that Jewish tradition was potentially both secular and national. Despite their commitment to secular Jewish identities and practices, however, many of the scholars identified with the movement, such as Leopold Zunz and Heinrich Graetz, had deep roots in Judaism and attempted to span the gap between the religious and secular branches of Jewish history. Significantly, they sought to create a national literary history so as to construct a nation.

That fraught relationship between the identity of the Jew and the identity of the nation continued into the twentieth century. The Frankfurt school theorists, Theodor Adorno and Max Horkheimer, placed the unassimilable Jewish other at the center of their meditation on modernity, *Dialectic of Enlightenment*, arguing that the structural position of the Jew highlighted the disastrous conclusions of Enlightenment conceptions of universality: that is, totalitarianism.[5] Long before poststructuralists began iterating the politics of difference, the Marxist German-Jewish thinkers saw totalitarianism, particularly Hitler's brand of fascism, as the *telos*, or endpoint, of the swallowing of difference that had begun in the homogenizing maw of the Enlightenment. A half-century later, proponents and critics of multiculturalism were continuing to ask if enlightened liberal societies had room for difference. The term *multiculturalism* had been coined in the 1940s, not long after Adorno and Horkheimer had published their work; and it came to be used in its common sense in the 1970s, when Ozick and Bellow were writing their racially inflected Holocaust narratives. Nonetheless, the concept did not come into prominence as a discourse in America until the 1980s and 1990s, when Jewish American writers became even more self-conscious about their own position in multicultural debates and the ensuing culture wars.

Race and Literary History in Philip Roth's *The Human Stain*

Finding themselves in an ambiguous position during the culture wars of the 1980s and 1990s, Jewish American writers began to focus on discourses of cosmopolitanism, interracial identity, and transracial masquerade to express the anxieties attendant to their liminal position in American literary history and multicultural discourse. These preoccupations find their apotheosis in Philip Roth's novel *The Human Stain* (2000), in which the archetypical Jewish author manifests his vexed relationship to race and canonicity by articulating the concerns of the endangered Jewish intellectual and proponent of universal humanism through the mouth of an African American passing for a Jewish professor. Until recently, few scholars have attempted to study the responses of Jewish writers to their increasingly canonical status in an American literary environment focused on the particularity of racial and ethnic voices, even though writers such as Roth have played a pivotal role in articulations of literary ethnicity—what Mark McGurl calls "high cultural pluralism."[6] The result is a gap in the study of both contemporary American literature and critical race theory, an inherently comparative discipline dedicated to "uncover[ing] the ongoing dynamics of racialized power, and its embeddedness in practices and values which have been shorn of any explicit, formal manifestation of racism" (Crenshaw et al. xxix). Although early theorists of critical race theory were interested primarily in the ways in which the "dynamics of racialized power" were inscribed in legal practices and social values, later scholars such as David Palumbo-Liu and Walter Mignolo argue that the formation of literary histories have also been crucial to the implicit institutionalization of race.

In *The Culture Wars: The Struggle to Define America* (1991), James Davison Hunter began to articulate the link between multiculturalism and the culture wars, contending that the culture wars were defined by a collision between religious and secular interests to control the American public sphere. Although some of these battles for social dominance took place in the courts, many took place in or around cultural institutions such as universities and museums or around social practices such as marriage or family planning that had once been outside the purview of election-cycle politics. During the 1980s, however, progressive intellectuals and conservative interests began to fight over the "politicization of the curriculum" in universities (215). As a way to acknowledge the interconnections of racial and literary genealogies, critics who espoused multiculturalism argued fervently against what they saw as the univocality of the western canon. In their view, institutional revisions of the standards used to determine the value of literary works should be the corollary to affirmative action programs used to increase university diversity. They challenged the canon with books by writers from across the racial, ethnic, national, and gender spectrum, with the goal of fostering a diversity of viewpoints in higher education. This challenge to the canon, articulated by Barbara Herrnstein Smith, Harold Kolb, and others, posited the impossibility of a neutral literary sphere apart from the discursive shifts in value taking place in the world around the university.[7] In response, conservative opponents of multiculturalism argued vehemently against what they saw as the loss of a shared public discourse, claiming that "multiculturalism's hardliners, who seem to make up the majority of the movement, damn as racism any attempt to draw the myriad of American groups into a common American culture. For these multiculturalists, differences are absolute, irreducible, intractable" (Siegel 35).

Jewish American authors and intellectuals inhabited a particularly vexed place in these debates about whether to privilege difference or sameness, private or public loyalties, the canon or challenges to it. Novelists, in particular, had long been anxious about their hyphenated identity, a bind originating in what many saw as Jews' too successful integration into postwar America. It didn't help that "as early as the 1960s, influential critics [had] argued that American Jewish writing no longer counted as a distinct or innovative literary project, for younger Jews had grown so assimilated, so remote from traditional Jewish life, that only nostalgia kept it going" (Dickstein 168). As I have discussed in earlier chapters, pessimism about the position of the Jewish writer as an intermediary, simultaneously able to speak for the marginalized and for the average American, increased in the 1970s. By then, Bellow and Malamud, once quintessential American figures of modern ethnicized alienation, were no longer part of the literary avant-garde. When compared to the immediacy of racially identified authors and experimental postmodernists, their realist commitments and their eschewal of autobiography seemed to be outmoded.[8]

By the 1980s, the situation had become even more complex. Jews were now categorical symbols of successful acculturation into American society—so much so that Asian Americans, seen as similarly apt at incorporating themselves into the body politic, were being dubbed the "new Jews" (Liu 3). For instance, the Asian American protagonist of Gish Jen's *Mona in the Promised Land* (1997) believes that imitating her Jewish acquaintances in Scarsdale is the entryway into white America. In these years, many Jewish American writers feared that, within the framework of the burgeoning field of multicultural fiction, Jewish difference was no longer different enough. As Andrew Furman points out, Jewish American writers had a shaky hold on their outsider status and no clear criteria for establishing their identity as a discrete group rather than a loose collective.

PASSING, SO TO SPEAK: ROTH AND RACE

As an advocate of the independence of the authorial voice, stripped of allegiance to ethnic and familial affiliation, Philip Roth found multiculturalism particularly worrisome. He had long had the reputation of being the enfant terrible of American letters, the author of gleefully establishment-challenging works such as *Goodbye, Columbus* (1959) and *Portnoy's Complaint* (1969). Yet by the 1990s he had become less a figure for millennial alienation than a linchpin of the American canon.[9] Among detractors of the old boys' club of American letters, there was little difference between Roth and Updike, postwar writers of roughly the same age, a perception that resonates with Ozick's critical appraisal of Updike's Jewish Bech books (see chapter 3). The fact that Roth was Jewish and Updike a Protestant was nearly irrelevant. The books of both authors depicted well-heeled white members of the intellectual and socioeconomic elite. Both men were "past retirement age," far from the "multicultural literary fashions of the day," and "thoroughly trashed by feminists" (Max). According to Sven Birkerts, by the 1990s, both Roth's and Updike's work (along with the work of fellow postwar American writers Saul Bellow and Norman Mailer) had become "weak, makeshift and gravely disappointing to all who believed that these novelists had a special line on the truth(s) of late modernity." Roth, like his literary alter egos, had once gained identity from challenging the standards of white Protestant America, posing as an antidote to the stuffy mores of the bourgeoisie. But in an era of rising multicultural and feminist literary critique, he was coming to embody the status quo he had once sought to undermine. To many of his critics, Roth was just another old white man.

This de-ethnicizing, this whitening, of Roth was appropriate in a number of ways. He had long been ambivalent to being deemed a representative man. Like Bellow, he often purported to reject both religious and national identity in favor of a more universal classification as a writer.[10] In "Writing about Jews," first published in *Commentary* in 1963 and later in *Reading Myself and Others* (1975), he rails against his appointed role as spokesman for the Jewish tribe. Addressing the many Jews who have criticized him for not giving "a balanced portrayal of Jews as we know them," he argues that fiction cannot and should not be concerned with representing the whole of a people: "what fiction does and what the rabbi would like it to do are two entirely different things. The concerns of fiction are not those of a statistician—or of a public-relations firm. The novelist asks himself, 'What do people think?'; the PR man asks, 'What *will* people think?'" (48, 50). The Jewish writer is expected to ask himself, "what will the goyim think?" in a manner never required of the Gentile writer in America (50). Yet even as he resents the imperative to write *as* a Jew for an imagined *goyische* audience and with the possibility of anti-Semitism always in mind, Roth relishes the possibility that his work has the capacity to speak to Jews who are unimpressed by the tired pieties of rabbis and other Jewish communal leaders. Roth ends his essay by asking if the question might be with "who is going to address men and women like men and women, and who like children." For a postwar Jewish audience in search of a touchstone for Jewish identity, the "stories the novelists tell" have become more persuasive than "the sermons of some of the rabbis." The Jewish writer is becoming the true conscience of the race precisely because "there are regions of feeling and consciousness in [his stories] which cannot be reached by the oratory of self-congratulation and self-pity" (63).

This ambivalence about speaking for the Jews is a central component of Roth's work and provides a fascinating parallel to the anxiety about speaking for the other expressed by writers such as Bellow, Ozick, Malamud, and Hettie Jones. Roth, too, has felt most comfortable speaking the self (especially the Jewish self) through the voice of an other, as he does so effectively in *The Human Stain*. This strategic racial ventriloquism is not as disconnected to his literary project as he would have us believe. Despite his protestations about rejecting the coercive pull of the first-person plural, he has discomfited his many Jewish critics precisely because he has persisted in portraying a racialized Jewish difference.

In his "American trilogy," published between 1997 and 2000, Roth manifests a particular preoccupation with race and the whitening of Jewish identity. The first book in the trilogy, the historically conscious and panoramic novel *American Pastoral* (1997), highlights the squalor of Roth's beloved Newark after the race riots and white flight of the late 1960s. In this shifting racial landscape, the reader witnesses a transformation in how the writer represents the effects of racial unrest on a city and in how he represents Jewish racial identity. The male antiheroes of his earlier works—Neil Klugman of *Goodbye, Columbus*, Alexander Portnoy of *Portnoy's Complaint*, and Roth's frequent literary alter ego Nathan Zuckerman—are depicted as dark, racially intermediary figures who share the carnality of the stereotypical Negro and occasion miscegenation anxieties in the parents of the white women they date. In contrast, his portrayal of Jewish identity in *American Pastoral* is suffused with anxiety about the gradual whitening of Jewish identity after the 1960s. Swede Levov, the novel's protagonist, is a WASP masquerading as a Jew.[11] His nickname plays off his Aryan features: he is blond and blue-eyed, a vaunted athlete, and a cannily diplomatic presence, nothing like the Portnoys and Zuckermans who peopled Roth's fictional landscape in the previous decades. In *The Plot against America* (2004), the third book in the trilogy, Roth returned to the Jewish racial profile in America, detailing the attempts of the fictional Roth clan to demonstrate their commitment to the WASP ethos of land and liberty while American fascists foment German-style racial anti-Semitism. But as Walter Benn Michaels points out in his criticism of the novel, Roth imports the racism and segregations experienced by the Jewish characters in *The Plot against America* from the Jim Crow South rather than Germany (*The Trouble with Diversity* 51). The writer uses what he perceives to be the ambiguous whiteness of Jews in America as a site from which to critique race and ethnicity in the United States.

Between *American Pastoral* and *The Plot against America*, Roth published *The Human Stain* (2000), his deepest investment in representing the complexities of race in America. Coleman Silk, the tragic hero, is a black man passing for white. At the age of eighteen, he leaves his home in New Jersey and, with it, his commitment to the racial and familial affiliations with which he has been raised. Silk joins the navy, where he learns that his light complexion allows him to pass for Greek American or Arab American. As he sloughs off the anchor of his race, Silk also decides to get the image of an anchor tattooed on his arm; it becomes his "human stain," the only material reminder of the past he has discarded.

Postwar America is newly in love with the Jewish people, whom they've just helped to save from total annihilation in Europe. Now that he's left the navy, Silk decides to become Jewish himself, employing his intimate knowledge of northern New Jersey's large Jewish population to effectively impersonate the articulate Jewish intellectuals who surround him in his classes at New York University. As a graduate student in classics, he meets a Jewish woman, Iris Gittelman, and marries her for "that sinuous thicket of hair that was far more Negroid than his own," a shrewd decision that will preempt future questions about the hair texture of his offspring and thus his own origins (136). He gets a job, first as a classics professor and later as dean of faculty, at Athena College, a small liberal-arts school in New England, bastion of white America. The tale of *The Human Stain* begins when Silk, about to retire after a long and successful career as a professor and a white man, returns to the classroom and is accused of racism.

Roth's novel engages with race and its interconnections with literary history in a number of ways, most strikingly through the trope of passing and the way in which the writer uses the secret of Silk's blackness to legitimate his critique of multiculturalism. Passing has a lengthy history in American literature. Since at least the nineteenth century, when the "one-drop rule" essentialized racial identity into an entity that transcended the visible and located itself in the imagined interiority of blood, the literature of passing has sought to tell the stories of those who have managed to opt out of their racial legacy. Despite Roth's self-conscious engagement in this literary tradition, however, we need to distinguish between his character Coleman Silk and the haunted protagonists of earlier narratives, such as Nella Larsen's *Passing* (1929) and James Weldon Johnson's *Autobiography of an Ex-Colored Man* (1912). Like Silk, Clare Kendry of *Passing* and the nameless protagonist of Johnson's novel are trickster figures who play with the notion of the unitary self by assuming and rejecting multiple identities. Nonetheless, they are tormented by the genealogies to which they've lost access, whereas Silk is not entirely at odds with himself. Unlike Larsen's and Johnson's protagonists, he inhabits the role of a white person with relative ease. Although Roth does reveal his secretive character's worried machinations, he does so mostly to indicate the deep sense of pleasure that Silk experiences at the thought of escaping from the shackles of "the coercive, inclusive, historical, inescapable moral *we* with its insidious *E pluribus unum*" into "the raw I with all its agility" (108).

Importantly, Roth's use of passing differs from the way in which earlier authors used it because it is no longer the highly charged description of a transracial move. It has become something far vaguer, a trope for describing a host of social and emotional metamorphoses. Once, the concept of passing fell into what Catherine Rottenberg calls a "subversive–recuperative binary," in which it either disorients or reifies racial categories (433). More recent considerations of passing have concentrated on how it can be used to complicate our ideas of identity, racial or otherwise, a more fluid notion reminding us that identity is both process and performance. The discourse of passing emphasizes that race, like gender, as Judith Butler formulates it in her notion of "performativity," only comes into existence in the ways in which we perform it and through the discourses that constitute it (94).

This concept of passing as performative—and thus of race as de-essentialized—is central to Roth's use of the trope. Throughout *The Human Stain*, he emphasizes the fact that Coleman Silk's passing is performative on multiple levels. Strikingly, in a novel about various kinds of education, Roth suggests that whiteness is a state of being, which his protagonist can learn through careful ethnographic analysis of white mores and adherence to the cultural standards of white America. In the perverse *Bildungsroman* that is Silk's life story, childhood in a predominantly Jewish New Jersey town has given him the means to learn a particular brand of white identity.[12] His flawless performance of this identity, coupled with his all-out embrace of western universal humanism and its masterworks, eventually make him appear *whiter* than many of his colleagues at Athena College. Whiteness, Roth seems to tease, is a fluid state that one can perform too well.

Silk's choice to pass as a Jewish white man, who just a few decades earlier would have been distinctly out of place in the wealthy WASP world of Athena, adds another layer of impersonation to his performance of whiteness and a comparative cast to Roth's exploration of race. As Daniel Itzkovitz points out, Jews have often been associated with "racial chameleonism," a facility for mimicry and adaptation seen as characteristic of this wandering race and related to the racial ventriloquism that is a hallmark of contemporary Jewish American writers ("Passing Like Me" 39).[13] During the early years of the twentieth century, many believed that Jews were able to mask difference beneath a cloak of apparent sameness. If, indeed, they were "naturals" at passing, then Jewishness might hold "significant implications for the evolution of a modernist cultural logic that was at once race-conscious and unable to locate the exact nature of racial difference" (37).

The fact that Jews in America remained both immutably different and supremely adaptable to the ever-shifting tenets of whiteness marked them as uniquely anxiogenic cultural entities, and concerns about the difference hiding in the midst of white America couldn't help but seep into early twentieth-century literature. Jews were often portrayed as harbingers of the inauthenticity of modernity, and they functioned as figures for successful passing in many narratives by African American authors. Lori Harrison-Kahan points out that Jewish "chameleonic" figures appeared in most of the best-known passing narratives of the Harlem Renaissance, including "Walter White's *Flight* (1926), Nella Larsen's *Passing* (1929), Jessie Fauset's *Plum Bun* (1929), and the republication of James Weldon Johnson's *The Autobiography of an Ex-Colored Man* (1912, 1927)" (*The White Negress* 84). These narratives portrayed Jews as enviable; for unlike blacks, who were entirely "lost to their people" when they renounced their racial designation, they managed to move between the roles of outsider and insider with comparative ease.

Roth, too, highlights the complexity of the Jewish racial profile in America through his conflation of passing into whiteness and passing into Jewishness. He is not alone in his preoccupation with this characteristic. As Harrison-Kahan points out, contemporary tales of racial passing often adopt the figure of the Jew as a fundamental, rather than a peripheral, component of the narrative. In many such works, African American characters don Jewish identities as their means of passing into whiteness. Harrison-Kahan asserts that multicultural passing narratives, such as Danzy Senna's *Caucasia*, look to the ambiguous racial position of Jews in America as a convenient metaphor for the multiplicity attendant to racial identity in a post-binary era. She suggests that Jews are tropologically useful for these authors, as they were for authors in the first half of the twentieth century, because Jews are simultaneously intermediary figures poised between racial designations and, after World War II at least, indisputably white. The category of Jewishness in contemporary narratives of passing adds "a third term to the typically black-and-white schema of US race relations . . . [and] deploy[s] Jewishness to expose the social construction and plurality of whiteness as well as to challenge existing theories of mixed race identity that rely on binary configurations" (22).

In *The Human Stain*, there is often such a slippage between passing and Jewishness as metaphors for racial indeterminacy. Silk's neighbor is writer Nathan Zuckerman, a regular character in Roth's work. Early in the book, Silk chooses to tell him the story of his trials at Athena College. The men are spatially and racially adjacent, which Roth makes clear by emphasizing that only an outsider to Athena's New England aristocracy is fit to hear and, later, tell the black man's story. Further, Silk himself passes for "one of those crimp-haired Jews of a light yellowish skin pigmentation who possess something of the ambiguous aura of the pale blacks who are sometimes taken for white" (15–16). Jews, he recognizes, are an intermediary race, a waystation of sorts on the road from black to white. When Silk was growing up, his father believed that Jews were models of assimilation for middle-class blacks, "like Indian scouts, shrewd people showing the outsider his way in, showing the social possibility, showing a colored family how it might be done" (97).

By making Silk black and Jewish at different moments, Roth taps into the liminal Jewish racial history in America, a theme he has long favored. Nonetheless, he doesn't write about the indeterminacy of Jewish identity primarily as a way to imagine a utopian, post-binary racial landscape. Instead, he uses Silk's performance of Jewishness to work out the vexed place of the Jew and the Jewish writer in the multicultural canon. Passing, which disavows visible difference in favor of a willed sameness, undermines the stakes of multiculturalism as it was practiced at the time Roth was writing *The Human Stain*. In particular, it plays with multiculturalism's central argument: that recognition by another is the precondition of identity. Passing, by contrast, is predicated on invisibility.[14] As Carole-Anne Tyler points out, passing is only visible if it is a failure.

Throughout the novel, Roth uses the valences of passing to pose potent questions about how racial and ethnic discourses affect the literary sphere. In addition to challenging the prevalent discourse of multiculturalism, however, his use of the trope emphasizes his own anxieties about his decision to pass as "a writer" rather than "a Jewish writer," a choice he discusses in "Writing about Jews." Might an ethnic writer or intellectual pass so successfully into the canon that he no longer retains any hold on his former particularity, the substance of his voice? Can a passing individual be lost not only to his people but to himself and his audience? Is there always a loss in passing from difference into sameness? Silk is troubled by these questions about authenticity and voice, the consequences of his decision to pass, and his reliance on and discomfort with his own performance come to haunt him.

Roth's novel includes a nonhuman character, a young orphaned crow named Prince, who becomes a figure for Silk's mimicry and playful impersonation. Prince lives at the edge of the college town, haunting the parking lot of the local post office and diving in to pick off the barrettes of little girls, until he is rescued by the Audubon Society.[15] But all attempts to reintroduce the crow back into his natural environment fail; as an Audubon Society volunteer puts it, "he doesn't know the crow language" (242). Prince's attempts to play at being just another crow are thwarted by the "human stain" left behind in his speech, the result of "being hand-raised" (242). He is indelibly marked by his time among human beings, his otherness obvious to other crows, even if he can't hear the difference himself.

Faunia Farley, Silk's mistress, likes to visit Prince at the shelter. She sees something familiar in him, recognizing that "the human stain" is the necessary result of congress with another: "Impurity, cruelty, abuse error, excrement, semen—there's no other way to be here" (242). While her rumination on the crow functions as one of many rejoinders to those 1990s multiculturalists (and anti-Clintonites) who sought an impossible purity, it also links the crow to her lover. Prince's "human stain" highlights the perils inherent in Silk's move between races (242). His passing, like that of the protagonists in Larsen's and Johnson's narratives, can never be entirely successful. He is marked in ways he does not realize, ways that leave large swathes of the world and of his own interiority illegible to him. It becomes increasingly clear in *The Human Stain* that all acts of passing—like all acts of translation—occasion a loss.

The Human Stain of Identity

In *The Human Stain*, Roth uses a racially intermediary character to question the possibility of evading the universal human stain of mixture by assuming a particular racially or ethnically affiliated "we."[16] Like David Hollinger's *Postethnic America: Beyond Multiculturalism* (1995), also written during the heyday of identity politics, the novel posits a reinvestigation and progressive deconstruction of racial and ethnic categories so as to strip them of their social and epistemological weight, asking us to embrace cosmopolitanism rather than multiculturalism.[17] Although Silk's passing is at the heart of *The Human Stain*, the fact that he is white or black, Jewish or Christian, is remarkable unimportant in the universe of the novel. He is defined primarily by his intellectual and generational affinities, from his love of classical literature and big band music, to his wholesale embrace of Viagra, to his discomfort with what he sees as the feminist posturing of Delphine Roux, a French poststructuralist who in the novel is both a harbinger of the death of humanism and a representative of the multicultural academy's emasculating power.

Critical accounts of *The Human Stain* often lose sight of the fact that Roth's novel is not only a novel about race but also one about literary history and the Jewish academic in the multicultural academy. When we first meet Silk, he has long since made his decision to pass as a white man. Before the novel opens, he has spent years as a professor and academic dean. In the opening chapters we learn that he is now teaching a few last courses before retiring from the academy, and he is preoccupied with the waning standards of the student body. After many years of fashioning himself into an urbane Jewish intellectual seeking to wake up the musty academic establishment, he finds himself struggling to interest his students in the genealogy of western literature that begins with Homer as well as in what they perceive as its outmoded humanistic values.

Yet in the canonical works he teaches, Coleman sees himself. For obvious reasons, he is particularly drawn to Homer's story of Achilles, a hero felled by a secret infirmity. The story of Oedipus also resonates with him, for the purity of the professor's blood is at stake, as the epigraph for *The Human Stain* makes clear. It comes from Sophocles's *Oedipus the King* and marks the moment when Oedipus is seeking a means to cleanse himself. He asks Creon, "What is the rite of purification? How shall it be done?" and Creon replies, "By banishing a man, or expiation of blood by blood" (1). Even the name of Athena College has figurative significance in the professor's life. The goddess Athena was the product of a motherless birth, having sprung fully formed from the skull of her father Zeus, as if she were an idea of perfect male generativity. Her birth is a metaphor for Silk's freedom from his own mother and her race.

Even as they give meaning to his life, Silk's attachments to these myths and masterworks alienate him from those around him. Long a popular teacher, he has suddenly found himself in the 1990s unable to communicate with his students or comprehend the changing academic landscape at Athena. Having rejected his own racial genealogy in favor of the family of western literature, he now speaks in a language that his young students cannot translate. The tragedy of *The Human Stain* centers around these issues of language and translation and the ability to mask the private self by passing into the lingua franca of universal humanism.

"Midway into his second semester back as a full-time professor . . . Coleman sp[eaks] the self-incriminating word that would cause him voluntarily to sever all ties to the college." Five weeks into the semester, when two students have not deigned to show up for class, Silk "open[s] the session by asking, 'Does anyone know these people? Do they exist or are they spooks?'" His joke is woefully misinterpreted. The two missing students, "who [turn] out to be black," hear about his use of the word *spooks*, a pejorative for African Americans, and submit a complaint.[18] The new dean of faculty calls the distinguished professor into his office, and Silk is shocked to discover that he faces charges of racism. As he later explains to Zuckerman, "I was using the word in its customary and primary meaning: 'spook' as a specter or a ghost. I had no idea what color these two students might be." While it is clear that Roth is mocking administrators and students for misconstruing the aging professor's color-blind use of the word, he simultaneously clarifies that Silk's word choice is blind and "self-incriminating" in other ways (6). The word *spooks* holds the spectral "human stain" of his racial heritage as well as his repudiation of his lineage and his flight into what he has perceived to be the transcendent realm of the intellect.

Silk's passing is not entirely successful. Like Faunia Farley, his inappropriate love interest, he is, in a sense, illiterate—unable to read correctly and respond to signs in the world around him. He believes that he has committed himself to an extra-ideological universe of literature and ideas, where race and the body don't matter. But his students and the newly multicultural academy have not made a similar commitment. For, if Silk is felled by an instance of tragicomic parapraxis, he is also "undone by a word that no one even speaks anymore" (334). By saying aloud the word *spooks* and, with it, his guilt at hiding himself, he also speaks of a time when the valences of words were different. He is not only punished for transgressing the boundaries of race but also castigated for adhering to outmoded standards. Silk is unable to measure the shifts in an academic world that would now reward him for the racial difference he once saw as a hindrance. Blackness, as Roth portrays it, has become a commodity of considerable worth: after all, when his students accuse him of racism, Silk requires the intervention of his replacement, Herb Keble, who draws on the power of his epistemic location as an African American man in the multicultural academy to speak on Silk's behalf.[19] The private has become instrumental in the public world of Athena College, and Silk finds himself smack in the middle of an era in which "ethnic is in."

The intertwined themes of teaching and speaking play a central role in *The Human Stain*. The catalyst for Silk's fall begins in the classroom, and the novel is filled with educators. Near the end of the novel, his sister Ernestine (the character who lets Zuckerman into the secret of her brother's race) points out that their family generation has been comprised of teachers, from the award-winning educator and civil rights leader Walter, to the renegade intellectual Coleman, to the pious and dedicated schoolteacher Ernestine herself. Their father, a Pullman waiter, was also an educator of sorts. The siblings trace their interest in education from his stentorian urge to sing the praises of Shakespeare even as he served food to white diners on a train. By focusing on teachers, not to mention middle-class blacks' allegiance at midcentury to the ideals of western civilization, Roth presses us to consider the epistemology and institutionalization of race—how we know ourselves racially through the teachers and texts that instruct us.

Eric Sundquist and Ross Posnock provide cogent analyses of *The Human Stain*, but both focus on the tale's racial component rather than the academic narrative. Sundquist even goes so far as to place the two storylines into an Aristotelian hierarchy of sorts, reading the racial passing narrative as tragedy, the academic one as comedy (513). Yet the two narrative threads are bound together, a fact that accounts for much of the novel's potency. As Pamela Caughie argues in *Passing and Pedagogy*, the ethics of passing outside one's own subject position was a pressing concern for academics in the multicultural classroom, where anxiety "led just about everyone, it seems, to question who has the right to engage in certain practices, who can cross over and for what purposes, or who can speak as, for, and from what positions" (15).

In the novel's skirmishes over race and the academy, the character of Delphine Roux plays a critical role. She and Silk are set up as contrasting, if similarly self-destructive, characters with differing literary and racial allegiances. Silk stands for hybridity and mess, while Roux represents the "ecstasy of sanctimony" that characterized the 1990s, a period of "calculated frenzy" when "a president's penis was on everyone's mind" (2, 3). The polemical force and genuine meanspiritedness behind Roth's depiction of Roux reveal his contempt for the shifting intellectual landscape she signifies.[20] Like Silk, she is theatrical in her allegiances, performing feminism and racial sensitivity while concealing her secret prejudices and desire for sexual submission. Near the end of *The Human Stain*, as she is writing a personal ad, she worries over how to phrase it so as to avoid getting responses from black men. When she accidentally sends the ad to her departmental colleagues (a moment of subconscious self-sabotage similar to Silk's use of *spooks*), she refuses to take responsibility, instead staging a break-in at her office and claiming that Silk has written and sent the incriminating text.

By creating a character who moves ably between the subject positions of black and Jew, Roth has launched a harsh critique of political correctness and the American puritan impulse. He has also outwitted critics who might argue that his portrayal of Roux and her harassment campaign are merely the cranky mutterings of an aging Jewish writer, another "old goat" "sadly out of touch" with the literary establishment (Max). His act of speaking through Silk is the ultimate act of speaking for the other and, perhaps, of speaking the self through the other, as Malamud often did in his own work. Silk can say things that Roth can't: the most vociferous critiques of the multicultural university come from Silk's mouth. While the narrator Zuckerman clearly blames the college administration for his friend's downfall, he, like Roth himself, ironically deflects responsibility for his criticism. Rather, he ventriloquizes, posing as a medium, a disembodied dummy, through which we hear the voice of the persecuted Silk. Roth has long been interested in the complexities of authorship and the authorial voice, but only in his later novels has he begun to experiment with the idea of author/narrator as ventriloquist, one who can pass fluidly among subject positions. *The Human Stain* is the most fully realized of these explorations.

Zuckerman's role as ghostwriter/ventriloquist is complicated. When he and Silk first meet, the professor asks the aging author to "write something for him," to act as his literary proxy by transcribing the tale of his firing from Athena College and the puritanical racial politics that have felled him and his wife, Iris (11). After Silk's ignominious death, Zuckerman accedes to that demand and decides to complete the professor's unfinished manuscript, *Spooks*, with which he has long been familiar. Silk had begun with the intention of writing a tell-all book about the events surrounding his dismissal, in particular his treatment at the hands of colleagues whom, as academic dean, he had been responsible for hiring. As Zuckerman soon recognizes, however, Silk could never have completed *Spooks*, precisely because the specter at the heart of his narrative is not political correctness or his absent students but himself. As Roth makes clear, Silk's adherence to the rhetoric of radical individualism, the ideology behind his successful passing, ultimately kept him from telling his story.

The life of *New York Times* literary critic Anatole Broyard (who died in 1998) may have served as a blueprint for Silk's character, a link that emphasizes the way in which "accepting the democratic invitation to throw your origins overboard" can affect an individual's ability to write (*Human Stain* 334). Like Silk, Broyard was an African American who began using his light complexion to pass for white during a stint in the military during World War II. Brett Ashley Kaplan contends that "because he demonstrated the performativity of race, Broyard offered a perfect model for Roth's main character" (125). The most significant characteristics that Silk and Broyard share, however, involve writing. An immensely talented writer, Broyard was long expected to become a great American novelist during the postwar era. Yet he was never able to deliver upon the promise of his first published fiction, even though all of literary New York eagerly awaited its follow-up. In "The Passing of Anatole Broyard," Henry Louis Gates suggests that he failed to live up to his early promise precisely because of the decision to conceal his race and his subsequent inability to establish a convincing narrative voice. To write effectively, Gates argues, Broyard "would have had to be a Negro writer, which was something he did not want to be. In his terms, he did not want to write about black love, black passion, black suffering, black joy; he wanted to write about love and passion and suffering and joy. We give lip service to the idea of the writer who happens to be black, but had anyone, in the postwar era, ever seen such a thing?" (207). As a result, Broyard silenced himself at an early age, becoming instead, as Gates suggests, a thinly veiled figure in works by a number of well-known postwar authors. Thus, by linking Silk's story with Broyard's, Roth transforms his novel from a simple critique of the imperative to write as a black writer or a Jewish writer into a far more ambivalent document about the inextricability of racial and literary genealogies. Despite Roth's clear sympathy with Silk's universal humanist aspirations, he nevertheless insists that Silk's choice, like Broyard's, converts him from writer to character, simultaneously depriving him of a voice and making him a tragic figure akin to those who passed into whiteness in the literature of the Harlem Renaissance.[21]

The Human Stain pokes holes in the puritan ethos of late twentieth-century American society, a judgment-hungry culture that sought to prevent inappropriate sexual liaisons (such as those between Faunia and Silk, Bill Clinton and Monica Lewinsky) while trapping writers and intellectuals into what Werner Sollors might call their "descent relations" (*Beyond Ethnicity* 6). Although *The Human Stain* may appear to be one of Roth's least Jewish novels, it nonetheless indexes a fraught moment in the histories of comparative racialization, American Jewish literature, and Roth as an American Jewish author. It questions the position of the Jew in both the canon and the ethnic landscape of multicultural America.

In a rare interview to celebrate the novel's publication, Roth bristles at interviewer Charles McGrath's intimation that the book is "about issues of race and of Judaism and of where the two intersect." Instead, he argues that his protagonist's decision to pass for white by passing for a Jew is merely "a cunning choice that successfully furnishes him with a disguise in the flight from his own 'we.'" Even as this statement deflects the assertion that *The Human Stain* is yet another instance of his "writing about Jews," it marks another step in the deracialization of the Jew in America. If, as Roth contends, Silk's "choice has nothing to do with the ethical, spiritual, theological or historical aspects of Judaism, . . . has nothing to do with wanting to belong to another 'we,'" Jewish identity, which the novelist has long pilloried for being an inescapable "we," has been transformed into an archetypical white identity, a release from the collective rather than the trail of recriminations and immutable affiliation that Jewishness had once been for this self-consciously American writer.[22] Silk's choice to pass into Jewishness to escape "his own 'we'" emphasizes not only the postwar shift in Jewish racialization but also the paradoxical nature of race in America: the notion that race is impossible to evade yet, with the right performance, can be "passed." This collision undergirds the tragedy of Coleman Silk and animates Roth's attempts to understand the position of the Jew, long a figure for the successful ideal of American self-fashioning, in a literary sphere that no longer prizes the individual stripped of allegiance to his past.

How much does literary history intersect with racial history? In *The Human Stain*, Roth explores this question via the ethical interpenetration of writing and race during an era in which the understanding of both was changing. Who has the right to write the story of another? Do we each have a right to write our own story, apart from the original myths of our families and races? Sollors argues in *Beyond Ethnicity* that all American literature is ethnic literature, formed around the dialectic of consent and descent he discerns at the heart of the nation's symbolic imaginary. If we follow Sollors, then *The Human Stain* is a prototypically American narrative, situated at the crossroads of consent and descent, the limits of self-fashioning and the inescapability of the past. It is also what Sollors calls elsewhere an "interracial narrative," one that troubles essential notions of race by refusing the black-white binary system (*Neither Black nor White yet Both* 4). Roth's "interracial" narrator speaks to the writer's sense of irony: a black man performing Jewishness is accused of racism and becomes a spokesman for the vexed position of the Jewish intellectual and author in our multicultural age, "the man who decides to forge a distinct historical destiny, who sets out to spring the historical lock, and who does so . . . only to be ensnared by the history he hadn't quite counted on" (*The Human Stain* 335–336).

In the 1990s, Roth, like Silk, faced the perils of his life-long insistence on the importance of self-authorship, of eschewing the past and its racial obligations. *The Human Stain* reflects his own pessimism but also envisions a new kind of multicultural literature situated at the intersection of races rather than in a system of racial binaries. While critiquing multicultural politics, the novel is also Roth's attempt to write himself into the newly identified multicultural canon. Long a devotee of teasing out the connections between American and Jewish history, not to mention the bonds between national and personal myths,

Roth created, in *The Human Stain*, a felicitous exploration of the way in which private narratives shape public life and vice versa, a concern central to multicultural discourse.

In her study of the "interethnic imagination" in contemporary American fiction, Caroline Rody looks at how literary forms can exist in the interstices between ethnic groups and ethnic voices. While her book focuses on how Asian American authors engage with the idea of the interethnic and speak about themselves through their relationship to others, her concept is equally appropriate to the Jewish canon and its relationship to race and the literary voice. For writers such as Roth, the multicultural canon being developed during the culture wars was a site of exclusion, even though its stakes had in some ways been set by the pluralist discourses of postwar Jewish writers. By adopting the voices and bodies of racialized others, these writers had attempted to reclaim their own vocal difference and unique place in American literary history.

As I discussed earlier in this chapter, Mark McGurl sees Roth, Bellow, and Malamud as forerunners of the literary school he dubs "high cultural pluralism," and his book introduces the concept by invoking Roth's strange career:

> Another way to get at the impressive typicality of the figure of Philip Roth would be to note how, seen against the forty-year backdrop of the field he has inhabited, he can seem to figure either as a culturally conservative white male writer, staunchly upholding high modernist literary values, or, as was more plainly the case in the 1960s, as a conspicuously "ethnic" writer ("The Jew You Can't Permit in the Parlor") who introduces cultural difference into that system. Braiding these roles together, he could be said to hold in suspension the elements of the form of postwar literary fiction that I will call high cultural pluralism, which combines the routine operation of modernist autopoetics with a rhetorical performance of cultural group membership preeminently, though by no means exclusively, marked as ethnic. (56)

Although McGurl uses Roth to typify a certain type of writer and writing, in reality, Malamud, Roth, and Bellow (whom Bellow himself ruefully characterized as the "Hart, Schaffner & Marx of literature" to connote the trio's increasing commodification as Jewish writers) have played an unusual role in American letters (Shenker 46). Although they are accounted for under McGurl's system, they seem to vex some of its arguments. The way in which they have been absorbed into the American canon has left them in a marginalized position vis-à-vis other writers who are dubbed as ethnic. How do we understand Jewish American writers, many of whom continue to have a profound interest in racialized otherness even as they have become canonical "American" authors? Where do these writers fit into the larger narrative of contemporary American literature? In his introduction to *The Ethnic Canon*, David Palumbo Liu contends that the process of canon formation has profoundly political implications. He suggests that ethnically or racially marked literary works are absorbed into the canon only after a process of neutralization that smoothes out the texts' ideological rough edges. Post-1967 Jewish American literature continues to sit awkwardly between the conventional canon and "the ethnic canon," disrupting both the neutralizing process of canon formation and the narrative of postwar American literature.

CHAPTER 5

Race, Indigeneity, and the Topography of Diaspora

The Genealogy of the Diasporic Writer

Like Philip Roth, who used his African American character Coleman Silk as a way to articulate ideas about Jewish racialization and the Jew in the canon, contemporary Jewish American writers and artists have often turned to various others in their effort to speak to and about their ambivalent reactions to the waning of Jewish difference. For some of these writers and artists, speaking for others has also been a way to talk about divisive issues in contemporary Jewish life, such as Israel, Zionism, and the role of race in Jewish self-fashioning in a secular diaspora. Recent contentious debates about the role of American academic organizations (for instance, the American Studies Association and the Association for Asian American Studies) in the boycott and divestment from Israel movement, not to mention renewed conflict between Israel and Gaza, have divided the American Jewish community and displaced conflicts about the Jewish state's future from Israel to the United States. Moreover, the controversy around the firing of scholar Steven Salaita, whose work compares America's violent dispossession of Native Americans with Israel's relationship to Palestinians, has shown not only the power of analogy in critical responses to Israel but also the continuing relevance of Jewishness (as concept and lived experience) in America's culture wars.[1]

Munich and the Jewish American Genealogical Imperative

Munich (2005), a cinematic collaboration between writers Tony Kushner and Eric Roth and director Steven Spielberg, opens with a fragmentary re-creation of the 1972 massacre of Israeli athletes at the Olympic Games in Munich, carried out by members of Black September, a newly organized terrorist organization. As in his celebrated World War II epic, *Saving Private Ryan* (1998), Spielberg spares his viewers no detail of the violence. However, in contrast to that film, which opens with an intimate anatomy of the bloodshed on Omaha Beach, *Munich* parcels out the violence slowly, by way of the flashbacks and dreams of the film's tragic protagonist, Avner, a Mossad agent who is hunting down "the architects of the . . . massacre." The film marries snippets of violence-to-come (an Israeli athlete holding the door against the intrusion of Black September, documentary footage of newscasters covering the hostage situation) with scenes of the athletes' and terrorists' families sitting around their television sets, their faces flickering with lurid images from the screen.[2] Viewers begin to sense that Kushner, Roth, and Spielberg, among their other goals, are critiquing the media's role in disseminating images of violence in the late twentieth century.[3] By juxtaposing images of Arab families' grief over their lost loved ones with scenes of Jewish families' reactions to news of the athletes' capture and death, the scenes encourage us to identify with both groups. We are prodded to embrace universal humanistic ideas about the commonality of all subjects, which, the film suggests, might help us to end the seemingly eternal conflict between Arab and Jew.

Gilberto Perez argues that the medium of film works by encouraging identification between the audience and the characters. If we accept his argument, then we might say that *Munich* asks its viewers to identify in multiple directions, in a manner that undermines conventional distinctions between "terrorist" and "terrorized."[4] At the same time, its scenes of suffering kin introduce another issue that haunts both the film and contemporary Jewish American aesthetics more broadly: the role of race and genealogy in maintaining the particularity of Jewish collective identity in a manner that troubles the conventional identity between Jewishness and Jewish territory after Israel.

As I mentioned in my discussion of the *Wissenschaft* movement in chapter 4, Jewish art and literature have been alternately denigrated and praised for their inherently deterritorialized, transnational character. During the eighteenth century, the Enlightenment philosopher Voltaire composed screeds against the possibility that Jewish art could contribute anything worthwhile to European culture. In 1850, the composer Richard Wagner went even further, writing that Jews were incapable of authentic artistic production because they lacked the particularity of national *genius loci*, a central tenet of nineteenth-century German Romanticism.[5] Influenced by Johann von Herder's earlier writings on art and *Volksgeist* (national character), this idea that land and racial memory combine to produce a viable art and culture also fed into a broader nineteenth-century anxiety about nationhood, one of the elements that catalyzed the Zionist quest for a Jewish home.[6]

Today, as evidenced in Gilles Deleuze and Félix Guattari's *Kafka: Towards a Minor Literature* (1986), that attitude has been nearly reversed. Theorists see Jewish diasporic literature and the figure of the Wandering Jew as models of ideal supranational or exilic literary production. Nonetheless, as Shaul Magid points out, "the ongoing conversation about Israel and the Diaspora, both in the academy and beyond, still largely centers on familiar dichotomies, categories formulated in the early years of the Zionist movement: center/periphery, geulah/galut, home/homelessness, power/powerlessness, and, of course, sovereignty/anti-Semitism" (194).[7] These "familiar dichotomies" have been particularly pervasive in American discourse, where many Jews, both inside and outside the academy, continue to privilege Israel in their self-conception, however little they might actually know about the nation or its history. For some American Jews, the foundation of the nation-state of Israel and the return to what many deem the Jewish Promised Land have reterritorialized the Jewish imagination, negating the possibility that diaspora can remain as meaningful a category for interpreting or producing Jewish art and literature.[8]

In *Munich*, Spielberg, Kushner, and Roth make a pointed argument against Israel's primacy. The movie shows that, for Jewish American writers and artists, the foundation of Israel has done little to decrease the power of diaspora as either idea or lived experience. One way to explore this theme is through the concept of *diasporism*, a term coined by Anglo-American visual artist R. B. Kitaj in his "First Diasporist Manifesto" (1989) and developed in later incarnations of his manifesto. Kitaj's diasporism argues for the power of exile, cosmopolitanism, and marginality in the creation of art—a kind of at-home-ness with homelessness. This diasporic identity, he contends, provides an entryway for comparing the Jewish experience with those of Armenian, African, Cambodian, and even Palestinian diasporas. It also provides a space for self-critique—what Kitaj calls "an unfolding commentary on its life-source, the contemplation of a transience, a *Midrash* (exegesis, exposition of non-literal meaning)" (37).

Kitaj's close friend Philip Roth has alternately explored and satirized a related diasporism for similarly self-reflexive ends, particularly in his novel *Operation Shylock* (1993). The postmodern saga features a battle between the writer Philip Roth and a counterfeit Roth, whom the real Roth playfully dubs Moishe Pipik to connote his role as mischief maker. Pipik propagates a ridiculous diasporist project in Roth's name: to avoid being killed by Arab antagonists or become the oppressors rather than the perennially oppressed, Ashkenazi Jews must leave Israel and return to their true homes in Eastern and Central Europe. The novel juxtaposes a faux diasporism with Zionism to point out the ridiculousness of any ideological system based on the concept of return and the problems of the Jewish artist caught in between. No perfect solution exists to the problem of diaspora. No space exists in which Jews can be entirely safe from danger and the problem of others. As Roth and his doppelgänger Pipik suggest, the self is always constructed in relation to an other, whether that other is a member of another ethnic or national group or just another version of the self.

For twenty-first-century Jewish American writers and artists such as Steven Spielberg, Tony Kushner, Eric Roth, Michael Chabon, and Ben Katchor, diasporism of a kind has similarly become both a site for critique and a ground on which to build a meaningful secular Jewish identity. These artists resist the temptation to place Israel without question at the center of their Jewishness. They unite the importance of identifying a supranational geography for Jewish identity with postwar concerns about the waning of Jewishness as a racialized identity.

Kushner and Spielberg, as well as Eric Roth, one of the film's original scriptwriters, are archetypical but vastly different diasporic Jewish artists; and their combined project, *Munich*, attests to the preoccupation of twenty-first-century American Jews with questions of genealogy, race, and belonging. The film's creators challenge the assumption that Zionism is the master narrative of Jewish identity as well as its unselfconscious privileging of the mythology of return. Although they explore the possibilities and politics of return throughout the film—particularly in the obsessive and ultimately futile attempt to remember the traumatic past by re-creating the circumstances of the Munich attack—family and family lineage become the metaphors through which they examine the valences of identity and groundedness for contemporary American Jewry. Their engagement with kinship, bloodlines, and Jewish identity also suggests that the film's perspective is more ambivalent than it might at first seem. Anxieties about waning Jewish racial difference and Jewish particularity in diaspora converge with concerns about the place of Zionist understandings of the Jewish nation in contemporary Jewish life. As the filmmakers engage with and criticize the place of family and tribal dynamics in the foundation and racialization of the nation, they imagine a form of Jewish "racial" identity that transcends the strictures of shared geography.

The protagonist Avner's own genealogy and provenance are tied to the importance of defining and creating a homeland for the Jews. His father, an Israeli war hero, is the absent center of *Munich*. Although the father does not appear in the film, he exists just offstage; like the biblical idea of the Promised Land, he is a reminder of the authenticity of Zion lost since the early days of Israel's war of independence. Relying on the legacy of this heroism, Golda Meir, Israel's prime minister, asks Avner to lead a motley group of intelligence experts and assassins to track down Black September. Wary of being valued only because of his famous parent, Avner asks Meir if she seeks his help because he is "the son of a hero." She jokes that he need not worry: "your mother is who you resemble" (24). Her suggestion that the young Mossad agent is softer and more feminine than his hypermasculine Zionist father is particularly insulting (despite, or because of, its being voiced by a woman) in the context of Israel's longstanding valorization of military might and machismo.

Meir's remark foreshadows Avner's complex relationship to maternity and its links to his conceptions of race and nation. As his wife, Daphna, points out, he was "orphaned" at a young age, left by his mother to fend for himself in a kibbutz after his father went missing during war. Daphna cynically notes the results of this early desertion: "So she put you in the kibbutz and abandoned you. And now you think Israel is your mother" (26). Avner's substitution of nation for mother is significant: it is his fealty to this idea of the Jewish nation that compels him, with much discomfort, to agree to violently avenge Israel. It also highlights the problematic ways in which territory has been racialized and gendered in contemporary conceptions of Jewish identity. Traditionally, Jewishness is passed down matrilineally, transmitted from mother to child and maintained by endogamy, circumcision, and other bodily markers of difference. Now, however, it necessitates a more complex racial and gender politics. While Avner accepts the role of his mother in transmitting Jewishness to him, he must reject any sign of femininity or feminized exile in himself to become the rightful son of his father and fatherland. Through such depictions of gender and engendering, Kushner, Roth, and Spielberg comment on the vexed place of family in understandings of diaspora. For even as matrilineal Jewishness is privileged in certain racial conceptions of Jewish identity, Jews are plagued by anxieties about masculinity and power, inflamed by their encounter with European modernity and the questioned manliness of the shtetl Jew.[9] As an antidote to this fragile masculinity, the figure of Israel is contrasted to a conception of diaspora as feminine, and the violent agents in *Munich* share and often embody this vision of Israel as metaphor for maleness.[10]

This gendering of diaspora and Promised Land is not new. Historians Michael Stanislawski and Moshe Zimmermann have written about the deep interpenetration of masculinity and *fin de siècle* Zionism. At the Second Zionist Congress in 1898, Max Nordau, Theodor Herzl's second-in-command, called on his followers to create a *Muskeljudentum*, a muscular Judaism and a muscular Jewish body to go with it. This healthy and always masculine-identified Judaism would be the "opposite of the typical Galut (Diaspora) Jew: weak, frail, despised, doing his *Luftschaefte* (unproductive business)" (Zimmermann 13). The distinction between diasporic Jewry and *Muskeljudentum* is central to the gender dynamics of *Munich* and to the rhetoric of Jewish militarism favored by the counterterrorist officials in the film.

Increasingly, *Munich* contrasts the domestic sphere, identified with femininity and the private domain of the family, with masculine duty and the public realm. Avner's assassinations of the suspected terrorists are interspersed with visits to Paris to meet the shadowy members of Le Group, a family-run underground organization whose help he needs to complete various killings.[11] At various points in the film, he waits to meet his contact Louis in front of a Parisian shop window. The window, glowing and warm in contrast to the often-rainy midnight streets on which Avner and Louis meet, frames a display of a well-appointed and cozy kitchen waiting for a family to inhabit it. Tormented by the recognition that he cannot live in such a space until he finishes avenging Israel, Avner soon learns that Le Group itself is such an ideal family. He pays a visit to their compound, an aging mansion in rural France, and meets Papa, the benevolent de facto leader, who explains Le Group's credo: no allegiance to any government or ideology beyond that of the family. He agrees to help find the members of Black September but only if he can conceive of the Jews not as a nation but as an extended family in search of reparations for centuries of abuse.

The Holocaust plays an important, if implicit, role in *Munich:* the film is set in the early 1970s, when the 1967 Six Day War hung over all discussions of Israel and rhetoric in Israel and America linked the Holocaust to fears that Israel's Arab neighbors would annihilate the nation. Appropriately, when Avner expresses doubts about becoming an agent of Israel's bloodlust, his own mother arrives to drive the metaphor of the mother country home, pressuring him to avenge both his Jewish national family and the members of their immediate family who perished in Europe during World War II. As she entreats him to avenge the grandparents, aunts, and uncles lost in the Holocaust, she also stresses the need to place the public family of Jews above his own nuclear family, a move symbolized in her *kibbutznik* rejection of the traditional family unit in favor of a decentralized and collective means of raising children.

As Meir and other Israeli officials make clear, Avner's decision to become an Israeli assassin will require him to leave Daphna, "the only home [he] has ever had," for several years, abandoning her when she is pregnant—much as his mother once abandoned him. Moreover, because the nation will need to disavow participation in avenging the Munich attack, Avner will officially no longer exist in Israel, so he must displace his pregnant wife, moving her from the motherland of Israel to Brooklyn, a classic symbol of Jewish diaspora. As the date of their child's birth approaches, the pair ruefully discusses how this move to America will transform their baby into yet another one of the world's many "homeless Jews" (67). Their anxiety reflects Avner's recurring worries about how to maintain an authentic, at-home Jewishness and is central to the way in which the film addresses the issues facing Jews in contemporary diaspora. The importance of whether one is born in Jewish-owned territory or into the undesirable condition of *galut*, or exile, becomes tantamount. The Jews in *Munich* argue over their *sabra* credentials, reserving the derogatory *yekke* to describe the Jews of Israel who were not born in the nation or are unable to properly identify with Israel as motherland. *Sabra* is a Hebrew word for a cactus-like plant, and it is used to connote native Israelis, whose tough exterior masks their vulnerable center, whereas *yekke* is a Yiddish-inflected label for German or Western European–identified Jews. The contrast between the terms emphasizes the continuing hegemony of ideas about native or authentic Israeli-ness. Those who are viewed as autochthonous, native to the land, are contrasted with those who live in diaspora, a condition of inauthenticity where Jews mask their otherness by donning European "yekke" (jackets or clothing).

The farther the assassins are from Israel, the more engaged they become in proving their ties to the land. Most of the violence in *Munich* takes place in Western Europe and is carried out by western-identified Jews, whose anxieties about the purity of their Jewish lineage seem to fuel their blood thirst. Steve, a blond-haired, blue-eyed, South African Jew, is particularly unapologetic about killing Arabs, stating that "the only blood that matters for [him] is Jewish blood" (116). Even Avner's purportedly impeccable sabra credentials are more symbolic than real, given the absence of his hero father, his fledgling connection with his icy mother, and his adolescent exile to Frankfurt. However, as Spielberg, Roth, and Kushner make clear throughout the film, Avner's fraught relationship with his parents' adopted homeland and his contested indigeneity drive him to cement his relationship to Israel; shedding the blood of others often becomes an attempt to prove his adherence to the nation's ideology. The filmmakers tie the question of who is born truly Jewish to a larger one: when a nation builds *echt*-Jewishness on claims of authenticity and the mythology of Jewish autochthony, what is it creating? Steve's claim that "only Jewish blood matters" is catalyzed not simply by the Holocaust and fears of imminent Jewish extinction, much less by adherence to a religious idea of Jewish chosenness, but by something far more chilling—a belief that the spilling of another's blood is the only way to buttress the matter of one's birthright.[12]

The filmmakers juxtapose Jewish and Palestinian beliefs about connections among race, violence, and land as a way to meditate on the repercussions of both groups' claims to autochthony. In a pivotal scene, Le Group provides a safe house in Athens for Avner's counterterrorist faction, but members find that they are sharing it with a Palestinian unit sent to Greece to protect the very man they've come to kill.[13] To keep the peace, the Israeli agents pretend to be members of a European Communist terrorist cell, and the men agree to inhabit the same safe house. By playing with the idea of doubling and the double, the scene dramatizes the similarities between the groups. The Israeli agents recognize that they are being double-crossed by Le Group, which truly has no allegiance to one nation over another. At the same time, they see many of their own struggles and identifications reflected in the Palestinian men, including the increasingly global influence of America and American popular culture.[14] Although they fight over the radio dial (the diasporic Jews want to listen to The Temptations' "Papa Was a Rolling Stone" or the Staples Sisters' "I Know a Place" while the Palestinians seek more traditional Middle Eastern music), they eventually agree to listen to Al Green's "Let's Stay Together," a love song that ironically brings together two groups who will attempt to kill each other by the end of their stay in Athens. As the song plays and the other group members sleep, the faux-Communist Avner and the Palestinian leader Ali discuss their conceptions of home. Avner teases Ali about his fantasies of return to "a country [he] never had" and his poetic attachment to the materiality of the past, his "father's olive trees . . . the crappy village he came from . . . chalky soil and stone huts" (102, 103). In answer, Ali invokes the Jews and the nineteenth-century discourse of nationalism that inspired them to seek Israel. For the Communists, the ideal future is an international, cosmopolitan one, a world without nations. But Avi contends that "[you] European reds . . . don't know what it is not to have a home." The Palestinians "want to be nations." For them, as for the Jews, "home is everything" (103).

The question of where to locate Jewish home is central in *Munich*. Although an attack on Israeli citizens catalyzes the action of the film, most of it takes place in Europe, for centuries the site of Jewish exile and the birthplace of the Jewish question. The film ends in America, as Avner fails to gain recognition from the Israeli government officials whom he once thought of as his family. Unable to connect with his wife and child—his true kin—after his years of violence on behalf of Israel, he storms the Israeli embassy in New York and demands an audience with the men who had hired him.[15] Finally an official visits him, and Avner begs for "proof that every man [they] killed had a hand in Munich." The official evades the question, arguing that Avner had "killed for the sake of a country you now choose to abandon. The country your mother and father built. That you were born into." The official suggests that Avner worries about the men he has killed because his identity is no longer fixed to a nation of his own. If he wants to ease those anxieties, he must agree to work in and for Israel. Only then will he "officially exist" and return from "exile" (160). When Avner refuses to return to Israel, the official clearly no longer feels any tie to him. In the last moments of the film, Avner invites him to share dinner with his family in Brooklyn: "You're a Jew. You're a stranger. It's written someplace or other, I'm supposed to ask you to break bread" (161). The official sadly shakes his head and says no. With this rejection of the shared kinship of Jews as strangers, *Munich* marks the failure of the Promised Land to unite Jews and solidify Jewish identity. The moment is striking, given Spielberg's triumphant embrace of Israel at the end of *Schindler's List*. In *Munich*, however, he speculates about creating a new genealogy for Jewish identity, one that rescues the more benign, exilic attributes of Jewish group identity from the myth of return.

Zionism was a nineteenth-century ideology that instrumentalized the biblical relationship to Zion as a myth of autochthony; and as Spielberg, Roth, and Kushner make clear, twentieth-century Jews have used land-based identity politics to protect their claim to Israel. In *Munich*, the myth of shared autochthony replaces any genuine shared religious or cultural practice. Yet even though the film begins with an exploration of the role of the family in upholding the nation, it ends with an idea of how genealogy might provide an alternative as a model for group identity. The filmmakers' solution to the Jewish question is particularly interesting because it both critiques the importance of racialized ideas of birthright in the maintenance of land and upholds a sense that custom and identity are entangled with race.

Despite the tortured history of Jewish racialization, culminating in the Nuremberg Laws that marked Jews as a separate, degenerate race, numerous critics are working to reclaim diaspora and transcend territorially based identity politics through a corporeally defined Jewishness.[16] Kushner, Roth, and Spielberg are not the first to speculate about how to subvert the reified hierarchy between diaspora and Promised Land, the age-old antipodes of Jewish identity. In exploring ideas of nation and nationlessness, Ranen Omer-Sherman's *Diaspora and Zionism in Jewish American Literature* gives equal weight to both terms, particularly as they pertain to early twentieth-century Jewish fiction and poetry. Nine years before *Munich* was released, brothers Daniel Boyarin and Jonathan Boyarin wrote "Diaspora: Generation and the 'Ground' of Jewish Identity," a meditation on finding a Jewish identity within the long history of Jewish dispersal. Like the filmmakers, the Boyarins see genealogy as an antidote to the territorial conception of Jewishness that has gathered power since the Six Day War. Early in their essay, they assert that the "ground" of group identity can be situated on either "a common geographical origin" or "[a] common genealogical origin" based on "generation" (693). The Boyarins argue that the decision to locate Jewish collective identity in a geographical "myth of autochthony" has had vast repercussions, not only validating dispossession and racism but also undermining the progressive possibilities of Jewish diaspora and the unique customs and ideologies that have arisen as a result (699). The brothers differentiate between genealogy and autochthony as narratives of Jewish collective identity. While autochthony posits land as the origin for group identity and belonging, genealogy—the group cohesion that persists in diaspora—relies on an intangible notion of identity in shared practice and belief and, strikingly, the body.

To support this idea, the Boyarins argue for the Bible's engagement with nomadism and the long history of Jews who have maintained their identity through performative practices and the marking of bodily difference (such as circumcision, kosher laws, and endogamy). Like Coleman Silk in Philip Roth's *The Human Stain*, the brothers conceive of race as performative and embodied. In contrast to what many proponents of land-identified Jewishness argue, they assert that "the biblical story is not one of autochthony but one of always already coming from somewhere else." God's covenant with Abraham is seen as meaningful precisely because he suggests that land does not only belong to those who are native to it. In fact, the "traditional Jewish attachment to the Land, whether biblical or post-biblical, provides a self-critique as well as a critique of identities based on notions of autochthony" (715). According to the Boyarins, even in the Bible there are two poles of Jewish identity: one that favors exile, critique, and

Mosaic nomadism; another that favors the foundation of a Jewish state or permanent dwelling. A genealogical idea of Jewish identity that posits "descent from a common ancestor" as a precondition of Jewishness is race-based without being racist, "an extension of family kinship and not its antithesis and thus on the side of wilderness and not on the side of Canaan" (717). "Race is here on the side of the radicals; space, on the other hand, belongs to the despots" (718).

According to the Boyarins, anxieties about using a genealogical model to understand group identity center around the association of genealogy with race as well as a related Christian discomfort with any model that is descent- rather than consent-based. But they contend that the conception of race they put forth as a model for Jewish identity is unrelated to contemporary understandings of race. Instead, Jewish race or "generation" is consonant with "forms of identification typical of nomads, those marks of status in the body" that keep Jewish communal identity from becoming state- or nation-based (718).[17]

But what does it mean to ground Jewish identity in generation, as the Boyarins do, rather than in a "myth of autochthony" (699)? Their emphasis on generation takes much from early twentieth-century historian Simon Dubnow's theorization of Jewish identity. In *Nationalism and History: Essays on Old and New Judaism*, he wrote that the concept was key to understanding how the Jews could carry their "national spirit" through thousands of years of exile. Like many other historians of his generation, Dubnow was devoted to a Hegelian model of history as one of supersession, or overcoming. The fact that Jewishness was passed down by generation rather than through alliance to a state allowed it to function as the apotheosis of his tripartite model of group-national identity. The inheritance of Judaism from mother to child, regardless of a homeland, enabled Jews to pass beyond the first stage of national development, what he termed the "tribal" stage, as well as the second "political territorial" stage, and then finally to arrive at the third and most advanced, the "cultural-historical or spiritual" stage (100). "One may become a member of some artificial, legal or social-political grouping, but it is impossible for a person 'to be made' a member of a natural collective group, of a tribe, or people, except through mingling of blood (through marriage) in the course of generations, through the prolonged process of shedding one's nationality" (102).

Most startling in the intersection between Dubnow's and the Boyarins' supranational theories of generation and diasporic Jewish identity is their shared acceptance of a model of descent relations defiantly based on race. Their use of the Jewish diaspora to articulate how genealogy might work as the unifying force in group identity becomes a radical means of troubling the concept of identity based on fixity in space rather than on the ground of generation—what the Boyarins define as "a kinship with other people who happen to do certain things" in common (704). This definition is important because it challenges the assumption that the language of genealogically based culture or identity is always racist.

The language of genealogy provides an important corrective to racialist models of thinking without undermining the identifications, strategic or otherwise, that allow groups such as women and people of color to make claims for rights, recognition, or collective belonging.

The Boyarins' use of genealogy also attempts to rescue Jewish diaspora from its contemporary associations with imperialism, which have been famously articulated by Stuart Hall. He differentiates between imperial and progressive forms of diaspora: the imperial posits the possibility of a return to the homeland, whereas the progressive accepts the condition of exile. In search of an example of the first concept, he not surprisingly chooses the Zionist model, calling it "backwards-looking" and politically regressive (225). To the Boyarins, however, it is possible to use Jewish diaspora in precisely the opposite way—as a tool and an argument against territorializing discourses of identity. How might this deterritorial model provide a blueprint for Jewish American writers? The answer is of profound importance to all writers and critics who are invested in maintaining their communal ties without using those ties to support racism or race-based oppression.

Diaspora and Topos in Jewish American Literature

In *Munich*, Avner's decision to make a new home in Brooklyn represents one solution to how to find a home that is not national or nationalist. Here, Spielberg, Roth, and Kushner have followed a long line of diasporic artists offering numerous incarnations of a home-in-diaspora. The concept has increasingly become a topos in Jewish American literature. Traditionally defined by its sense of placelessness, diaspora is now a site in which Jewish American writers root their investments in Jewish identity and their speculations about the Jewish future. In the works of contemporary writers such as Tony Kushner, Ben Katchor, Philip Roth, and Michael Chabon, diaspora is a place that is both ontological and real. It is a figurative space from which to question the imperative to view Jewish identity as grounded only when there is Jewish ground beneath Jewish feet; it allows them to critique the common vision of diaspora as peripheral and Israel as central to definitions of Jewish identity. This diaspora has also become a geographical place—from Roth's satirical vision of a return to the space of Eastern Europe in *Operation Shylock* (1992), to Kushner's obsession with the blank geography of Antarctica in *Angels in America* (1990), to Katchor's depiction of the upstate New York Ararat of Major Mordecai Noah in *The Jew of New York* (1998), to Chabon's creation of a Yiddishland in Alaska in *The Yiddish Policemen's Union* (2007). They and many other contemporary Jewish American writers evince a growing preoccupation with delineating new promised lands, ones that are not located in an always deferred future time and place but are already present and delivered—situated firmly in galut spaces and identities.

Often these authors map alternative geographies for Jewish identity, creating fictional versions of what the anthropologist Benedict Anderson calls "imagined communities"—quasi-national spaces defined by imagined affinity and shared practice more than actual geographical boundaries.

The problem of representing diaspora in Jewish American literature since the foundation of Israel has an interesting history. In the years just after the nation's official recognition, popular literature such as Leon Uris's *Exodus* (1958) focused on the triumphs of Israel's foundation. In the early 1970s, novelists such as Bellow and Malamud traced the contours of the American Jewish imagination of diaspora in the period after the Six Day War, but their investigations were built on a simple premise: Israel was the ultimate home of the Jews. Bellow's Sammler reaches the pinnacle of his existence only when he travels to Israel to report on the war. Malamud's Lesser discovers that, in an America no longer hospitable to the Jewish race, he is the eternal Wandering Jew. But for Jewish American writers working during the past twenty years, this negative image of diaspora has shifted greatly. How does their renewed interest in diaspora allow us to sketch an alternate topography on which to build a meaningful Jewish identity? How can we account for the power of landlessness in the terrain of the Jewish American literary imagination? What are the ethical valences of using racial ventriloquism to critique Zionism? And how do these writers link diaspora to questions of race, difference, and otherness?

Like Spielberg, Roth, and Kushner's *Munich*, Ben Katchor's *The Jew of New York* and Michael Chabon's *The Yiddish Policemen's Union* scrutinize the concept of a Jewish homeland. The difference is that both Katchor and Chabon are profoundly invested in the idea of Jewish geography. The Yiddish-inflected spaces they imagine are both land-based and fundamentally diasporic. Their Jewish characters are never fully at home in the spaces they inhabit, even as they inhabit them with frenzied devotion. By pitting Jews against Native Americans, they nod to Palestinian dispossession but also emphasize the ways in which the Wandering Jew and the land-bound native peoples are often simplistically reduced to allegories for exile and indigeneity respectively. This is particularly true in the American context, as James Clifford has suggested. Likewise, in "America's Indian, Europe's Jew: Modiano and Vizenor," Jonathan Boyarin juxtaposes the role of Jews in Europe with that of Native Americans in the United States, pressuring the nature of allegorical thinking even as he exposes productive nodes of comparison between the two groups.[18] Just as late twentieth-century Jewish American writers of the 1970s–1990s used African American characters as a way to speak about their own waxing and waning sense of Jewishness as a racial identity, early twenty-first-century writers, such as Chabon and Katchor have used Native American characters as a way to articulate their anxieties about the connection between race and nation in both Israeli politics and the American investment in Israel. Chabon and Katchor create a diasporist place for an increasingly imperiled Jewish identity.

Both *The Jew of New York* and *The Yiddish Policemen's Union* appeared during a period of great flux in American culture—just after the rise of multiculturalism and the culture wars and during growing conflicts between critics and proponents of Israel just before and during the Second Intifada. As the writers make clear in these novels, those who seek a Jewish homeland "must confront and negotiate tensions between diasporic and indigenist narratives of the land" (Casteel, *Second Arrivals* 78). They must also accept the ways in which exile and indigeneity are profoundly linked. In the work of both novelists, Jews dispossess Native Americans to claim a native relationship to the land and to end their centuries of dispersal. By doing so, they undermine their own condition of internal exile and the claims of difference that have long been identified with it.

An Imaginary Ararat: Jewish Bodies, Jewish Homelands, Native American Identity

In *Adventures in Yiddishland: Postvernacular Language and Culture*, Jeffrey Shandler analyzes the increased circulation of Yiddish as cultural currency now that the Jewish mother tongue has become largely "postvernacular." According to him, despite the plummeting numbers of native Yiddish speakers since the decimation of European Jewry, the language of the shtetl has maintained a vibrant existence and has deep importance in Jewish identity and self-fashioning. The decline of Yiddish as a medium for daily communication correlates with an increase in the language's importance on "its secondary, or meta-level of signification—the symbolic value invested in the language apart from the semantic value of any given utterance in it" (4).[19] Notably, it provides a symbolic structure around which postwar diasporic Jews can cohere. Those who wish to maintain ties to Yiddish create an imaginary linguistic community, a space Shandler calls "Yiddishland." A play on Anderson's "imagined communities," Yiddishland as a space is more fictive than real, yet it is profoundly meaningful for those who opt to live within its smudged geographical and emotional boundaries.

To explain his idea, Shandler points to "Guidebook to a Land of Ghosts" (1997) by Jewish American novelist Michael Chabon, first published in the Library of Congress magazine *Civilization* and later reprinted in *Harper's*. The article is a mournful paean to the guidebook *Say It in Yiddish* (1958), a postwar dictionary of common Yiddish phrases that imagines an impossible land where the *mameloshen* (mother tongue) is spoken on every street corner and in every citizen's home. Yet according to Shandler, not only does the essay fail to account for the continuing power of Yiddish as a spoken language in ultra-Orthodox and other extant Jewish communities, but it also ignores the guidebook's true importance: that it allows Jews to "conjure a homeland for Yiddish, with its implications of indigenousness, territoriality, and even sovereignty" (33). Throughout history Yiddish has been associated with marginality and the transience of the Wandering Jew, yet in its postvernacular mode the language finally has found a resting place in the imagination of Jews who are resuscitating it and the world of their antecedents.[20] What Shandler does not specifically state is that, in contrast to Israel, Yiddishland provides a space for often-secular diasporic Jews who are uncomfortable about grounding their Jewish identity on land mapped out by the Zionist project in the Middle East.

Ironically, although Shandler criticizes Chabon's piece to undergird his own assertions, he does not fully explore the illustrations that accompany the article, which in both *Civilization* and *Harper's* is accompanied by the intricate drawings of Ben Katchor. In contrast to the text, Katchor's images of an ersatz home for Yiddish and Yiddish speakers, complete with Hebrew-lettered factories, cinemas, telephone booths, and ferry boats, create a Yiddishland much like the one Chabon invokes in his exploration of the guidebook. In this set of drawings, and throughout his oeuvre, Katchor intimately imagines a communal space for diasporic, pluralistic, contemporary Jews who are searching for a place to call home. For instance, Julius Knipl, the protagonist of many of Katchor's best-known comic strips (published in the *Forward* since 1988), is a nostalgic real estate photographer charged with capturing the ever-vanishing landscape of such a space. Through Knipl's alert gaze and clicking shutter, Katchor depicts an unnamed *Yiddishkeit* utopia centering on the sepia-toned cafeterias and small businesses of a Jewish neighborhood located half in the past, half in the present. In his strips for the urban design magazine *Metropolis*, he is similarly preoccupied with imagining the spaces that might be inhabited by Jews who, like himself, were raised in New York by Socialist, Yiddish-speaking parents—Jews who were raised to see the city as a haven.

Yet it is in his 1998 graphic novel, *The Jew of New York*, that Katchor most closely renders a Jewish space akin to Shandler's Yiddishland.[21] The novel takes New York City as a model for a diasporic groundedness in the Boyarins' mode, a place where the Wandering Jew can put down roots and find community. Katchor uses the space of the city (as well as an unlikely Promised Land to which some of its denizens attempt to escape) as a way to engage in debates about Jewish territoriality and sovereignty. Simultaneously, he explores the thorny position of the contemporary American Jew and the need to speak about Jewish problems via the bodies and voices of others, a concern that has been central to the post-1967 Jewish American writers I've discussed in this book.

The Jew of New York is Katchor's black-and-white ode to real-life Major Mordecai Noah and his band of fellow urban Jews, who were intent on forming "a new Jerusalem" in rural upstate New York during the early nineteenth century.

It is also a metafiction, a novel that tells Major Noah's story through a play written about him: an anti-Semitic satire that narrates the tribulations of a thinly veiled caricature of Noah named Major Ham. The play, which shares the name of Katchor's novel, introduces readers to the tale of a great American failure. "Tired of seeing a nation of seven millions of people, rich and intelligent, wandering about the world," Noah posts signs all over New York City advertising a new utopian community (6). He calls it Ararat, after the mountain on which many believe Noah's ark landed after the deluge. Soon he has gathered a ragtag group, and together they travel into the hinterlands outside of Buffalo to found a Jewish homeland. But once the itinerant Jews get a glimpse of the deprivations of life outside the city, they give up on the project.

Katchor opens *The Jew of New York* by imagining a Yiddish readership for the story to come. After playfully transliterating the book's title into the Hebrew characters of written Yiddish, he introduces the tale's cast of characters: Nathan Kishon, a *shoykhet* (kosher butcher), who is mistaken for a Native American after living in the wilds of upstate New York; the wily salesman Mr. Marah; Nathan Ketzelbourd, a Jewish woodsman who mocks Ararat's settlers for naïvely attempting to construct a homeland so far from their true home in the city; and Enoch Letushim, an "Oriental Jew" from Palestine, who tries to sell his assimilated American brethren burial soil from the Holy Land so that they can return to their biblical home in death, if not in life. Katchor renders these disparate schemers and dreamers as paper dolls, drawing in dotted lines to guide scissors, a metafictional technique that draws attention to the constructed nature of the novel's world. At the same time, these cut-outs undermine the omniscience of Katchor as author, calling on the reader to participate in the subversive spirit of the text and engage the dolls in a finger-puppet performance. Alongside the Yiddish words and Hebrew letters that appear throughout the text, the paper dolls demonstrate Katchor's desire to create a community of readers who are intimately involved in building the world of the novel.

After introducing his characters, Katchor describes the play that shares the book's name, an anti-Semitic satire that has taken the New York theater world by storm. When members of the New World Theater Company meet to mull over the 1830 theater season, they discuss the need to please the audience by adhering to a popular formula. Each season, they assert, should have an Indian play, a patriotic play, and a comedy. This season, "The Jew of New York," "a thinly-veiled burlesque of the life, to date, of Major Mordecai Noah" will provide the comic relief the citizens of New York so desperately need (4). Samson Gergel, the company's scenic director and sole Jewish member, is drafted to add Hebrew verisimilitude by "bringing out those effects which would most excite an audience" (1). He laments the fact that he will be participating in a performance of stereotypical Jewish identity, marveling that in order to play an exaggeratedly

Jewish version of Mordecai Noah, "the actor, Daizy, will transform himself into a caricature of this eminent citizen—a 'Major Ham' with a 'ghetto stoop' visible from the highest balcony" (4).

By positioning "The Jew of New York" within *The Jew of New York*, Katchor participates in the postmodern experimentation favored by many recent graphic novelists, notably Art Spiegelman in his innovative *Maus* (1986). But such contrivances also appear in earlier literary fiction, such as Malamud's *The Tenants*, which features a novel within a novel. Like Spiegelman, who interweaves multiple texts into the larger body of his novel, Katchor composes *The Jew of New York* by melding a number of tales and texts. He juxtaposes the story of the play "The Jew of New York" with tales told from the point of view of several different Jews of New York and disrupts the novel's narrative with playbills, pamphlets, and advertisements inserted into the body of the text. At the same time, the play at the heart of Katchor's tale emphasizes the fact that the graphic novel-to-come will not simply be a lighthearted rendition of Major Noah's career but a chance for Katchor to meditate on themes of Jewish identity.[22] The play titled "The Jew of New York" stages an exaggerated and categorical Jewish identity, as the definite article in its title suggests. Likewise, the larger body of the graphic novel titled *The Jew of New York* performs a certain notion of Jewishness, one that is in conversation with contemporary debates about race and ethnicity.

Katchor's novel abounds with texts meant to elucidate the typical character of a New York Jew. He re-creates them in painstaking visual detail: advertisements for the utopian community that Noah and his followers plaster all over Manhattan; the playbill for "The Jew of New York," promising a rare insight into the mind of a real, live Jew; a pamphlet comparing the characteristics of the Jews with those of the Native Americans in the upstate wilds; and an advertisement for the Hebrew-speaking Native American the Jews discover. Significantly, this highly material text depicts the abject bodies of both "the Jew of New York" and the city of New York. In contrast to the saccharine re-creations of old Jewish New York that appear in the work of many Jewish artists, Katchor's renderings include the often grotesque details of daily life.[23] They feature obsolete objects and individuals: the corpse of a wandering Jewish madman stuffed and put on display in a museum because he is thought to be a rare South American tiger; an ecstatic religious writer who lapses into seizures while cataloguing the onomatopoeic sounds of diners farting and spitting at a local restaurant (and who composes a massive exegesis on the origins of the Yiddish word for belching, *greptz*); a failed entrepreneur who refuses to wear clothing or sleep indoors; and the stooped Willy Lomanesque characters who reappear throughout the text, desperate to sell charred or broken goods pulled from their pockets. The novel is, quite literally, graphic. Katchor illustrates these bodies and tells their stories in relentless, exhaustive detail; he is adamant about using the medium of the comic to create a fully fleshed Jewish space akin to Shandler's Yiddishland.

There is something distinctly political about Katchor's visual and literary rendering of the bodies that litter the world of *The Jew of New York*. From the first pages of his text, he explicitly constructs a metaphorical connection between the body of the Jew and the body of the city. On the book's inside front cover, Katchor has drawn a map of the nineteenth-century city as a clear body of sorts. Depicting the plans of the Lake Erie Soda Water Company to fill Lake Erie with seltzer to aid digestion, it is a pictorial representation of just one of the utopian schemes that flourish in the novel. The company creates this map to demonstrate that its arteries can fuel the effervescing vitality of the urban space. The body of the city, however, is not healthy. While *The Jew of New York* begins with this optimistic blueprint for a distinctly Jewish civic project, it ends with the company's failure and "an enquiry into its profligate behavior" (100). Accordingly, the back cover of *The Jew of New York* depicts the broken vessels and torn up ground of the failed company, allegory for the failed national project at the book's heart.

Throughout the narrative, Jews are portrayed as more embodied than are the Christians who surround them on the streets of New York. In the nineteenth century, exaggerated depictions of Jewish physiques abounded in popular media, drawing attention to their purported racial otherness as well as to their supposedly animalistic side. Katchor's drawings play with this long history of Jewish caricature. He imagines the beefy Nathan Kishon, arguably his central character, as a ritual slaughterer who goes native in upstate New York after following the charismatic Noah. In one memorable scene, unable to sleep in a bed after returning to the city, Kishon lumbers out to sleep on the grass outside his boardinghouse, where a passerby mistakes him first for an animal and then for an Indian. Katchor represents this moment both visually and verbally, encouraging us to identify with the passerby in recognizing the slow transformation of Kishon from city-dweller to native.

In his depiction of Kishon's mentor Ketzelbourd, a true Wandering Jew who works as a fur trader upstate, Katchor extends this identification between the corporeal Jew and the untamed. Ketzelbourd becomes obsessed with the beavers whose pelts he trades; and when he discovers that they are nearing extinction, he enters into a state of extreme mourning that Katchor draws as a metamorphosis into animal form. Ketzelbourd's obsession culminates in his melancholic attempts to impersonate one of the animals. To indicate the intense identification between Ketzelbourd and the animal world, the artist depicts the trader after his death, stuffed and on display in a museum, transformed by the gaze of the spectator into a wild animal. At the same time, by juxtaposing Ketzelbourd with the artificial Jews of New York as they perform their identity onstage and the purported member of one of the Lost Tribes of Israel staging his Jewishness in Hiram's Museum, he leaves his reader with the sense that impersonation and a search for authenticity through impersonation are at the heart of the identities of all the Jews of New York, just as they were in Roth's *The Human Stain*.

Katchor's tale takes place during the great era of religious fervor known as the Second Great Awakening, and throughout the text the writer sacralizes the material world. For instance, apart from its role in impersonation, the body takes on an added valence in *The Jew of New York* as a site of worship. Yosl Feinbroyt, an eccentric religious zealot and amateur linguist, translates the sounds of belching and farting into a lexicon for transcendence. The health-mad members of the community of New Afflatus worship oxygen. Dr. Emil Vinyack's Compulsory Hotel offers cures for both epilepsy and passion. Ketzelbourd, the mourning fur trader, develops an idiosyncratic system of worship that involves praying before the image of John Jacob Astor and masturbating before images of a Sarah Bernhardt–like stage actress. Kabbalistic daydreams find their way onto the handkerchiefs the characters use to wipe their noses.

Significantly, Katchor explores Major Noah's preoccupation with the similarities between the bodies of the Jew and the Native American. By focusing on these racialized bodies, the writer attempts to re-create Noah's interest in the Lost Tribes of Israel and the broader nineteenth-century fascination with biological definitions of race that focused on physiognomy as a barometer for measuring difference and value. Katchor repeatedly depicts a pamphlet and a lecture that draw comparisons between the physical appearance of Native Americans and Jews. Early in the novel, middleman Isaac Azareal remembers a lecture in which it is said of the Indians, "They are all very like Jews, in appearance and voice, for they have large noses and speak through the throat" (3). Vervel Kunzo, a representative from the Berlin Society for the Culture and Science of the Jews, muses about a similar pamphlet while swimming around the boundaries of New York City. Katchor is not merely courting historical accuracy in this emphasis; the parallel between these two dispossessed communities recurs throughout the book. As Samuel G. Freedman has argued, the issue of the ethical imperative of a Jewish homeland in Israel was a pivotal one in American Jewish self-definition during the second half of the twentieth century.[24] Katchor uses the space of his graphic novel to draw parallels between the physically coded difference of Native Americans and Jews and engage in a potent conversation about territorial dispossession and American Jewish self-definition. His emphasis on their racial similarity links to the Palestinian question in Israel: even as observers forecast continuing bloodshed, many are quick to point out the irony that Palestinians and Jews are both Semites.

Katchor's attention to the imagined physical difference of Native Americans and Jews asks us to consider how racial and ethnic otherness has been measured, not only in the nineteenth century but also in 1990s America. As questions of canonicity and representation, affirmative action, ethnic difference, and political correctness fueled debates between Americans on the right and left, the question of Jewish difference became meaningful for Jewish artists and intellectuals in novel ways. Were Jews best represented by Allan Bloom and the neoconservative

Jewish writers at *Commentary* magazine, linchpins of the mainstream canon and bulwarks against the perceived encroachment of ethnic political interests on mainstream (mainly white and male) American art and culture?[25] Or was there something unavoidably different about "the Jew," as anti-Semitic scribblers such as the playwright of "The Jew of New York" have asserted, something that a Jew writing from the left might seize upon? Had Jews become the ultimate American success story, the whitewashed model minority, as Eric Liu calls them in his 1990s meditation on Asian Americans as "the new Jews"? Or was it possible to recover the Jewish difference from mainstream America in the American Jews' past and their formerly marginalized position? Can a politics of failure vie with the existing Jewish American politics of success? These questions provided the context for *The Jew of New York*, as they did for *The Human Stain*.

The relationship between Jews and Native Americans becomes Katchor's means of commenting on this anxiety. Elim-min-nopee, a Native American "rescued from the wilds of Upper New York State" and sold to a hungry theater audience as a member of a Lost Tribe of Israel, is one of the artificial Jews who people his invented landscape (66). The tribesman's name, a play on the name of the Lenape tribe and a brilliant meta-linguistic joke on the alphabet (L-M-N-O-P), is only one of the selling points of the show.[26] As Katchor writes in an advertisement for Elim-min-nopee's recitation, "An authentic Jewish synagogue has been erected from wood, at great expense, for this performance" (67). The recitation "in perfect Hebrew! By a rare and living member of one of the lost tribes of Israel!" is, like the play "The Jew of New York," a calculated performance of Jewish identity pitched to the people of New York—Jewish and non-Jewish. By juxtaposing these two playbills, Katchor suggests the performed nature of Jewish identity in the world his characters inhabit.

A few pages earlier, Katchor has described another character, Isaac Azarael, "a fine example of a Jew raised and now happily thriving in the free air of our republic," who is holding forth on both Elim-min-nopee's appeal and the power of the image of "a new Jerusalem discovered in the wilds of New York State." Everyone in New York City, it seems, is in search of an authentic chosen people. The Jews dream that a community of Hebrew-speaking Indians, untainted by contact with modernity, exists as "a New Jerusalem." As Azarael says of this dream, "By comparison, we, the Jews of the old world, appear to have been thoroughly corrupted by European culture and are Jews in name only" (59). In a different way, Enoch Letushim, the so-called Oriental Jew from Palestine selling soil from the Holy Land, also demonstrates that authentic Jewishness is a commodity with infinite worth for Jews and non-Jews. Letushim (whose name means "hammered" or, more metaphorically, "sharp and forbidding") recounts how visitors to Jerusalem are preyed on by "unscrupulous guides [who] lie in wait for credulous pilgrims who are eager to learn the historical and religious significance of the ground upon which they happen to be standing at the moment" (47). The

Jew from Palestine praises New York City because it is not haunted by this sort of authentic biblical past. New York, in contrast to Jerusalem, is dominated by commerce and the new to such an extent that Letushim finds it difficult to get any clear history of the landscape that surrounds him. In one scene, he asks a porter for the history of the particular corner of Broadway on which he is standing. The porter lists a series of business establishments and the nothingness that was there before them; for anything earlier, he suggests, "you'll have to ask an Indian" (48). Just as Major Noah's New World attempt to found a New Jerusalem is bound to fail, so, too, is any enterprise designed to get at the essence of identity or the origins of history in America; and this politics of failure is at the heart of the Jewish American literary enterprise after 1967.

Katchor's Jews of New York are situated between assimilation and separatism, and his focus on their search for an American homeland is part of the uniquely contemporary nature of his project. By using Mordecai Noah as both hero and foil, he creates not just a meta-fable but one based on actual historical accounts. Historian Jonathan Sarna calls Noah "the first man in history to confront and grapple boldly with the tensions between [Jewish and American identities]." He sees these tensions as "rooted in American Jewish history" and similar to those "faced by all minority groups which seek to preserve a measure of their identity while integrating into a larger, and at times hostile, mass society" (ix). Noah's scheme to found a community devoted to "both Jewish self-government and subservience to American law" was characteristic of his proto-pluralist aims (132). He saw his city as an ideal marriage of God's chosen people and God's chosen nation and invited the upstate Indians to join his New Jerusalem, claiming that the groups shared an identity and outlining their many common physical attributes and traditions. His argument was, at least in part, an instrumental one. As Sarna explains, "he understood that if the Jews and the Indians were one people, the Jews were then both 'the first people in the old world'—the ancestors of Christianity—and 'the rightful inheritors of the new'" (136).

In the 1980s and 1990s, when Katchor was creating *The Jew of New York*, debates were igniting over the melting-pot definition of American ethnicity, an idea that Anglo-Jewish writer Israel Zangwill had first proposed in the twentieth century and that Horace Kallen and other American Jewish proponents of cultural pluralism subsequently theorized.[27] Jonathan Freedman points out the deep investment that Jewish writers and thinkers had in ideas about ethnicity while noting the ways in which those discourses have since come under fire.[28] Does being an American require the melting of ethnic difference? As Katchor was writing, the question was becoming increasingly urgent. His representation of the imagined community of Ararat addresses this complicated relationship between ethnic/racial difference and Americanness. Noah and the other New York Jews in the novel are both marked as racially different and celebrated as paradigmatically

American. As Katchor slyly suggests, they are as American as the original settlers who displaced them.

In *The Jew of New York*, Noah is described as a patriot and a war hero. He regales his followers with tales of seeing the elderly Ben Franklin as a child. At the same time, in the play about his life, "The Jew of New York," he is transformed into a caricature, Major Ham, a bent and misshapen Jewish creature motivated more by ego than by civic spirit. Similarly, his upstate community has a complicated relationship to America and Americanness. Noah sees Ararat as not only a mythical home for the universal Wandering Jew but also, as his advertisements make clear, a distinctly American space protected by the nation's commitment to pluralism. The community's cornerstone notes the date of its foundation (in the month of Tishri, in the year 5585) and points out that this is fifty years after the date of American Independence. By linking the Jewish calendar date with a central American event, the foundation of Ararat is situated in both Jewish and American history.[29]

Katchor is not the first Jewish artist to compose an elegy to the New York City of the past. As Hasia Diner suggests in her study of the Lower East Side, Jewish American literary and visual artists have often fastened onto an imagined former Manhattan composed of internecine streets, culinary exotica, and collective poverty. In their often-sentimental renderings, they attempt to construct a conduit to an era that they imagine to be more authentically Jewish than the present is.[30] Their own parents might have defined success as an ability to escape the world of their forebears, yet these third-generation Jewish artists attempt a backward flight, retreating into a notion of the past that functions as an antidote to the upwardly mobile (and presumably empty) ideology and assimilation of their parents. Yet even though many representations of past Jewish urban life are romantic rehearsals of ethnic stereotypes and celebrations of the ghetto, beneath the maudlin nostalgia is a desire to recover the urban Jew's long-lost position as cultural and political outsider in America, one that is similar to the motivations behind Shandler's Yiddishland.

Like other celebrated Jewish American artists such as Will Eisner and Art Spiegelman, Katchor depicts Jewish bodies through the medium of the comic, which he has described in an interview with Alexander Theroux as the ideal mode for "mixing words with concrete images." His detailed drawings of the abject body of the Jew in nineteenth-century New York recover the lost position of Jew-as-outsider, and his representation of bodies within the text as well as the body of the text itself have political weight. Katchor's innovative combination of images and words allows him to create a Jewish world unto itself. By showing Jews at home in a world that is both Jewish and American, where ethnicity is in flux, he works against the image of the Jew as rootless. Moreover, by choosing a visual medium, he challenges a belief that Jews as a people are unable to produce an authentic art because they do not possess a nation of their own. Like the proponents of postvernacular Yiddish, he creates a picture of nineteenth-century New York that is also a blueprint for today's Jew of New York, the paradigmatic diaspora Jew.

Katchor himself points to the influence of a popular nineteenth-century genre, the historical romance, on *The Jew of New York*. In his preface to *The House of the Seven Gables* (1851), Nathaniel Hawthorne famously describes the genre, which he differentiates from the novel:

> When a writer calls his work a Romance . . . he wishes to claim a certain latitude, both as to its fashion and material, which he would not have felt himself entitled to assume, had he professed to be writing a Novel. The latter form of composition is presumed to aim at a very minute fidelity, not merely to the possible, but to the probable and ordinary course of man's experience. The former—while, as a work of art, it must rigidly subject itself to laws, and while it sins unpardonably, so far as it may swerve aside from the truth of the human heart—has fairly a right to present the truth under circumstances, to a great extent, of the writer's own choosing or creation. If he thinks fit, also he may so manage his atmospherical medium as to bring out or mellow the lights and deepen and enrich the shadows of the picture. (3)

Hawthorne's use of the genre allows him to depict the Puritans not as historically specific actors but as figures through which he addresses conflicts in his own present, commenting on authority, divinity, and the nation's relationship to the past.[31] Similarly, Katchor uses a picture of Jewish identity in nineteenth-century New York "to claim a certain latitude" in representing the possibilities for renewed diasporic Jewish community in the late twentieth century, melding the visual and the literary into "an atmospherical medium . . . to bring out or mellow the lights and deepen and enrich the shadows of the picture" in *The Jew of New York*.

Indigeneity, Sovereignty, and the Place of Jewish Identity

In Michael Chabon's 2007 novel *The Yiddish Policemen's Union*, the dream of a Jewish Promised Land is also alive and well and located squarely in territory normally thought of as diasporic. The novel was originally titled *Hotzeplotz*, a reference to what Chabon says is the "Yiddish expression 'from here to Hotzeplotz,' meaning more or less the back of nowhere, Podunk, Iowa, the ends of the earth" (Underway 115). The novel creates a someplace out of the blank space of this nowhere. Much like Philip Roth's *The Plot against America* (2004), it is a speculative history that reimagines postwar Jewish life.

In Chabon's novel, a temporary Yiddish-speaking settlement for Jewish refugees is established in Sitka, Alaska, in 1941. Seven years later the burgeoning state of Israel is destroyed after an unsuccessful struggle for independence. As a result, a flock of Jewish refugees move to Sitka, a city primarily inhabited by the native Tlingit population. Chabon's Judaized Sitka is fanciful but based on the ghost of historical fact. In 1939, members of Roosevelt's cabinet recommended that the many Jewish refugees from Europe be housed in the Alaskan territory, then mostly undeveloped and uninhabited (except for its Native population). The plan never came to fruition, but *The Yiddish Policemen's Union* imagines what would have happened if it had. Certainly, Chabon's interest in this fictive asylum, like Roth's in *The Plot against America*, is a response to the effects of the Holocaust on world Jewry. Yet while both imagine a universe in which that decimation did not happen, Chabon goes a step further and negates the need for Israel. In an interview, he explains that "the book explores the idea of a world with no Israel, where Jews are moved completely onto a side track of history, unlike now, where ... this little country of 5 million people dominates the headlines and gets an insanely disproportionate amount of world attention—and grief" (Eskenazi).

As it is for Katchor in *The Jew of New York*, failure is at the center of Chabon's diasporic imagination. In *The Yiddish Policemen's Union*, the roles of European Jews and those who escaped Europe for Palestine before the Second World War are reversed: the early Zionist inhabitants are forced to flee to America when their stab at independence fails. Although they attempt to cling to the dream of a spoken Hebrew "brought over by the Zionists in 1948"—"some spiky dialect, a language of alkali and rocks"—they are soon speaking Yiddish, a more viable tongue in Chabon's Alaska. In Sitka, "those hard desert Jews tried fiercely to hold on to [Hebrew] in their exile but, as with the German Jews before them, got overwhelmed by the teeming tumult of Yiddish, and by the painful association of their language with recent failure and disaster." It is Zionist ideals, both territorial and linguistic, that are associated with "failure and disaster," not the culture of diasporic Jewish life (286). Nonetheless, when the novel opens, the sovereignty of this Jewish utopia is threatened: Sitka is set to revert back to American ownership, leaving its Jewish inhabitants scrambling for an alternative place to call home. The book is constructed as a meditation on the many, often futile ways in which the rootless Sitka residents address their anxiety about the loss of their diasporic community. While it adopts the specifically Jewish mythology of the Promised Land, it also, like the work of many Jewish American writers, uses the bodies and voices of others to think through the pressing concerns of American Jews. Despite a longing to be elsewhere, the Jews of Sitka are deeply engaged with the geography of their own intermediary space between America and sovereignty.

The Yiddish Policemen's Union focuses on the travails of Meyer Landsman, an alcoholic detective in search of the killer of Mendel Shpilman, a man who may or may not have been the Messiah.[32] Landsman's name is simultaneously ironic and sincere; while he spends much of the novel isolating himself from his fellow *Landslayt* (the Yiddish word for inhabitants of the same village or geographic region), he is also the reader's tour guide to the landscape of Sitka, which Chabon delineates in painstaking detail. When we meet Landsman, his wife has kicked him out of their home, and he is living on Max Nordau Street in what he calls the "exile" of the Hotel Zamenhof (9). Like many of the names Chabon chooses, the street's and the hotel's are significant. Max Nordau, the co-founder, with Theodor Herzl, of the World Zionist Organization, is juxtaposed with linguist L. L. Zamenhof, the inventor of Esperanto, who hoped that a universal language would promote peaceful coexistence between disparate peoples. Yamenhof was also a Yiddishist and published the first grammar of the Yiddish language in 1879.[33]

As it was for Katchor, Yiddish is a vital element of Chabon's commitment to representing a successful diasporic community. Like Esperanto, it works to create a community defined outside the boundaries of the nation, yet it does not remain aloof from the American culture that surrounds it. Passersby marvel at "the raucous frontier energy of downtown Sitka, the work crews of young Jewesses in their blue head scarves, singing Negro spirituals with Yiddish lyrics that paraphrased Lincoln and Marx" (30). Children watch a television show that "comes from the south and is shown dubbed into Yiddish ... [about] a pair of Jewish children who look like they might be part Indian and have no visible parents" (38). To emphasize this hybridity, Chabon often entangles Yiddish with English. Rather than call his gun a "piece," as a hardboiled noir detective might, Landsman calls it a "sholem," suggesting that the gun can establish a "peace" of an entirely different kind (2). Simultaneously, Yiddish works to create a coherent community of Jews. The Sitka dwellers communicate primarily in Yiddish but switch into what they call "American" when they are around an outsider, using the *mameloshen*, or mother tongue, to cement their sense of group identity (6).

By integrating Yiddish so thoroughly into the novel, Chabon participates in a longstanding conflict about the viability of a Yiddish-speaking diasporic community after the Holocaust. In fact, part of the impetus for the novel was Shandler's criticism of his mournful ode to the guidebook *Say It in Yiddish*. In an interview with Jon Wiener, Chabon explains:

> The point of the essay in *Harper's* was to try to speculate on where you could go with *Say It in Yiddish*. Realizing there was no actual place where you would need this book, I tried to dream up some imaginary destinations where such a book might come in handy. And I dwelled a little bit on this Alaska thing in that essay, this proposal once that Jewish refugees be allowed to settle in Alaska during World War II, just for a paragraph. But I found I couldn't get it out of my head.

According to Michel de Certeau, places "place" those who live in them; by indexing an individual's position in space and in relation to a constellation of other individuals, they reinforce identity.³⁴ Thus, even as Sitka is a geographical place, it is also a discursive space in which Chabon thinks through the possibilities and problems of diaspora.³⁵ Chabon's shift in titles from *Hotzeplotz* to *The Yiddish Policemen's Union* emphasizes the novel's focus on spaces both imagined and real. The title of the novel refers to Landsman's only means of identifying himself after he is stripped of his police badge: a tattered membership card in the imaginary Yiddish Policemen's Union. The card itself is a canny invocation of the fictive yet urgent nature of communal identity as well as a sly nod to the *Landsmanschaften* that many Jewish immigrants joined to remind them of their European homelands.

The novel itself becomes a similar sort of space for working out questions of identity. Chabon has long been famous for his experiments with genre. In contrast to many writers of literary fiction, he dips into and between genres such as the comic book and the science fiction novel or, as in *The Yiddish Policemen's Union*, the generic conventions of the gumshoe detective novel.³⁶ Chabon reinforces his commitment to cross-pollination by marrying a Jewish tale with Yiddish inflections and biblical undertones to a prototypically American set of linguistic and narrative rules: the staccato dialogue, the hyperbolic plot devices, and the layers of deception that characterize the midcentury detective novel. He says that his choice of the genre arose from a desire to make the imaginary diasporic space of Sitka intensely real, just as Raymond Chandler's intimate tracery of the contours of Los Angeles is central to his portrayal of antihero detective Philip Marlowe. "[To] present [this world] in toto to the reader," he realized that he "was going to need a narrative framework that enabled [him] to have access to every aspect and layer of that world." The panoptic gaze of the detective, as well as his aloofness from and complicity with the world around him, become metaphors for the diasporic negotiation between worlds. Although "[an] omniscient narrator, a Dickensian narrator, probably would have worked also, . . . this detective figure who is able to go anywhere, see anything, talk to anyone, . . . [whose] badge gets him in any door, . . . understands the inner workings of his society . . . [and] knows which wheels are getting the most grease." To Chabon, "it seemed like the right choice for a figure to be a guide for the reader into this Jewish inferno" (Wiener).

As the reader's Virgilian guide, Landsman can move among and critique a variety of Jewish geographies in Sitka. His role also allows Chabon to intensify the thematic tension between rootlessness and territory in the Jewish imagination and the perilous results of cleaving to separateness. In search of Shpilman's killer, Landsman heads to the island of the Verbover Hasidim because he has heard that Shpilman might be the son of the Verbovers' leader. We learn that the Verbover sect "started out, back in the Ukraine, black hats like all the other black hats, scorning and keeping their distance from the trash and hoo-hah of the secular world, inside their imaginary ghetto wall of ritual and faith." After the destruction of their group, the rebbe and his family fled to the island refuge, where "he found a way to remake the old-style black-hat detachment," carrying "its logic to its logical end, the way evil geniuses do in cheap novels."[37] In this Promised Land, the rebbe "built a criminal empire that profited on the meaningless tohubohu beyond the theoretical walls, on being so flawed, corrupted, and hopeless of redemption that only cosmic courtesy led the Verbovers even to consider them human at all" (99).

Throughout the novel, Chabon probes at the ethics of the Verbovers' dream of sovereignty and the way in which their insularity constructs an idea of the other. Their crimes are myriad, and even their commitment to religion is about boundaries and not belief. They employ a "boundary maven" named Itzik Zimbalist to keep others out of their territory and help them evade Talmudic laws, such as the proscription against carrying things outside the home on the Sabbath, by building symbolic walls with string in and around the community. Preoccupied with the return of the Messiah, the rebbe casts out his son, Mendel Shpilman, when he discovers that he is gay, a transgression against community mores. Finally, intent on reconstructing the Temple in Jerusalem, the Verbovers plot to blow up the Arab holy place, the Dome of the Rock, to facilitate the resurrection of a Jewish Zion. In Chabon's hands, the Verbovers function as ideal metaphors for the perils of Jewish land obsession. Diaspora, messy and predicated on contact, is undermined by the boundary building of the island Jews, and the meaning and ethics of Jewishness itself are lost in the Verbovers' way of life. Yet as Nora Rubel has pointed out, the Verbovers also function as others in the world of *The Yiddish Policemen's Union*. Just as Saul Bellow opens *To Jerusalem and Back* with an anxious representation of a secular Jew's encounter with orthodoxy, Chabon, via Landsman, manifests a deep discomfort with the visual and cultural difference of the Hasidim. Rubel suggests that Landsman's "feelings echo those of many contemporary American Jews" (101). His aversion to the Verbovers, although logical, given their behavior in the world of the novel, indicates the chasms that exist inside the American Jewish community.

Throughout the novel, Chabon engages with identity and authenticity in diaspora through a broader portrayal of race, genealogy, and dispossession in Sitka. As in *Munich*, questions of birth continue to recur. Landsman is in exile at the Hotel Zamenhof because he has destroyed his relationship with his wife after their tortured decision to abort their chromosomally damaged baby. Shpilman, anointed a Messiah by his rebbe father, is cast off the Verbovers' island because he is gay and will not marry and maintain the family line. The residents of Sitka fear that they are members of a dying race. In fact, the only male character who is able to successfully reproduce is Ber Shemets, whose wife Esther-Malke is repeatedly pregnant during the course of the book.

Ber is Landsman's sidekick and adopted brother. Half Jewish and half Tlingit, he joins the family after Jews murder his Tlingit mother during the "Synagogue

Riots," when "eleven Native Alaskans were killed in the rioting that followed the bombing of a prayer house that a group of Jews had built on disputed land" (43). A clear analogue for conflict between Jews and Palestinians in the West Bank and other contested areas, the riots leave the young "Bear," as he is then known, homeless. Ber's Jewish father is Landsman's uncle, and Ber comes to live with Landsman and his parents when it becomes clear that his father won't have him. Himself a canny impersonator, the uncle had "gone native" in Tlingit society during his youth, learning to "gaff a seal with a steel hook, through the eye, and to slaughter and put up a bear, and to enjoy the flavor of candlefish grease as much as that of schmaltz." Only later, after he had fathered Ber, was it discovered that "his study of Native culture and his trips into the Indianer-Lands were a beard for COINTELPRO work during the sixties" (42).[38] The uncle's role as a double agent emphasizes the instability of identity in Sitka.[39] It is also a nod to the lengthy history of Jewish racial passing, particularly in the Jewish relationship to African American identity during the 1960s—a theme with deep roots in post-1967 Jewish American literature and its commitment to racial ventriloquism. Landsman's uncle can become Tlingit, but he can also safely return to his Jewish identity before the riots begin, just as COINTELPRO operatives did throughout the era.

At first, Ber Shemets, whose Yiddishized name means "Little Bear," is a comical figure in the novel's universe because his performance of Jewishness does not match his racial phenotype: "[He] lives like a Jew, wears a skullcap and four-corner like a Jew. He reasons as a Jew, worships as a Jew, fathers and loves his wife and serves the public as a Jew. He spins theory with his hands, keeps kosher, and sports a penis cut (his father saw to it before abandoning the infant Bear) on the bias. But to look at, he's pure Tlingit" (44–45). In the minds of many Sitka residents, his appearance and the uncanny bubbling up of his racial otherness cancel his Jewishness. The visibility and immutability of race that emerge in Chabon's description jar with the novel's increasingly flexible definition of Jewish identity. As the only character to successfully define himself as both Jewish and Native American, Ber increasingly defies these fixed racial concepts; in his ethical identification with Jewish practice and generativity, he becomes the most authentically "Jewish" character in the novel, while also allowing Chabon to explore the relationship between indigeneity and diaspora.

Chabon has long been concerned about Palestinian rights in Israel. In 2008, he and his wife, novelist Ayelet Waldman, wrote about their fears in the newsletter of the organization Americans for Peace Now: "As Jews and Jewish novelists, we devote our lives to envisioning and imagining the world as we have inherited it and as we wish it might be. But all of that history and all those imaginings are endangered, *now*, by those who are committed to ensuring future bloodshed, violence and fear." In a 2010 *New York Times* op-ed piece about the Gaza flotilla, he followed up on that earlier article, calling for an end to Jewish exceptionalism.

Yet some critics, notably Ruth Wisse in *Commentary*, see his posture as both shallow and dangerous. She reads *The Yiddish Policemen's Union* "as the Arab alternative version of Jewish history, which erases Israel from the map of the world while simultaneously fantasizing a gigantic Zionist-American anti-Arab crusade." This narrative, she avers, "has been making inroads in the 'progressive' circles to which Chabon belongs." Moreover, "Chabon's mock-Yiddish reinforces the sentimental stereotype of the Jew as harmless refugee, one who does not threaten the peace of the world, or the peace of the Jews themselves, unless and until he fatally conspires to resettle the land of Israel."

Though one might take exception to Wisse's vitriol, *The Yiddish Policemen's Union* clearly links Tlingit displacement with Palestinian removal, even as it inscribes Jewishness onto Sitka's Native population. In this way, as Sarah Casteel points out, the novel is reminiscent of Canadian writer Mordecai Richler's *Solomon Gursky Was Here* (1989), a magical realist novel about a fabled Jewish adventurer and entrepreneur who explores the Arctic in the nineteenth century and becomes a hero in an Inuit community. Chabon's interest in exploring the relationship between indigeneity and diaspora connects him to a lengthy history of North American writers engaged with ideas of the frontier and its inhabitants. In her *Members of the Tribe: Native America in the Jewish Imagination*, Rachel Rubinstein argues that Jewish and American investment in Native American identity speaks to a long-term Jewish ambivalence about fitting in and standing out in America. The characters in *The Yiddish Policemen's Union* measure both their Americanness and their otherness against the Tlingit population, a common trope in American literature since long before the nation's westward expansion. In the end, Chabon supports these uneasy dialectics of contact over the Verbovers' choice to remain aloof from the world.

As an adult, Ber becomes increasingly religious as a means of dealing with his mother's murder. In contrast, many of the local Jews respond to Sitka's reversion to American control by clinging to the idea of the Promised Land: "They are like goldfish in a bag, about to be dumped back into the big black lake of Diaspora. But that's too much to think about. So instead they lament the loss of a lucky break they never got, a chance that was no chance at all, a king who was never going to come in the first place" (202). As the threat of reversion looms, the Jews plan ever more extreme ways of bringing about the end of diaspora: from Buckbinder the dentist, who creates a museum of eerily accurate scale models of the Third Temple to be created on the site of the Dome of the Rock; to the religious leaders, who attempt to breed red heifers to signify the Messiah's arrival and the end of days. This search for personal and communal identity in the wake of transience is the central theme of Chabon's novel. What is innovative about his rendering is the way in which he posits the acceptance and affirmation of transience and diaspora as an answer to the existential hand wringing attendant to lacking a place in the world. Landsman and his ex-wife, Bina Gelbfish, embody the acceptance of exile; they are part of the tribe of landless Jews who "carry their homes in an old cowhide bag, on the back of a camel, in the bubble of air at the center of their brains. Jews who land on their feet, hit the ground running, ride out the vicissitudes, and make the best of what falls to hand, from Egypt to Babylon, from Minsk to the District of Sitka, ... the kind of Jews who explain the wide range and persistence of the race" (155). After seeing the destruction wrought by the Verbovers' quest for land, the two agree that the only way of maintaining sanity in the contemporary world comes from finding an ethics rooted in transience.

Chabon ends *The Yiddish Policemen's Union* with two sentiments that evoke his diasporic ideal. First, he writes of Landsman's dawning realization that "there is no Messiah of Sitka, ... no home, no future, no fate but Bina. The land that he and she were promised was bounded only by the fringes of their wedding canopy, by the dog-eared corners of their cards of membership in an international fraternity whose members carry their patrimony in a tote bag, their world on the tip of the tongue" (411). This affirmation resonates with *Munich*'s call to find peace in relationships rather than in land. Like the imaginary Yiddish Policeman's Union of which Landsman is the sole member, it also suggests that all communities must partake of the imaginary to survive. Second, Chabon asks his readers to stop their stories from telling them. Landsman realizes that he has been unnecessarily exiled from Bina because of "the story that has been telling him for the last three years" since their baby was aborted (375). Shpilman, anointed as a potential Messiah, kills himself because he has been caught in the web of other people's stories, particularly those of the Promised Land and the restoration of the Temple. Next to his body, he leaves a chess board in a *Zugzwang*—"an end game" in which a player has to move but cannot avoid being checkmated—to express the situation. He has been forced to live out the fantasy of the Promised Land, to be moved around like a chess piece because of his father's obsessive desire to end the Jews' condition of transience. Chabon's topography of diaspora is most provocative in the ways in which it suggests future modes of telling our own stories and escaping those that others have told us.

In an article in *The Nation* called "The Imaginary Jew," William Deresiewicz laments the end of Jewish American literature. As writers move away from what Deresiewicz describes as an authentic Jewish identity rooted in religious tradition, immigrant neighborhoods, or a national imagination, their prose becomes less uniquely their own. In fact, he believes that contemporary Jewish writers such as Chabon write novels about the Jewish past because it's the only way they can recover any sort of context for Jewish identity.[40] Yet by imagining a Jewish future in diaspora, Chabon is suggesting a direction for Jewish American writing—one based on choice and the fashioning of alternative but historically informed geographies of Jewish identity. He is also indexing American Jews' changing attitudes about Israel. In *The Yiddish Policemen's Union*, he connects a continuing interest in the political and poetic possibilities of diaspora with an appreciation of the power of "emplacement" (Casteel, *Second Arrivals* 3).[41] Chabon is interested in what one character in the novel calls "the Eternal Return of the Jew and how it can be measured only in terms of the Eternal Exile of the Jew" (372). The poetics of Eternal Return, so prized in Jewish culture, remain meaningful only in a deferred state. For Chabon, all dreams of sovereignty are impossible dreams. Jewish culture is defined and kept vibrant only in zones of contact, negotiation, and hybridity. The one Jewish idea that fails in *The Yiddish Policemen's Union* is the airless dream of utopia—a universe without the mess of double agents, failing marriages, and native communities with whom one must share the land. The conclusion is clear: it is only without a land that we can find a home; it is only with the other that we can find ourselves.

Coda

To begin to resemble the other, to take on their appearance, is to seduce them, since it is to make them enter the realm of metamorphosis despite themselves.
—Jean Baudrillard

The Uses of Jewish Exceptionalism

In May 2010, Israel attacked six civilian ships, known collectively as the Gaza freedom flotilla, that were attempting to break the blockade at Gaza to bring construction materials and humanitarian aid to the residents. The military operation was a public relations disaster for Israel, and a number of American writers and intellectuals weighed in on the subject. As I mentioned in chapter 5, Michael Chabon was among them, publishing a *New York Times* op-ed about the episode. His response was unusual, however, because it explored the concept of Jewish exceptionalism as it related to both Israeli and American Jewish identity. In his view, the most vociferous defenses and critiques of Israel all emanate from "the foundational ambiguity of Judaism and Jewish identity: the idea of chosenness, of exceptionalism, of the treasure that is a curse, the blessing that is a burden, of the setting apart that may presage redemption or extermination." For Jews throughout history, this idea has led to varied repercussions: "To be chosen has been, all too often in our history, to be culled."

Chabon's point is clear: Israel attempts to deflect critics with the myth of Jewish uniqueness, both biblical and post-Holocaust; Israel's detractors (sometimes including Chabon himself, as he admits in the op-ed) imagine that a Jewish nation should manifest a Jewish commitment to ethical behavior that is antithetical to the nineteenth-century nationalist project at the nation's heart. Nonetheless, while Chabon's op-ed was controversial when it was published, it evades a broad critical examination of the concept of exceptionalism and its power in Jewish, American, and Jewish American contexts. As Anthony Smith argues in his important *Chosen Peoples: Sacred Sources of National Identity*, Israel's sense of chosenness is not unique. There is a long history of nationalism that uses Judeo-Christian biblical claims of election to sacralize modern concepts of race, territory, and white supremacy. In U.S. history, for example, the rhetoric of exceptionalism has been central to the state's self-conception, expansion, and military and humanitarian intervention. From the beginning, the Puritans borrowed the imagery of biblical chosenness to suggest that they might function, as John Winthrop put it, "as a city upon a hill," an example unto other nations. The historian Deborah Madsen argues that early Americans saw themselves as the typologically preordained descendants of the Israelites.

It's important to note that 1492 was a pivotal year in both Jewish and American history, marking Spain's expulsion of its Jewish population and Columbus's "discovery" of the Americas.[1] The two histories were further joined in that cataclysmic year when Columbus, under the sway of fifteenth-century theories about the Lost Tribes of Israel, suggested that the indigenous populations he encountered in the New World might be members of those tribes. This Lost Tribes idea, later espoused by a number of North American settlers, peaked in the eighteenth and nineteenth centuries when American leaders and thinkers were in search of a discourse to support their claims of national chosenness and by-proxy indigeneity. The nineteenth-century fascination with the Lost Tribes theory was an early example of the way in which America linked its sense of exceptionality to an idea of Jewish difference.

As Jonathan Freedman contends, American and Jewish mythologies were further joined as the Ashkenazi Jewish immigrant narrative entered twentieth-century American culture. Its imagery of melting pots, Lower East Side factories, and Ellis Island became a "culturally validated synecdoche" for a host of other immigrant stories in a manner that often cancels out their diversity and richness (7). Eventually, as Eric Liu suggests, Jews became America's first "model minority," used, as Asian Americans would later be, to point out the failures of other minorities, primarily African Americans, to succeed in the nation's neoliberal political and economic landscape. This disjuncture between Jews and Americans of color gathered more steam after the Holocaust, when America buttressed its sense of exceptionalism and displaced guilt about its own history of genocide by drawing a stark contrast between American and European treatment of Jews.[2] As Nikhil Pal Singh asserts, "civic myths about the triumph over racial injustice have become central to the resuscitation of a vigorous and strident form of American exceptionalism—the idea of the United States as both a unique and universal nation—once thought mortally wounded by the Vietnam War and the divisive racial politics of the late 1960s" (17).

For Jewish writers, a sense of post-racial exceptionalism, along with an increased awareness of the link between Jewishness and Americanness, has had real and sometimes unwanted repercussions. Chabon wrote an op-ed for the *Times* not simply because he was a concerned, politically active citizen but because the role of Jews in Israel and America and the myth of Jewish exceptionalism have had profound effects on the Jewish imagination, particularly on how Jews imagine themselves in relation to others. Ironically, the marriage of Jewish interests with American hegemony has sacrificed one sense of Jewish difference for another. As I discussed in chapter 1, Jewish writers and intellectuals once saw themselves as having a special purchase on suffering that allowed them to speak for others who had suffered. An awareness of uniqueness encouraged them to engage in the art of appropriation, even as such appropriations were being discredited in postwar literary discourse. The gradual alliance between Jewish and American interests, as well as the success of Jews as model minorities, continued to exert pressure on Jewish writers to seek identifications with the other. Perhaps this is another aspect of the double-edged sword of exceptionalism that Chabon discusses in his op-ed.

As Chabon's career attests, an ambivalent relationship to Jewish exceptionalism, as well as an investment in the seductions and perils of literary appropriation and racial ventriloquism, are characteristic of many Jewish American writers, whether their political or aesthetic affiliations are avowedly progressive or conservative.[3] If, as I suggest in chapter 4, Jewish writers were protagonists in the culture wars of the 1980s and 1990s, they are currently central to the internal culture wars that have riven the Jewish community in America during the first decades of the twenty-first century. In 2000, Samuel Freedman's *Jew vs. Jew* predicted a crisis in American Jewish identity around the issues of religious observance, Israel, and political allegiance; and Jewish American writers may be the clearest lens through which to witness the "struggle for the soul of American Jewry" that he foresaw at the cusp of the new millennium (23).

Passing for a Jewish Writer, Talking about the Future of American Literature

As I have discussed, Chabon's desire to imaginatively engage with the other (in his case the native Inuit population, a clear analogue for Israel's displaced Palestinians) in order to speak about Jewish identity is a constitutive characteristic of much post-1967 Jewish American fiction. From Malamud's grappling with the place of the Jewish writer in a literary and social climate that increasingly valued the authenticity of the racialized voice in *The Tenants* to Hettie Jones's construction of a black-Jewish interracial narrative in *How I Became Hettie Jones* to Philip Roth's curmudgeonly commentary on the culture wars via the black Coleman Silk in *The Human Stain*, Jewish American writers have insisted on thinking through the complicated terrain of modern Jewish—and modern American—identity via the category of race. Yet the question of what it means to speak *as* a Jew and *for* others remains powerful and provocative, one not simply for self-identified Jewish American writers, but for a variety of American authors of various stripes. In turn, the question resonates with larger themes in twenty-first-century American culture, from contentious debates about whether indeed we have become a "postracial" society, to how much race matters in a digital era, to what role the politics of identity and the poetics of appropriation will play in the future of American fiction. Recent American fiction has become reinvested in Jewishness (or, rather, Jewish difference) as allegory and lived experience.

No trend in American letters more clearly demonstrates the continuing importance of Jewishness to contemporary conversations about race than does the recent rash of passing narratives involving Jews. Jess Row's 2014 novel *Your Face in Mine*, for example, considers the future of the appropriative imagination, focusing on the story of Martin Lipkin, also known as Martin Wilkinson, a Jewish man who elects to have "racial reassignment surgery" to become African American. Returning home after a family tragedy, Lipkin/Wilkinson's old high school band mate, Kelly Thorndike, runs into his transformed friend on the street. After letting him into the secret, Lipkin/Wilkinson hires Thorndike to compile an archive of his history and write his story. Although the novel is ostensibly the narrative of a white man who feels he can only authentically become himself by taking on the appearance and life of an African American man, Row opts to make Lipkin both white and Jewish before he becomes black.[4]

As Joshua Lambert points out in a review, this choice links the story of Lipkin/Wilkinson's surgical and spiritual transformation to the racial history of cosmetic surgery, particularly alterations to the Jewish nose and the desire to assimilate to hegemonic beauty ideals. Lipkin/Wilkinson's Jewishness also recalls Lori Harrison-Kahan's observation, which I mentioned in chapter 4, that Jewish characters often appear in narratives of passing to suggest a potential third racial category. At the same time, Jewishness functions differently in Row's twenty-first-century narrative from the way it does in the early twentieth-century texts that Harrison-Kahan is studying. In *Your Face in Mine*, Lipkin/Wilkinson's nominal Jewishness is the site of a lost authenticity as well as a marker of the impossibility of racial authenticity in a purportedly postracial age. Row cannily hides the word *kin* in both *Lipkin* and *Wilkinson*, for the novel is at heart a rumination on the fate of kinship in an era when few people retain ties to larger religious, ethnic, or cultural communities.

In *Your Face in Mine*, Row builds an analogy between Lipkin/Wilkinson's racial reassignment surgery and gender reassignment procedures and the psychological condition of gender dysphoria that compels people to modify their bodies to better reflect their perceived sense of gender. The alignment of race and gender suggests something fundamental about how Row views race—and perhaps about how we might productively include Jewishness in conversations about race without resorting to reductive essentialisms or anti-Semitic stereotypes. The historian Lisa Silverman suggests that it is useful to think about Jewishness and Jewish difference as functioning in a manner akin to gender. While linked in some ways to biological concepts of sex, gender transcends those limitations: one's gender and sex do not always travel along parallel lines, and gender is also constituted relationally. As Simone de Beauvoir has noted, woman is constructed as other in relationship to a notion of man as the universal or given. In reference to German Jewish culture, Silverman writes, "The boundaries between the constructed ideals of 'Jew' and 'non-Jew' operate similarly [to gender boundaries], becoming invisible once they are defined so that they can be involved as the framework of the ideal definitions of these categories. It is in performing Jewish difference that Jews and non-Jews invoke these boundaries in a process of self-identification that played a critical role in German Jewish culture" (29). Like both gender and race in Row's imagining, Jewishness in the American context invokes the boundaries between self and other to perform difference. This prototypical performativity functions as the blueprint for the sense of race that persists in *Your Face in Mine*—and in twenty-first-century American culture.

Alongside its provocative insights about race and gender, Row's novel implicitly questions the role of racial and ethnic identity in the formation of other bodies. As we have seen in Mark McGurl's exploration of high cultural pluralism in the corpus of postwar American writing, the notion of the authentic racialized voice, located in the raced body, has become central to a certain school of fiction. On one hand, Row's novel suggests that racial and ethnic identity are meaninglessness, functioning as a mess of floating signifiers, there for the taking. On the other hand, it also advertises the persistence of meanings that are attached to race and ethnicity, the continuing need to perform and proclaim race, whether as bodies or texts. It is the white Jewish Lipkin, not the white Protestant Thorndike who is willing to relinquish the privileges of whiteness to gain a fixed identity. Like other post-1967 Jewish and American writers, Row suggests that one needs to assume a voice that is not one's own in order to have a voice.

At the end of the novel, Thorndike has racial reassignment surgery to become Asian. In interviews, Row has suggested that this character, too, sees his WASP identity as incommensurate to the task of creating an authentic voice, literary or otherwise. The writer "traces some of his own questions about race to his time as a teacher in Hong Kong in the late '90s" and notes that the novel recalls "all of the times [he's] felt drawn to a particular racial identity: listening to hip-hop or reading books about Native American reservations or being in a Buddhist temple" (F. Lee). In *Your Face in Mine*, both Thorndike and Lipkin/Wilkinson believe that they can only speak for themselves when they learn how to pass for and speak as another.

As McGurl has shown, the idea that one needs to adopt the voice of an other to have a literary voice is a powerful one for postwar writers educated in the "write what you know" school. Ironically, as Jewish writers such as Roth, Ozick, and Bellow have made their anxious entry into the American canon, they have become, for a number of young American writers, symbolic of an earlier era of literary authenticity. This is clearly the case for Joshua Ferris, whose envy for the archetypical Jewish writer is at the center of his most recent novel, *To Rise Again at a Decent Hour* (2014):

> [The novel] starts from the question of whether there's a kind of private language and intimacy to religion that the mutt-y white guys like me are missing out on. And to some extent, I'm also thinking about the question of whether as a *writer* there's something I've missed out on. When you're an American novelist in 2014, at a point when Philip Roth has had a kind of apotheosis—has ascended to heaven even though he's still on earth—you realize the extraordinary richness he found in Judaism. I didn't grow up within that richness. I simply didn't have it. It cuts both ways, of course. There are writers who happen to be Jewish who get labeled as "Jewish writers" and would much rather be just writers. And here I am, lamenting the fact that I'm not a Jew! (J. Lee)

For Ferris and many other writers and intellectuals, Roth remains the archetypical American writer, one for whom "religion offers . . . a tradition both to be nurtured in and to fight against." In Ferris's view, "that nurturing and that conflict can produce great literature. Roth was given a lifetime of material from the fights he picked with Judaism—with the generation of Jews that raised him, with the generation that excoriated him, and finally with the generation that celebrated him." In contrast, Ferris contends, "I got a few potluck dinners and some basement training in Noah" (J. Lee). Ferris's idealization of the Jewish writer is fascinating because it gets at the continuing representation of Jewishness as a racial identity that one cannot escape regardless of religious identification or practice as well as Jewish writers' own ambivalence about becoming canonical American literary figures even as they maintain an association with racial authenticity.

As Updike does in *Bech: A Book*, Ferris carries this identification with Jewishness into *To Rise Again at a Decent Hour*, which explores issues of writing, identity, and Jewishness from the purview of the digital age, when all identities are stealable, amorphous, and fluid. The novel is the melancholic tale of Paul O'Rourke, a depressed dentist whose online identity is stolen by an unknown man. After creating a fake website for O'Rourke's dental practice, the thief assumes the dentist's identity on Twitter and Facebook in order to write screeds against modern-day "Amalekites," descendants of the biblical antagonists of the Jews. O'Rourke's struggle with this spectral online self, who may or may not be Jewish, catapults him and the novel into a meditation on religion, authenticity, anti-Semitism, and the Internet. Significantly, the battle with the online O'Rourke parallels O'Rourke's existing worries about authenticity and his obsessive pursuit of religion, particularly his desire to become "Jewish-ish" like his ex-girlfriend Connie is (304).

Throughout the novel, O'Rourke contrasts Judaism with Christianity, arguing that Jewishness functions more like a race than other religions do. Like the participants in Reddit's conversation about Jewishness, which I discussed in this book's introduction, O'Rourke inscribes a racialized essence to Jewish identity that he does not attribute to other religious groups.

> Whether you were born a Christian or a Jew seemed tantamount to the same thing from the perspective of the newborn, but growing up made all the difference in the world. A Christian could slough off his inherited Christianity and become an atheist or a Buddhist or a plain old vanilla nothing, but a Jewish person for reasons beyond my understanding, would always be Jewish, e.g. an atheist Jew or a Jewish Buddhist. Some of the Jews I knew, like Connie, hated this fact, but, as a non-Jew, I had the luxury of envying the surrender to fate that it implied, the fixed identity and tribal affiliations—which is why I minded the slander of being Jewish online less than the vile and outrageous insult of being Christian. (63)

Ferris sets the imagined rootedness of Jewishness—"the fixed identity and tribal affiliations" that recall Coleman Silk's anxious depiction of blackness in *The Human Stain*—against the digital ether in which identities can be quickly assumed and shrugged off. In an interview about the novel, he recalls, "[I was] interested in the way that the Internet creates a second world, a second reality. I mainly go about my business unobserved. I don't engage with social media. But when I go online, I can type my name into Google and see pictures of myself. I have an existence online that is not mine. There is a version of me out there that I'm not developing—that other people are developing on my behalf." The idea of the Internet as the engine of existential doubleness haunts both O'Rourke and Ferris himself, who contends that O'Rourke "is striving for a kind of sincerity. And the Internet—the reflections of himself he sees online—are part of the reason he can't find that sincerity, I think. He's too aware of himself as an actor in the world, and that stops him acting. He's an object rather than a subject. [His] great fear—and probably mine—is that it's no longer possible to be authentic in the way it was before the social internet came along" (J. Lee). As we have seen, Jewish representation in the twentieth-century has largely been the story of moving from object to subject of representation; perhaps, in the twenty-first century, the figures of the Jew and the Jewish writer are becoming aligned with a form of subjecthood that might act against this doubling and objectification of the self.

Ferris is not the only author to think through Jewishness in the Internet age—or to use Jewishness as a metaphorical antidote to the age. A number of

Jewish writers have also engaged with the viability of Jewishness as a meaningful, if still constructed, "racial" category. In *Super Sad True Love Story* (2010), Gary Shteyngart, whose rollicking fictions often employ racial stereotypes even as they seek to subvert them, looks at the fate of Jewishness in an undisclosed dystopian future. He imagines a time in which identities are mediated by technology, particularly the handheld device he calls the "äppärät." The äppärät and the äppärät owner share a total identity; people come to know each other through the "hotness" and credit scores that the äppärät streams above its owners' heads. Young people communicate entirely through text messages and email, and speak in a sexually charged and consumer-obsessed language of abbreviations and acronyms. They are put off by the smelly dust and must of books and prefer the clean anonymous surfaces of communication technologies. In this world, to paraphrase Marshall Berman, all that is solid melts into air.

Yet Shteyngart's narrator, Lenny Abramov retains a commitment to collecting and reading books, writing in a diary, and stoking his nostalgia for the European Old World. He is a romantic, and he is also achingly, stereotypically Jewish. In Shteyngart's dystopian digital future, ideas about race and ethnicity remain powerful. To Lenny, and to Shteyngart, the corporeality of his Jewishness is at the center of his resistance to the electronic mediations of the future. As in Ferris's and Row's novels, Jewishness is associated with a certain discourse of authenticity even as it can only be understood in reference to the body of another—in this case, the body of Eunice Park, Lenny's ethereal Korean American love interest, whose Asianness, in problematic ways, Shteyngart poses as more appropriate to the fast-paced technological ethos of the future.[5]

My rehearsal of these various contemporary texts does not suggest that Jewishness is *the* central topic of the novel during the past decade. Rather, I marvel at the continuing relevance of Jewishness as an idea and an identity for novelists, Jewish or not, who seek to address the compromised, polyglot nature of the self in the twenty-first century. The notion of the sometimes-racialized Jewish voice, as well as the propensity of Jewish writers to insist on speaking in voices not their own, remains a theme in our purportedly postracial era. While critics such as Ben Schreier have pointed out the increasing vacuity of the concept of Jewishness in American life, they miss the important point that race doesn't have to exist for it to matter greatly to those who claim or reject their racial identities. In the second decade of the twenty-first century, Jewishness continues to resonate with passing narratives and stories of racial ventriloquism, and novels and novelists remain preoccupied with questions of whether and how to speak in the voice of another, particularly when that other is of another "race." The continuing power of Jewishness, for Jewish and non-Jewish writers alike, is not simply evidence of a return to tribalism or a futile quest for authenticity in American culture. Instead, it is a profound statement on the symbolic resonance of the idea of voice for exploring race, representation, and the intersubjective nature of all identities. Jewish writers' urge to speak the self through the other—to ventriloquize—functions as a powerful reminder that we become who we are only in relation to others. The Jewish appropriative imagination also highlights the power and pitfalls of comparison. Identifying across racial boundaries can create genuine connections and allow us to think deeply about the artificiality of the categories that contain us. It can also function as a means of collapsing difference and silencing voices that need to be heard.

Our era is rich with identification-via-hashtag. Twitter and Facebook users assert *#jesuischarlie* and *#icantbreathe* to signal their sympathy for victims of terroristic violence. There is beauty in these identifications and their insistence that an American suburban dad can understand the plight of French satirists killed by Islamic militants, that a white teenager can comprehend the horror of police violence against African Americans. At the same time, these transnational and transracial identifications are only meaningful if they are fraught with ethical handwringing and an awareness of the limits of the empathic imagination. The work of Saul Bellow and Bernard Malamud, Hettie Jones and Michael Chabon, have long grappled with these delicate paradoxes of identity and identification. These Jewish American writers and intellectuals may sometimes speak in borrowed voices, but what they say continues to resonate in our world.

Notes

INTRODUCTION

1. Howe's suggestion that Zelig wants to "assimilate like crazy" is another example of how Zelig's supposed pathology is connected to his carnality, a common link in anti-Semitic stereotypes of the Jewish man, who has been rendered as both feminized (for instance, Jewish men have been said to menstruate) and predatory.

2. Traveling to France also dramatizes the differences between Jewish identity in America and Europe. In Europe Zelig's identity becomes fixed as a visibly Jewish one.

3. Complicated Jewish figures appear throughout the film. In a pivotal scene, Fanny Brice appears to serenade Zelig in an exaggerated Yiddish accent. This performance of Jewishness, however, is itself not entirely "authentic." After all, according to Barbara Grossman, Brice famously said that she "never used a Yiddish accent until Irving Berlin suggested she do so" (66).

4. While Rogin and Harrison-Kahan focus on the ethics of Jewish performances of blackface, Rachel Rubinstein's *Members of the Tribe: Jews in Native America* looks at how Jews in America figured their relationship to their own "tribe" via engagement with Native Americans in both literature and "redface" performance.

5. Both Silverman and Baron Cohen have performed in a type of blackface: Silverman on *The Sarah Silverman Show* and Baron Cohen in his depiction of Ali G. Interestingly, Baron Cohen wrote his senior thesis at Oxford on Jews and African Americans.

6. Walter Benn Michaels and Daniel Itzkovitz have argued that Jewish characters make guest appearances in modernist narratives precisely to undergird their nativist logic and the collision between the American embrace of radical individualism and anxieties about the nation's others-within attendant to the period.

7. In *Klezmer America*, Jonathan Freedman provides a brilliant account of the model minority discourse as it pertains to Jews and has been applied to Asian Americans, whom Eric Liu calls "new Jews."

8. Among other things, this shift is associated with a move away from understanding race and ethnicity via cultural pluralism, a species of discourse with which Jews have long been identified.

9. In "Not Really White—Again: Performing Jewish Difference in Hollywood Films Since the 1980s," Jon Stratton makes the point that critics have moved from understanding Jewish American identity through the prism of culture to that of performance (or, at times, performativity, in the sense that Judith Butler uses it). Some of the best recent studies of Jewish American identity and aesthetics have certainly born out Stratton's contention. Works such as Lori Harrison-Kahan's *The White Negress: Literature, Minstrelsy, and the Black-Jewish Imaginary* and Catherine Rottenberg's *Performing Americanness: Race, Class, and Gender in Modern African- and Jewish-American Literature* draw on Rogin's pioneering work in *Black Face, White Noise* to articulate Jewishness in relation to performance, both literal and symbolic.

10. A number of scholars have provided brilliant accounts of the history of Jewish racialization, particularly the transformation of Jews from ambivalently raced "Hebrews" at the turn of the century into unimpeachable "white folks" after World War II. Accounts that offer arguments about Jewish whiteness include Eric Goldstein's *The Price of Whiteness*, Karen Brodkin's *How Jews Became White Folks and What This Says about Race in America*, Matthew Frye Jacobson's *Whiteness of a Different Color* and *Roots Too*, and Rogin's *Black Face, White Noise*. Freedman's *Klezmer America* takes a different and very productive approach, focusing on the borders between Jewishness and other forms of otherness in America and on the pivotal role that Jews/Jewishness have played in theorizations of ethnicity.

11. In her essay, Seidman argues that secular Jewishness is characterized by identification with other forms of otherness, particularly those that center around questions of gender and sexuality.

12. I am also influenced by Jeffrey Melnick's nuanced account of "black-Jewish relations" in *A Right to Sing the Blues: African Americans, Jews, and American Popular Song*, which addresses the complex relationship between Jewish songwriters and composers and black performing artists.

13. I return to Arendt's "Reflections on Little Rock" in chapter 1.

14. In *They Knew They Were Right: The Rise of the Neocons*, Jacob Heilbrunn argues that many Jewish intellectuals moved inexorably to the right politically in part because of their anxiety about the New Left's challenges to the university system and to the canonical literary corpus with which they were so identified.

15. McGurl uses the phrase "the program era" to refer to the institutional dominance of the MFA program in postwar America and its effect on how we read and write fiction.

16. The concept of voice, however vaguely defined, continues to be central to scholarship on race and ethnicity. One of the central tenets of critical race theory is the notion of "voices of color," the idea that there is an authenticity to the voices of people of color that critical race theorists should access and usually embody if they are to appropriately carry out their work.

17. As McGurl himself points out, the importance of voice long predates its heyday in the high cultural pluralist works he identifies. In fact, as he notes, literary modernism had a "fascination with the artifice and mobility of personae, and was easily assimilable to later postmodern accounts of fractured and multitudinous subjectivity" (234).

18. In *The Dialect of Modernism*, Michael North uses the term *ventriloquism* to characterize modernist writers' preoccupation with adopting personae—particularly racially marked ones—in their work.

19. One need only think of the difference between Saul Bellow's early and late career work to see the transition that Jewish American authors made from anxiety about ethnic specificity to explicit Jewish identification.

20. I discuss this topic further in relation to Jewish writers and the idea of the canon in chapter 4.

21. For an example of how charges of essentialism factor into the work of scholars of Jewish American literature, see the work of Benjamin Schreier.

22. Michael Omi and Howard Winant's *Racial Formation in the United States: From the 1960s to the 1990s* remains a key text for many scholars studying race in contemporary America.

23. Werner Sollors places such symbolic identity at the center of his idea of ethnicity in his influential *Beyond Ethnicity*.

24. The link between queerness and Jewishness has been explored by Caryn Aviv and David Shneer in *Queer Jews*, by Warren Hoffman in *The Passing Game: Queering American Jewish Culture*, and by the contributors to *Queer Theory and the Jewish Question*, edited by Daniel Boyarin, Daniel Itzkovitz, and Ann Pellegrini.

CHAPTER 1 — THE POLITICS AND POETICS OF SPEAKING THE OTHER

1. *Commentary*'s decision to cut Arendt's critique of school desegregation came after a series of arguments between Arendt and the editorial forces at the then-avowedly liberal magazine. Refusing to take extensive suggested revisions or threats about needed content shifts into account when composing her final draft, Arendt created a rift between editorial factions that prefigured the magazine's future direction. Irving Howe picked up "Reflections" for *Dissent* when *Commentary* delayed its publication for almost two years, but ran an editorial disclaimer before the piece and two rebuttals from other writers after it, along with Arendt's famous preface.

2. In *Blacks and Jews in Literary Conversation*, Emily Miller Budick provides an indispensable analysis of the controversy surrounding Arendt.

3. For a fascinating account of the repercussions of the conflict between Arendt and Ellison, see Ross Posnock's chapter "Ralph Ellison, Hannah Arendt, and the Meaning of Politics" in the *Cambridge Companion to Ralph Ellison*.

4. A number of critics have addressed the allegorical power of "the Jew" as a figure in contrast to the multiplicity of experiences that comprise Jewishness—notably, Susan Shapiro's "Écriture Judaïque," which considers the erasure of the Jew in western discourse from a deconstructionist point of view; Daniel Boyarin and Jonathan Boyarin's exploration of the Jew as allegory in works from the New Testament to Jean-Luc Nancy's "Generation and 'the Ground' of Jewish Identity" (see chap. 5); Bryan Cheyette's *Diasporas of the Mind*; and Yuri Slezkhine's *The Jewish Century*.

5. Similarly, Jonathan Freedman explores how the Jewish experience of immigration often becomes a synecdoche for a variety of other American immigrant narratives. Making Jews stand in for others may effectively erase the specifics of those other experiences.

6. The fact that Arendt was a European Jew is significant because Jewish privilege in America was often structured around the idea of European Jewish suffering.

7. On the link between European colonialism and the Holocaust, see Arendt's *The Origins of Totalitarianism*.

8. See Michael Staub's *Torn at the Roots*.

9. Bellow's Herzog and Augie March were both Jewish-inflected everymen (see chap. 3).

10. Arendt was also invested in interracial marriage as a private means of addressing racial inequity, as opposed to the interventions of the federal government in Little Rock and elsewhere (see chap. 2). David Spitz ("Politics and the Realm of Being") and Sidney Hook ("Democracy and Desegregation") criticized her view that intermarriage was the

means of disorienting reified racial categories even though blacks themselves were not interested in intermarriage. According to the critics, she was again presuming to speak for the Negro by suggesting otherwise. In response, she wrote that "oppressed minorities were never the best judges on the order of priorities in such matters," further asserting her ventriloquial authority ("Response to Critics").

11. Ozick discusses the battle between Ellison and Howe in her 1972 "Literary Blacks and Jews," and Budick provides an eloquent introduction to these debates in *Blacks and Jews in Literary Conversation*.

12. The theme of Jews as owners, whether of tenement buildings or stores, comes up throughout African American narratives devoted to tensions between blacks and Jews. Baldwin famously writes of this tension in "Negroes Are Anti-Semitic Because They're Anti-White."

13. I use the term *black man* here because battles between black and Jewish writers and intellectuals were almost always couched in male-identified language and understood as a battle between masculine interests.

14. See Budick, *Blacks and Jews in Literary Conversation;* Eric Sundquist, *Strangers in the Land;* Adam Newton, *Facing Black and Jew;* Ethan Goffman, *Imagining Each Other;* and Wendy Zierler, "My Holocaust Is Not Your Holocaust."

15. In Yiddish, Levenspiel's name invokes both play or fakery and repetitive speech; the "spiel" he gives throughout *The Tenants* never changes. According to Malamud, the only other building Levenspiel owns is a decrepit tenement in Harlem, a connection he conceals.

16. Willie Spearmint becomes Bill Spear later in *The Tenants*, drawing attention not only to the man's aspirations to be another William Shakespeare but also to the purportedly primitive nature that Malamud suggests lies at the core of his literary hopes.

17. In his afterword, Paul Malamud points out that his father's novel is "prophetic" because it suggests that, despite the fantasies of good liberals, African Americans were not capable of integrating into the "American body politic" (in Davis 466).

18. For an exploration of the structural components of black autobiography and its links to conventions of the Puritan conversion narrative, see Werner Sollors, *Beyond Ethnicity*.

19. For more on this controversy, see Budick's *Blacks and Jews in Literary Conversation*, Sundquist's *Strangers in the Land*, and Davis's *Bernard Malamud*.

20. Unless otherwise noted, all quotations from the correspondence between Malamud and McPherson are drawn from their unpublished letters, archived at the Harry Ransom Center at the University of Texas, Austin.

21. The *Oxford English Dictionary* defines *the dozens* as "an exchange of insults engaged in as a game or ritual among black Americans."

22. As Steven G. Kellman argues in "*The Tenants* in the House of Fiction," the epigraphs draw attention to the self-conscious literariness of the work to follow, providing a point of departure for the author's "editorial intrusion" (169).

23. Here, I invoke the title of Robert Penn Warren's famous collection of interviews with civil rights leaders and black intellectuals, *Who Speaks for the Negro?*

24. Later, as conflict between the men increases, Spearmint again confronts Lesser about the Smith record. "'Lesser,' he said in a slow burn, 'why don't you give that record away or break it up or eat it? You don't even know how to listen to it'" (87).

25. Lesser's early allusion to his difficult childhood as a white kid in a predominantly black neighborhood recalls, perhaps intentionally, Norman Podhoretz's famous essay

about his own childhood in such a neighborhood, "My Negro Problem (and Ours)" (see chap. 3). Malamud's wife, Ann, has related that Malamud grew up with a close friend who was African American but that the pair eventually fell out (Davis).

26. The reference to Aeolus' bag is just one of the novel's many allusions to Romantic literature and culture and the Romantics' appropriation of classical tropes.

27. An early scene depicts Spearmint rebuffing Lesser, who has extended his hand in greeting.

28. Throughout *The Tenants*, Malamud uses feminine-identified images of water to signify Lesser's artistic practice.

29. Lesser's use of the word *abolish* to admonish Spearmint invokes the discourse of abolitionism as a way to embarrass Willie about his refusal of humanism.

30. The idea of the novel as a form that speaks borrows from Mikhail Bakhtin's concept of the novel as a dialogic, polyphonic space for the play of multiple voices.

31. This avoidance is literalized in Malamud's conflict with McPherson over the Jewish-sounding African American characters in the novel.

32. Sundquist notes that Malamud's frequent allusions to Spearmint as body and Lesser as ethereal Jewish mind recur in disturbing ways throughout *The Tenants* and bring to mind Frantz Fanon's (and others') critique of this particular racial Cartesianism.

33. Malamud's depiction of Irene further locates him in the realm of debates about black fiction. The works of Wright and Ellison (among others) demonstrate the long history of representing thorny sexual relationships between middle-class Jewish women and black men as a means of politicizing the relations between blacks and Jews.

34. Malamud's depiction of Irene, coupled with Spearmint's similarity to LeRoi Jones, suggest that the novelist may be referring to Hettie Cohen Jones, Jones's Jewish wife, whom he rejected when he became more committed to black separatism (see chap. 2).

35. Spivak writes of this sort of essentialism in her critique of the work of the members of the subaltern studies group. She argues that the historians of the collective run the risk of essentializing the identity of the peasants whose histories they hope to rescue. At the same time, she suggests that this essentialism must be understood and appreciated in light of the strategic political aims of the historians' project. We might make a similar appraisal of the work and aims of identity politics in America.

36. Interestingly, Malamud's never-completed final novel, *The People*, engages with the question of speaking for and through the other by representing the disappearing Native Americans, a growing concern for the author that correlated to his growing interest in the obsolescence of the Jew and the Jewish artist.

37. For exemplary Romantic works about the Wandering Jew, see William Wordsworth's "Song for the Wandering Jew" and Ahasuerus in Percy Bysshe Shelley's "Queen Mab." Richard Wagner's famous account of the impossibility of Jewish art appears in *Judaism in Music and Other Essays* (see chap. 4).

38. I write of this imagined Jewish artist as a male because of Malamud's clear assumption that the postwar Jewish artist for whom he speaks is male, one who stands outside the intensifying debates about ethnicity and women's rights.

39. There are echoes of Arendt in Ozick's language about what is or is not "taken for granted."

40. As Jerald Podair points out in *The Strike That Changed New York*, the growing economic and geographical isolation of urban African Americans contributed to the development of a black consciousness that defined itself in opposition to white culture and offered an important critique of it.

CHAPTER 2 — THE PERILS OF LOVING IN AMERICA

1. *Loving v. Virginia* 388 U.S. 1 (1967).
2. This point was central to Ruby Jo Reeves Kennedy's criticism in her 1964 review of *Intermarriage*.
3. For more on the centrality of Jews to this discourse, see Jonathan Freedman's *Klezmer America*.
4. For more on race, Jewish liberalism, and intermarriage, see Lila Corwin Berman's *Speaking of Jews*.
5. Not coincidentally, worries about Jewish intermarriage were often couched in the language of annihilation associated with the Holocaust. This same language also filtered into rhetoric surrounding the Six-Day War in Israel (see chap. 3).
6. As I will discuss, Dean Franco looks closely at this novel as autobiography in *Race, Rights, and Recognition*.
7. Werner Sollors's *Beyond Ethnicity* considers the role of exogamy in the imagination of ethnicity (see chap. 4).
8. In *The Merchant of Venice*, Jessica's intermarriage (and perhaps Jessica as a figure) can be seen as a metaphor for early modern anxieties about conversion and its capacity to throw the assumed fixities of identity and blood into crisis. Leslie Fiedler purposely placed the dyad of Shylock and Jessica at the center of his assessment of the importance of the figure of the Jew and Jewish exogamy in modern literature (*Love and Death in the American Novel*). To him, Jessica dilutes and in some way sanitizes her father's Jewishness.
9. Not incidentally, Fiedler also explores and rewrites the relationship between Ascha and Mervyn in his 1957 short story, "Nude Croquet," which reimagines the pair in a contemporary American context.
10. Mary Antin's *Promised Land* begins with "I was born, I have lived, and I have been made over. Is it not time to write my life's story? I am just as much out of the way as if I were dead, for I am absolutely other than the person whose story I have to tell" (xi).
11. Like Hettie Cohen and LeRoi Jones, Joyce Johnson and Jack Kerouac met in 1957, at the height of the Beats' success. Allen Ginsberg's *Howl* was published in 1956, Kerouac's *On the Road* in 1957.
12. Both Johnson's *Minor Characters* and Jones's *How I Became Hettie Jones* focus on reestablishing the voices of women of the Beat generation and look at the sustaining relationships among women of the period (including their own long-term friendship).
13. The statement's juxtaposition of "whitening" and "ethnicity" marks the confusion often present in attempts to contend with Jewishness. Should Jewishness be discussed in racial or ethnic terms? How does the vocabulary available for speaking about race and ethnicity, particularly in an American context, fail to articulate the position of Jews at various times in the nation's history?
14. Thompson's contrast between LeRoi Jones and Hettie Jones arises from her reading of LeRoi's *The Autobiography of LeRoi Jones by Amiri Baraka*, in which he refers to himself and his family as "brown" to designate their racial and economic position between "yellow" and "black" members of their race in 1940s Newark.
15. In her work on black female spectators and the "oppositional gaze," bell hooks examines the importance of who is allowed to be a looking subject and who is forced into being an object subject to the gaze of others. According to her, black women are usually

spectacle instead of spectator. Hettie Jones's representation of her own transformation into an object of others' gazes is a telling moment in her metamorphosis into a "raced" person at Mary Washington.

16. The subject of so-called Negro music in white America and the ethics of assimilation and appropriation are brilliantly explored in LeRoi Jones's *Blues People*, published in 1963.

17. Kimberlé Crenshaw's work on intersectionality and Riv-Ellen Prell's on Jewish women are particularly useful aids for thinking about Jewishness and gender in Jones's memoir.

18. Prell's *Fighting to Become Americans* considers the expectations for Jewish American women such as Jones.

19. Carter's sometimes-reductive reading of Ilka as a naïf runs up against similar limits.

20. Segal's later work continues to ponder the question of speaking for the other. In her story collection *Shakespeare's Kitchen*, she follows Ilka into later life and has her say to her boss at a think-tank: "I'm always interjecting my autobiography into the other person's story.... [I] mean to be expressing my sympathetic understanding, but all it does is take the conversation away from the other speaker."

21. In *Beyond Ethnicity*, Sollors points out that woman-as-greenhorn has long been a common trope in American fiction about the immigrant experience.

22. A woman whom Ilka meets at an employment agency tells her that "New York . . . is not America, like all you people always think" (8). After Ilka complains about not seeing the real America from her New York apartment, Fishgoppel sends her out west.

23. This sort of comparison aligns with Michael Rothberg's call for multidirectional memory in the appraisal of the Holocaust (see chap. 3).

24. In his celebrated study, *The Black Atlantic*, Paul Gilroy explores the links between African American and Jewish readings of the Exodus narrative.

25. Carter is a columnist for the *Harlem Herald*, reporting on the United Nations and other global and local matters.

26. In the same interview, Segal notes, "He was a spectacular raconteur but only a B-writer—as he knew. He was just a fantastic narrator and joke-teller but writing wasn't his means of communicating" (Johnson, "An Interview with Lore Segal").

27. In *The Beginnings of Jewishness*, Shaye Cohen looks at the origins of the matrilineal principle.

CHAPTER 3 — WHAT WE TALK ABOUT WHEN WE TALK ABOUT THE HOLOCAUST

1. Historian Hasia Diner disputes Novick's timeline in *We Remember with Reverence and Love*, arguing that the Holocaust played a far more central role in American Jewish life during the immediate postwar period than is commonly known.

2. I discuss literary voice and Mark McGurl's startling reappraisal of its role in postwar American literature in the introduction and chap. 1.

3. Wiesel's memoir, known in English as *Night*, was originally published in Yiddish as *Un di Velt Hot Geshvign* (And the World Remained Silent). Levi's work, known in English as *Survival in Auschwitz*, was originally published in Italian as *Se questo è un uomo* (If This Is a Man).

4. Hersey read the Holocaust through a number of Christian tropes, notably martyrdom. Anne Frank's *Diary*, too, was translated into English and became popular during the 1950s, especially in its stage-play form. Novick argues, however, that contemporary Jewish

critics such as Ozick have largely decried the story's early popularity, citing its "universalism" and its effacing of Jewish particularity (117).

5. For powerful interpretations of Holocaust memory and representation through the discourse of trauma theory, see Dominic LaCapra's *Representing the Holocaust;* Cathy Caruth's *Trauma;* and Shoshana Felman and Dori Laub's *Testimony.*

6. In the days before the Six Day War, Egypt amassed troops along its border with Israel and expelled peacekeeping forces from the buffer zone between the nations in response to conflicts between its ally Syria and Israel. On June 5, 1967, Israel launched a preemptive attack against Egypt and began a war against Egypt, Syria, and Jordan. As a result of the battle, Israel gained territory in the Sinai Peninsula, the Gaza Strip, the West Bank, eastern Jerusalem, and the Golan Heights. The results of this territorial gain are still felt in the Middle East: the lands garnered during the Six Day War are the most hotly contested and violent in the region.

7. A *succah* is a temporary dwelling place created by Jews to celebrate the holiday of Succot during the harvest season.

8. In Flanzbaum's even-handed anthology, *The Americanization of the Holocaust,* authors from various critical schools examine the pervasiveness of the Holocaust in American popular culture and daily life.

9. I make this argument in "Of Superheroes and Synecdoche."

10. In *Special Sorrows,* Matthew Frye Jacobson critiques the term *symbolic ethnicity,* so prevalent in the study of ethnic identity, for drawing a problematic dichotomy between the ethnic allegiances of immigrants and their purportedly more authentically ethnic countrymen (221).

11. For more on the ghetto archive, see Samuel D. Kassow's *Who Will Write Our History? Emanuel Ringelblum, the Warsaw Ghetto, and the Oyneg Shabes Archive* and David Roskies' *The Jewish Search for a Usable Past.*

12. Wiesel may be America's most prominent disseminator of Holocaust exceptionalism and the belief that the Holocaust survivor is in a unique ethical position. It is difficult to forget his 2003 appearance on network news broadcasts, where he gave his stamp of approval to the imminent Iraq War.

13. Recently, Quentin Tarantino took on these two fundamentally "American" disasters in his films *Inglourious Basterds* and *Django Unchained.*

14. Styron's choice to make Sophie Polish Catholic instead of Jewish is another example of how he transforms the Holocaust into an American, rather than a European, tragedy.

15. Although many people have written about *Mr. Sammler's Planet,* it has rarely been appraised as part of the American Holocaust canon. Sundquist's *Strangers in the Land* is a notable exception.

16. For more on the ghetto archive, see Samuel D. Kassow's *Who Will Write Our History? Emanuel Ringelblum, the Warsaw Ghetto, and the Oyneg Shabes Archive* and David Roskies' *The Jewish Search for a Usable Past.* Ozick also wrote *The Messiah of Stockholm,* an oblique Holocaust narrative borrowing from the life and work of Bruno Schulz, the author of *The Street of Crocodiles* (published in 1934 as *The Cinnamon Shops*) and a victim of World War II.

17. See Franco's recent *Race, Rights, and Recognition.*

18. Jews were pushed into mobile economic practices largely because they could not own land.

19. In a review of Updike's *Bech* books, Adam Kirsch notes that Ozick's 1976 short story "Levitation" might be read as a response to *Bech: A Book.* The story follows a Jewish-Christian

couple as they try and fail to host a dinner party for Manhattan's predominantly Jewish literary elite. As the Christian wife in the story stands by, her husband and his Jewish guests discuss the Holocaust and, in a moment of Chagall-like magical realism, float up toward the ceiling, leaving the wife alone on the ground. Kirsch's reading of the short story works particularly well alongside an appraisal of "A Mercenary" as a text with strong reservations about the role of the Holocaust in buttressing postwar Jewish American authenticity.

20. Ozick's story "Usurpation (Other People's Stories)" was a favorite of postmodern American writer David Foster Wallace, who used its first lines in his novella "Westward the Course of Empire Takes Its Way."

21. It is difficult to separate Ozick's reading of the African nation without a "written literature" from Bellow's oft-quoted and controversial comment that African tribes have produced "no Shakespeare." Bellow's first recorded utterance of this statement appears in James Atlas's profile of Allan Bloom, published in the *New York Times*. Alfred Kazin later took it up to criticize Bellow in a *New Yorker* piece called "Jews," to which Bellow replied in an angry editorial called "Papuans and Zulus" in the *New York Times*. Both writers have aligned themselves with the neoconservative Jewish intellectuals and writers at *Commentary* magazine. This self-identification complicates any approach to their work, although both disavow the influence of politics on their literary productions.

22. Here and in the chapter title, I invoke Englander's recent short story collection, *What We Talk about When We Talk about Anne Frank* (2012), which itself refers to the iconic Carver collection, *What We Talk about When We Talk about Love* (1981).

23. Many critics were surprised that during this era—when Bellow seemed to abandon some of his intellectual ambitions for political pursuits and the public sphere—he won the Nobel Prize for Literature and became a literary superstar.

24. Here, I distinguish between cultural pluralism, an ideology that celebrates slight ethnic differences while affirming the ideals of American liberalism, and racial or ethnic separatism, which came to prominence later in the twentieth century and embraces racial particularity over universalism. This distinction is particularly important in the universe of twentieth-century Jewish American authors such as Bellow and Ozick, who were comfortable with the cultural pluralism of their childhoods but not the separatism they saw in the post–civil rights, Black Power era.

25. Bellow was a noted Yiddishist and translated the work of Isaac Bashevis Singer, among others.

26. The protagonist as anthropologist is a familiar trope for Bellow. His degree was in anthropology, and he cheekily named his early literary magazine the *Noble Savage*. Often criticized for his focus on lush description over plot, he frequently structured his novels— from *Herzog* to *Henderson the Rain King*—as ethnographic explorations.

27. The figuring of Jew and black as mind and body is not a new formula. As Sundquist points out in *Strangers in the Land*, Frantz Fanon makes it a feature of his analysis in *Black Skin, White Masks*.

28. Bellow's portrayal of Sammler as either hunter or prey is one of the many ways in which the novel depicts New York City as a racially infused jungle, complete with stereotypes of primitivism.

29. This depiction of the sexuality of the Congo bush is particularly disturbing, given the long history of portraying Jews as perverse and overly carnal.

30. This quotation is often attributed to Irving Kristol, yet Wattenberg first uttered these lines about neoconservatism's roots to a reporter for the *Christian Science Monitor* in 1980. Like many origin stories, this one gets confused in the telling.

31. Bellow wrote one of the first glowing reviews of *Invisible Man* in the pages of *Commentary*, soon after the novel was published. According to Herbert William Rice, Ellison also composed parts of the unfinished *Juneteeth* at Bellow's house (137).

32. Atlas relates the story of this lost manuscript in his biography of Bellow. According to Atlas, Bellow's friends referred to the manuscript as "White No More."

33. See *A Political Companion to Saul Bellow*, edited by Gloria Cronin and Lee Trepanier, for more on this controversy.

34. Gruner funds Sammler in his travels to Israel during the 1967 conflict.

CHAPTER 4 — THE JEW IN THE CANON AND THE CULTURE WARS

1. I place this rupture in the eighteenth and nineteenth centuries because, while the ideals that led to the Emancipation of the Jews originated in the western Enlightenment and the French Revolution of the eighteenth century, they did not filter into Eastern Europe and catalyze the Haskalah, or Jewish Enlightenment, until the mid-nineteenth century.

2. For an interesting articulation of the notion that Jews possess a supranational spiritual nation, and one that disorients traditional Zionist conceptions of the need for a Jewish nation-state, see Simon Dubnow's *Nationalism and History* (discussed in detail in chap. 5).

3. David Biale, Michael Galchinsky, and Susannah Heschel outline this collision between Jewish writers and intellectuals and the ideas of multiculturalism in their introduction *to Insider/Outsider*.

4. The challenge that the Jew once posed for the European nation-state is often compared to the contemporary collision between the Muslim and western civilization; see, for example, Gil Anidjar's *The Jew, the Arab*. Without explicitly making such a point, Ian Buruma's *Murder in Amsterdam* (about the murder of filmmaker Theo Van Gogh and the rise of controversial "liberal" politician Ayaan Hirsi Ali) analyzes the Muslim challenge to Europe in terms once used to refer to the continent's "Jewish question."

5. In *Mr. Sammler's Planet*, Bellow makes a similar, if more reactionary, point in his depiction of the end result of the Enlightenment (see chap. 3).

6. Andrew Furman's *Contemporary Jewish Writers and the Multicultural Dilemma* is a notable exception.

7. Heschel makes a similar point, using the *Wissenschaft* scholars as proto-multiculturalists, in "Jewish Studies As Counterhistory."

8. Published in the early 1970s, both Bellow's *Mr. Sammler's Planet* and Malamud's *The Tenants* are racial dystopias—elegies for the privileged roles of the Jewish writer and intellectual in an increasingly racialized literary landscape. They are also critiques of the increasing commercialization of American culture and the postmodern culture to which it gave rise.

9. Roth's *Goodbye, Columbus* was criticized less for the novella at its center than for a number of its short stories, particularly "Epstein" and "Eli, the Fanatic."

10. When Bellow was asked if he thought he was awarded the Nobel Prize as a Jewish writer or an American writer, he replied that he thought he had won simply for being a writer. The discomfort of being defined as a Jewish writer (particularly as it pertained to his response to the Holocaust) runs thematically throughout his work, and his ambivalent response to his Jewishness prompted his lengthy correspondence with Ozick (now in the Saul Bellow archives at the University of Chicago). Atlas quotes liberally from these

letters in his biography of Bellow, and many appear in a recent compendium of Bellow's correspondence.

11. Arguably, *American Pastoral*, like *The Human Stain*, is a novel about passing—in this case, between Jewishness and whiteness.

12. Silk's first experiment with passing for white occurs at the behest of his Jewish childhood boxing coach, who tutors him in how to appear to be other than his own race.

13. Itzkovitz's title invokes *Black Like Me* (1961), journalist John Howard Griffin's account of passing for a black man during an extended trip through the segregated south.

14. This aspect of the discourse of passing—its mobilization of metaphors of difference and sameness—is also resonant in tales of passing for another gender or sexuality.

15. Silk and Zuckerman also linger on the edges of town. Roth often plays with this split between center and periphery in *The Human Stain*.

16. Here, Roth also distances himself from some of the more conservative opponents of multiculturalism, who long for a similar purity in discourse.

17. Jews have had a long and often negative association with cosmopolitanism.

18. An interesting intertext for Roth's use of *spooks* comes from Sam Greenlee's *The Spook Who Sat by the Door* (1973), a novel about an African American CIA operative who leaves the agency to join a black separatist group. The title plays on the pejorative use of the term to describe both African Americans and spies and suggests that the black operative sits by the door of the CIA office, functioning as a token minority rather than a real player.

19. Keble is also deemed the only appropriate person to eulogize Silk at his funeral and relegitimize him in the eyes of his former colleagues.

20. Roux also represents a castrating contrast to earth mother Faunia.

21. Roth became embroiled in a distinctly twenty-first-century conflict about the origins of *The Human Stain* when he challenged Wikipedia over the content of the novel's Wikipedia page, which asserted that Broyard was the inspiration for Silk. Roth's conflict with Wikipedia was a fascinating portal into changing ideas about authorship in the digital age but also a provocative statement on how totally Roth embraces the idea that he controls his characters and the proper interpretation of his their origins. Is this another case of Roth speaking for a black man rather than letting the man speak for himself?

22. Karen Brodkin analyzes these shifts in the spheres of private and public racial identification in *How Jews Became White Folks and What That Says about Race in America*.

CHAPTER 5 — RACE, INDIGENEITY, AND THE TOPOGRAPHY OF DIASPORA

1. Steven Salaita's *The Holy Land in Transit* makes this analogy between Native American and Palestinian dispossession.

2. The film narrates the Munich massacre through the dreams and "memories" of someone who was not present during the violence, an approach that hints uncomfortably at the idea of a Jewish collective unconscious, a theme consonant with many other vicarious renderings of the Holocaust. For more on this topic, see Gary Weissman's *Fantasies of Witnessing*.

3. The film also clarifies the way in which technology globalizes violence and makes it unreal through repetition, two central tenets of the postmodern criticism of mass media.

4. The affiliation between Black September members and the Israeli intelligence men is emphasized in a scene that flashes their photographs.

5. In *Das Judentum in der Musik*, Wagner wrote of the Jew's inability to produce a *Volk* art (see chap. 4).

6. For more on Herder's ideas, see his *J. G. Herder on Social and Political Culture* in which he states, "It is nature which educates families: the most natural state is, therefore, *one* nation, an extended family with one national character" (324).

7. Magid points out that "the focus on Zionism and Israel in American Jewish education is crucial in determining the place of Israel in the diasporic imagination and, more important, the self-fashioning of Diaspora Judaism in a post-state era" (195).

8. I have chosen to lowercase *diaspora* to avoid reinforcing the exceptionality of the Jewish diaspora.

9. For more on the history of gender in Jewish culture, see the work of Paula Hyman, Riv-Ellen Prell, and Daniel Boyarin, to name only a few scholars working in this productive area.

10. James Clifford comments on the gender dynamics of diaspora in his essay "Diasporas," and Naomi Seidman explores this process as it pertains to Jewish language politics in *A Marriage Made in Heaven*. Recently, theorists have noted how frequently women workers form the majority of certain nations' diasporic communities—for instance, the Philippines diaspora.

11. The filmmakers make their strongest claims about the importance of family in this section of *Munich*, which is also the portion most often criticized for taking liberties with the historical facts.

12. For more on the effect of Holocaust rhetoric on American Jewry after the Six Day War, see Peter Novick's *The Holocaust in American Life* as well as chap. 3.

13. Greece is often depicted as the cradle of western civilization and the birthplace of ideas about nation and exile.

14. The idea of double-crossing is important in *Munich*, emphasizing the problem of trust and the significance of family allegiances.

15. In a particularly heavy-handed moment, Avner's sexual encounter with his wife mingles with images of the Munich massacre.

16. Critics such as the Boyarins argue that the problematic issue is the possession of power by a group that appeals to its mythical rights to land.

17. This idea of a Jewish race somewhat unselfconsciously adopts the conventional idea of the Jews as "the chosen people" whose conceptions of tribal identity, whether territorially or genealogically based, might be a beacon for other post-national collectives.

18. Clifford makes a similar point in "Diasporas."

19. Moreover, as Anita Norich points out in "On the Yiddish Question," Yiddish, "now considered primarily through the language of memory and mourning, defended as a significant part of the Jewish past, . . . is analyzed without—in the most literal sense—being understood" (146).

20. The importance of Yiddish as a trope for displacement and extraterritoriality cannot be overestimated.

21. Katchor's *The Jew of New York* was serialized in the *Forward* in 1992 and 1993, and its popularity led him to create full-length work.

22. In an extended interview with Alexander Theroux, Katchor discusses how his interest in philosophy and the realm of ideas has influenced his comics—notably, how theory organizes space in *Julius Knipl, Real Estate Photographer: The Beauty Supply Shop District*.

23. As historian Beth Wenger makes clear, New York City, particularly the Lower East Side of Manhattan, has been a site for Jewish nostalgia and the idea of an authentic Jewish

past since the early twentieth century. Ben Shahn depicted such a world in many of his paintings, and Irving Howe looked back mournfully on this lost era in *World of Our Fathers*. Hollywood, too, has fastened onto the Jewish past in films such as *Hester Street* (1975), *Crossing Delancey* (1988), and *Liberty Heights* (1999).

24. In *Wrestling with Zion*, edited by Tony Kushner and Alisa Solomon, noted Jewish American academics, writers, and artists on the left discuss the repercussions of this rift.

25. Allan Bloom's *The Closing of the American Mind* became a rallying cry in the academic culture wars and also a sore spot for many Jews on the left.

26. Elim-min-nopee's name also invokes the specter of tribal genocide that hangs over *The Jew of New York*, with "Elim" suggesting the elimination of the Lenapes.

27. At the turn of the century, Israel Zangwill wrote the melodrama *The Melting-Pot* about three generations of a Jewish family and their experience of assimilation. His play was a hit with American audiences in 1908 and 1909.

28. In *Klezmer America*, Jonathan Freedman traces the trajectory of the ethnic as an idea central to Jews and Jewish thought, particularly in the Anglo-American context.

29. "Mapping Ararat: An Imaginary Digital Homelands Project" at the University of Toronto reimagines what Noah's Ararat project might have looked like if it had been successful (http://www.mappingararat.com).

30. Hasia Diner's *Lower East Side Memories* analyzes the neighborhood's place in Jewish nostalgia and history.

31. In *Sublime Desire*, Amy Elias adapts the idea of the historical romance into a genre rich with meaning for contemporary texts.

32. Shpilman's last name, which means "player" in Yiddish, is significant because his days center around playing chess and his life becomes a puzzle that Landsman must decode to solve his murder.

33. For more on Zamenhof, see Alexander Korzhenkov's *Zamenhof: The Life, Works, and Ideas of the Author of Esperanto*.

34. "A place is the order (of whatever kind) in accord with which elements are distributed in relationships of coexistence. It thus excludes the possibility of two things being in the same location. The law of the 'proper' rules in the place: the elements taken into consideration are beside one another, each situated in its own 'proper' and distinct location, a location it defines. A place is thus an instantaneous configuration of positions. It implies an indication of stability"(de Certeau 14).

35. Marc Auge's concept of a "non-place" is also relevant to Jewish Sitka; he exhorts anthropologists to study the non-places of cash machines, supermarkets, and airports in which much of postmodern existence is lived.

36. Chabon wrote a genre fiction manifesto in his introduction to the 2005 edition of *The Best American Short Stories* and expanded those ideas in his book of essays, *Maps and Legends*.

37. This teasing meta-commentary on genre is common in Chabon's work.

38. COINTELPRO was an FBI counterintelligence initiative enacted to subvert purportedly dangerous dissident political factions in the United States. It is most famous for its 1960s-era infiltration of leftist groups, such as the Black Panthers and the Weathermen.

39. Shpilman also engages in a sort of impersonation. When he is found dead at the beginning of the book, in his own exile at the Hotel Zamenhof, he is living under an alias, the name of a famous chess player, Emmanuel Lasker.

40. Chabon's interest in the Jewish past is also evident in *The Amazing Adventures of Kavalier and Clay*, which explores Jews and the comics industry in the wartime United States.

41. See Julian Levinson's *Exile on Main Street* for a work that follows the mutually constitutive relationship between diasporic Jewish and American literary traditions during an earlier period.

CODA

1. Sarah Phillips Casteel addresses the centrality of 1492 in "Sephardism and Marranism in Native American Fiction of the Quincentenary" and elsewhere. John Docker's *1492* argues that the year also marked a rupture in the history of diasporic cultures because it heralded the end of Spain's medieval golden age, when Jews, Muslims, and Christians lived together in a cosmopolitan and cooperative culture with ties across the Mediterranean.

2. For many complicated reasons, the relationship between Israel and the United States remains a special one, although charges to that effect often recall uncomfortable anti-Semitic tropes of Jewish economic and state control straight out of the hoax document known as the "The Protocols of the Elders of Zion" (1903).

3. Chabon tends to relate Jewishness to otherness in American culture—whether it's queerness in *Wonder Boys, The Mysteries of Pittsburgh*, or *The Amazing Adventures of Kavalier and Clay* or blackness in *Telegraph Avenue*.

4. As in Row's novel, Jewish American author Joshua Cohen's *Witz* engages with Jewishness and authenticity through passing, this time by suggesting that, once Jews themselves have died out, the door will be open for Gentiles to "become" Jewish, performing Jewishness via consumption in a manner similar to that of many secular Jews today.

5. In Jewish writer Ben Marcus's *The Flame Alphabet*, Jewishness inhabits a similarly deconstructive role. In his dark vision, Jews are pariahs, living in exile along the edges of society and practicing their religion in secret, much as the marranos did.

Works Cited

Aarons, Victoria. "The Outsider Within: Women in Contemporary Jewish-American Fiction." *Contemporary Literature* 28.3 (1987): 378–393. Project Muse. Web.
Aczel, Richard. "Throwing Voices." *New Literary History* 32.3 (2001): 703–705. Project Muse. Web.
Adorno, Theodor, and Max Horkheimer. *Dialectic of Enlightenment*. Palo Alto, CA: Stanford UP, 2002. Print.
Alcoff, Linda. "The Problem of Speaking for Others." *Cultural Critique* 20 (Winter 1991–1992): 5–32. Project Muse. Web.
Anderson, Benedict. *Imagined Communities: Reflections on the Origins and Spread of Nationalism*. New York: Verso, 2006. Print.
Anidjar, Gil. *The Jew, the Arab: A History of the Enemy*. Palo Alto, CA: Stanford UP, 2003. Print.
Annie Hall. 1977. Film.
Antin, Mary. *The Promised Land*. New York: Penguin, 2012. Print.
Arendt, Hannah. *The Origins of Totalitarianism*. London: Allen & Unwin, 1958. Print.
———. "Reflections on Little Rock." *Dissent* 6.1: 45–56. Web.
———. "Response to Critics." *Dissent* 6.2: 179–181. Web.
Atlas, James. *Bellow: A Biography*. New York: Modern Library, 2002. Print.
———. "Chicago's Grumpy Guru." *New York Times Magazine*. 3 January 1988. Web.
Auge, Marc. *Non-Places: Introduction to an Anthropology of Supermodernity*. New York: Verso, 2009. Print.
Aviv, Caryn, and David Shneer. *Queer Jews*. New York: Routledge, 2002. Print.
Azoulay, Katya Gibel. *Black, Jewish, and Interracial*. Durham: Duke UP, 1997. Print.
Bakhtin, Mikhail. *The Dialogic Imagination*. Austin: U of Texas P, 1982. Print.
Baldwin, James. "Negroes Are Anti-Semitic because They're Anti-White." *Collected Essays*. Ed. Toni Morrison. New York: Library of America, 1998. 739–748. Print.
Benbassa, Esther, and Jean-Christophe Attias. *The Jew and the Other*. Trans. G. M. Goshgarian. Ithaca, NY: Cornell UP, 2004. Print.
Benn Michaels, Walter. *Our America: Nativism, Modernism, and Pluralism*. Durham: Duke UP, 1997. Print.
———. *The Trouble with Diversity: How We Learned to Love Identity and Ignore Inequality*. New York: Holt, 2007. Print.

Bellow, Saul. *The Adventures of Augie March.* New York: Viking, 1953. Print.
———. *Dangling Man.* New York: Vanguard, 1944. Print.
———. *Henderson the Rain King.* New York: Viking, 1976. Print.
———. *Herzog.* New York: Viking, 1964. Print.
———. *Letters.* Ed. Ben Taylor. New York: Penguin, 2012. Print.
———. "Looking for Mr. Green." *Collected Stories.* Ed. Janis Bellow. New York: Penguin, 2013. Print.
———. "Man Underground." *Commentary.* June 1952. 608–610. Web.
———. *Mr. Sammler's Planet.* New York: Viking, 1970. Print.
———. "Papuans and Zulus." *New York Times.* 10 March 1994. Web.
———. *Seize the Day.* New York: Viking, 1964. Print.
———. *To Jerusalem and Back.* New York: Viking, 1976. Print.
Berman, Lila Corwin. "Sociology, Jews, and Intermarriage in Twentieth-Century America." *Jewish Social Studies* 14.2 (2008): 32–60. JSTOR. Web.
———. *Speaking of Jews: Rabbis, Intellectuals, and the Creation of an American Public Identity.* Berkeley: U of California P, 2009. Print.
Berman, Marshall. *All That Is Solid Melts into Air: The Experience of Modernity.* New York: Simon & Schuster, 1981. Print.
Berman, Paul. Introduction. *Blacks and Jews: Alliances and Arguments.* Ed. Paul Berman. New York: Delacorte, 1994. Print.
Bhabha, Homi. "Of Mimicry and Man." *The Location of Culture.* London: Routledge, 1994. 121–131. Print.
Biale, David, Michael Galchinsky, and Susannah Heschel. Introduction. *Insider/Outsider: American Jews and Multiculturalism.* Berkeley: U of California P, 1998. 1–16. Print.
Bird, Christine. "The Return Journey in *To Jerusalem and Back.*" *MELUS* 6.4 (1979): 51–57. JSTOR. Web.
Birkerts, Sven. "Roth, Mailer, Bellow Running Out of Gas." *New York Observer.* 13 October 1997. Web.
Bloom, Allan. *The Closing of the American Mind.* New York: Simon & Schuster, 2012. Print.
Boyarin, Daniel. *Unheroic Conduct: The Rise of Heterosexuality and the Invention of the Jewish Man.* Berkeley: U of California P, 1997. Print.
Boyarin, Daniel, and Jonathan Boyarin. "Diaspora: Generation and the 'Ground' of Jewish Identity." *Critical Inquiry* 19.4 (1993): 693–725. JSTOR. Web.
Boyarin, Daniel, Daniel Itzkovitz, and Ann Pellegrini, eds. *Queer Theory and the Jewish Question.* New York: Columbia UP, 2003. Print.
Boyarin, Jonathan. "America's Indian, Europe's Jew: Modiano and Vizenor." *Boundary 2* 19.3 (1992): 197–222. Project Muse. Web.
Branch, Taylor. "Blacks and Jews: The Uncivil War." In *Bridges and Boundaries: African Americans and American Jews.* Ed. Jack Salzman, Adina Black, and Gretchen Sullivan Sorin. New York: Jewish Museum, 1992. 50–69. Print.
Brodkin, Karen. *How Jews Became White Folks and What That Says about Race in America.* New Brunswick: Rutgers UP, 1998. Print.
Brown, Charles Brockden. *Arthur Mervyn.* Kent, OH: Kent State UP, 2002. Print
Budick, Emily Miller. *Blacks and Jews in Literary Conversation.* Cambridge: Cambridge UP, 1999. Print.
Buruma, Ian. *Murder in Amsterdam: Liberal Europe, Islam, and the Limits of Tolerance.* New York: Penguin, 2007. Print.
Butler, Judith. *Gender Trouble.* London: Routledge, 2006. Print.

Carson, Clayborne. "Blacks and Jews in the Civil Rights Movement: The Case of SNCC." *Bridges and Boundaries: African Americans and American Jews*. Ed. Jack Salzman, Adina Black, and Gretchen Sullivan Sorin. New York: Jewish Museum, 1992. 36–49. Print.

Caruth, Cathy. *Trauma: Explorations in Memory*. Baltimore: Johns Hopkins UP, 1995. Print.

Carver, Raymond. *What We Talk about When We Talk about Love*. New York: Vintage, 1989. Print.

Casteel, Sarah Phillips. "Jews among the Indians: The Fantasy of Indigenization in Mordecai Richler's and Michael Chabon's Northern Narratives." *Contemporary Literature* 50.4 (2009): 775–810. Project Muse. Web.

———. *Second Arrivals: Landscape and Belonging in Literature of the Americas*. Charlottesville: U of Virginia P, 2007. Print.

———. "Sephardism and Marranism in Native American Fiction of the Quincentenary." *MELUS* 37.2 (2012): 59–81. JSTOR. Web.

Caughie, Pamela. *Passing and Pedagogy: The Dynamics of Responsibility*. Champaign-Urbana: U of Illinois P, 2007. Print.

Cayton, Horace. *Long Old Road: An Autobiography*. Seattle: U of Washington P, 1974. Print.

Chabon, Michael. *The Amazing Adventures of Kavalier and Clay*. New York: Random House, 2000. Print.

———. "Chosen, but Not Special." *New York Times*. 5 June 2010. Web.

———. Introduction. *The Best American Short Stories*. New York: Houghton Mifflin, 2005. xiii–xvii. Print.

———. "Guidebook to a Land of Ghosts." *Civilization*. June/July 1997. Web.

———. "The Language of Lost History." *Harper's* (October 1997): 32–33. Print.

———. *Maps and Legends*. New York: Harper Perennial, 2009. Print.

———. *The Mysteries of Pittsburgh*. New York: Morrow, 1988. Print.

———. *Telegraph Avenue*. New York: Harper, 2012. Print.

———. "Underway." *The Believer*. August 2003. 115. Print.

———. *The Yiddish Policemen's Union*. New York: Harper, 2007. Print.

Chabon, Michael, and Ayelet Waldman. Untitled article. Newsletter of Americans for Peace Now, 2008. Web.

Cheyette, Bryan. *Diasporas of the Mind*. New Haven: Yale UP, 2013. Print.

Clarke, John Henrik. *William Styron's Nat Turner: Ten Black Writers Respond*. Westport, CT: Praeger, 1987.

Clifford, James. "Diasporas." *Cultural Anthropology* 9.3 (1994): 302–338. Web.

Cohen, Joshua. *Witz*. Chicago: Dalkey Archive, 2010. Print.

Cohen, Shaye. *The Beginnings of Jewishness*. Berkeley: U of California P, 2001. Print.

Combahee River Collective. "The Combahee River Collective Statement." Circuitous.org. Web.

Connor, Stephen. *Dumbstruck: A Cultural History of Ventriloquism*. Oxford: Oxford UP, 2001. Print.

Crenshaw, Kimberlé. "Mapping the Margins: Intersectionality, Identity Politics, and Violence against Women of Color." *Stanford Law Review* 43.6 (1991): 1241–1299. Print.

Crenshaw, Kimberle, Neil Gotanda, Gary Peller, and Kendall Thomas. Introduction. *Critical Race Theory: The Key Writings That Formed the Movement*. New York: New Press, 1996. xiii–xxxi. Print.

Cronin, Gloria, and Lee Trepanier, eds. *A Political Companion to Saul Bellow*. Lexington: UP of Kentucky, 2014. Print.

Davis, Philip. *Bernard Malamud: A Writer's Life*. Oxford: Oxford UP, 2007. Print.

de Certeau, Michel. *The Practice of Everyday Life*. Trans. Steven Rendall. Berkeley: U of California P, 2002. Print.

Deleuze, Gilles, and Félix Guatarri. *Kafka: Towards a Minor Literature*. Minneapolis: U of Minnesota P, 1986. Print.

Deresiewicz, William. "The Imaginary Jew." *Nation*. 28 May 2007. Web.

Dickstein, Morris. "The Complex Fate of the Jewish-American Writer." *Nation*. 4 October 2001. Web.

———. *A Mirror in the Roadway: Literature and the Real World*. Princeton: Princeton UP, 2005. Print.

Diner, Hasia. *Lower East Side Memories: A Jewish Place in America*. Princeton: Princeton UP, 2000. Print.

———. *We Remember with Reverence and Love: American Jews and the Myth of Silence after the Holocaust, 1945–1962*. New York: NYU P, 2009. Print.

Django Unchained. 2013. Film.

Docker, John. *1492: The Poetics of Diaspora*. London: Bloomsbury, 2001. Print.

Dubnow, Simon. *Nationalism and History: Essays on New and Old Judaism*. New York: Meridian, 1961. Print.

Elias, Amy. *Sublime Desire: History and Post-1960s Fiction*. Baltimore: Johns Hopkins UP, 2001.

Eliot, T. S. "Tradition and the Individual Talent." *Selected Essays*. New York: Harcourt, Brace, 1950. Web.

Ellison, Ralph. *Invisible Man*. New York: Random House, 1952.

———. "The World and the Jug." *Shadow and Act*. New York: Random House, 2011. 107–143. Print.

Englander, Nathan. *What We Talk about When We Talk about Anne Frank: Stories*. New York: Knopf, 2012. Print.

Eskenazi, Stuart. "Historical What-Ifs Key to Chabon Novel." *Seattle Times*. 17 November 2003. Web.

Fanon, Frantz. *Black Skin, White Masks*. Trans. Richard Philcox. New York: Grove, 2008. Print.

Felman, Shoshana, and Dori Laub. *Testimony: Crises of Witnessing in Literature, Psychoanalysis, and History*. New York: Routledge, 1992. Print.

Ferris, Joshua. *To Rise Again at a Decent Hour*. New York: Little, Brown, 2014. Print.

Fiedler, Leslie. *The Jew in the American Novel*. New York: Herzl, 1959. Print.

———. *Love and Death in the American Novel*. New York: Criterion, 1960. Print.

———. "Nude Croquet." *Esquire* (September 1957): 134–148. Print.

Flanzbaum, Hilene, ed. *The Americanization of the Holocaust*. Baltimore: Johns Hopkins UP, 1999. Print.

Franco, Dean. *Race, Rights, and Recognition: Jewish American Literature Since 1969*. Ithaca, NY: Cornell UP, 2012. Print.

Frank, Anne. *The Diary of a Young Girl*. New York: Bantam, 1993. Print.

Freedman, Jonathan. *Klezmer America: Jewishness, Ethnicity, Modernity*. New York: Columbia UP, 2008. Print.

Freedman, Samuel G. *Jew vs. Jew: The Struggle for the Soul of American Jewry*. New York: Simon & Schuster, 2000. Print.

Furman, Andrew. *Contemporary Jewish Writers and the Multicultural Dilemma: Return of the Exiled*. Syracuse, NY: Syracuse UP, 2001. Print.

Gans, Herbert. "Symbolic Ethnicity: The Future of Ethnic Groups and Culture in America." *Ethnic and Racial Studies*. 2.1 (1979): 1–20. Print.

Gates, Henry Louis. "The Passing of Anatole Broyard." *Thirteen Ways of Looking at a Black Man*. New York: Random House, 1997. Print.
Gilman, Sander. *The Jew's Body*. New York: Routledge, 1991. Print.
Gilroy, Paul. *The Black Atlantic: Modernity and Double Consciousness*. Cambridge, MA: Harvard UP, 1993. Print.
Ginsberg, Allen. *Howl and Other Poems*. San Francisco: City Lights, 2001.
Glaser, Jennifer. "Of Superheroes and Synecdoche: Holocaust Exceptionalism, Race, and the Rhetoric of Jewishness in America." *Jewish Rhetorics: History, Theory, Practice*. Ed. Janice Fernheimer and Michael Bernard. Worcester, MA: Brandeis UP, 2014. 231–248. Print.
Glazer, Nathan, and Daniel Patrick Moynihan. *Beyond the Melting Pot*. Cambridge, MA: MIT Press, 1970. Print.
Goffman, Ethan. *Imagining Each Other: Blacks and Jews in Contemporary American Literature*. Albany: SUNY P, 2000. Print.
Goldstein, Eric. *The Price of Whiteness: Jews, Race, and American Identity*. Princeton: Princeton UP, 2006. Print.
Gordon, Albert I. *Intermarriage—Interfaith, Interracial, Interethnic*. Boston: Beacon, 1994. Print.
Greenlee, Sam. *The Spook Who Sat by the Door*. Detroit: Wayne State UP, 1990. Print.
Griffin, John Howard. *Black Like Me*. New York: Signet, 1996. Print.
Grossman, Barbara. *Funny Woman: The Life and Times of Fanny Brice*. Bloomington: Indiana UP, 1991. Print.
Hall, Stuart. "Cultural Identity and Diaspora." *Identity: Community, Culture, Difference*. Ed. Jonathan Rutherford. London: Lawrence & Wishart, 1990. 222–237. Print.
Harrison-Kahan, Lori. "Passing for White, Passing for Jewish." *MELUS* 30.1 (2005): 19–48. JSTOR. Web.
———. *The White Negress: Literature, Minstrelsy, and the Black-Jewish Imaginary*. New Brunswick, NJ: Rutgers UP, 2011. Print.
Hawthorne, Nathaniel. Preface. *The House of the Seven Gables*. Boston: Osgood, 1876. 2006. iii–vi. Web.
Heilbrunn, Jacob. *They Knew They Were Right: The Rise of the Neocons*. New York: Doubleday, 2008. Print.
Herder, J. G. *J. G. Herder on Social and Political Culture*. Trans. F. M. Barnard. London: Cambridge UP, 1969. Print.
Herrnstein Smith, Barbara. *Contingencies of Value: Alternate Perspectives for Critical Theory*. Cambridge, MA: Harvard UP, 1988. Print.
Hersey, John. *The Wall*. New York: Knopf, 1950. Print.
Herskovitz, Melville. *The Myth of the Negro Past*. Boston: Beacon, 1990.
Heschel, Susannah. "Jewish Studies As Counterhistory." In *Insider/Outsider: American Jews and Multiculturalism*. Ed. David Biale, Michael Galchinsky, and Susannah Heschel. Berkeley: University of California, 1998. 101–115. Print.
Hoffman, Warren. *The Passing Game: Queering American Jewish Culture*. Syracuse, NY: Syracuse UP, 2009. Print.
Hollinger, David. *Postethnic America: Beyond Multiculturalism*. New York: Basic Books, 1995. Print.
Hook, Sidney. "Democracy and Desegregation." *New Leader*. 21 April 1958. Web.
hooks, bell. "The Oppositional Gaze." *Black Looks: Race and Representation*. Boston: South End, 1992. Print.

Howe, Irving. "Black Boys and Native Sons." *Dissent* 10 (1963). Web.
———. Introduction. *Jewish American Short Stories*. New York: Signet, 1977. 1–17. Print.
———. *The World of Our Fathers*. New York: Galahad, 2001. Print.
Hungerford, Amy. *The Holocaust of Texts: Genocide, Literature, and Personification*. Chicago: U of Chicago P, 2003. Print.
Hunter, James Davison. *The Culture Wars: The Struggle to Define America*. New York: Basic Books, 1991. Print.
Hyman, Paula. *Gender and Assimilation in Modern Jewish History: The Roles and Representation of Women*. Seattle: U of Washington P, 1995. Print.
Inglourious Basterds. 2009. Film.
Itzkovitz, Daniel. "Notes from the Black-Jewish Monologue." *Transition* 105 (2011): 3–20. Project Muse. Web.
———. "Passing Like Me: Jewish Chameleonism and the Politics of Race." *Passing: Identity and Interpretation in Sexuality, Race, and Religion*. Ed. Maria Sanchez and Linda Schlossberg. New York: NYU P, 2001. 38–63. Print.
Jacobson, Matthew Frye. *Roots Too: White Ethnic Revival in Post–Civil Rights America*. Cambridge, MA: Harvard UP, 2005. Print.
———. *Special Sorrows: The Diasporic Imagination of Irish, Polish, and Jewish Immigrants to the United States*. Berkeley: U of California P, 2002. Print.
———. *Whiteness of a Different Color: European Immigrants and the Alchemy of Race*. Cambridge, MA: Harvard UP, 1998. Print.
Jen, Gish. *Mona in the Promised Land*. New York: Knopf, 1996. Print.
Johnson, Drew. "An Interview with Lore Segal." *Bookslut*. December 2011. Web.
Johnson, James Weldon. *Autobiography of an Ex-Colored Man*. New York: Boston, Sherman, French, 1912. Print.
Johnson, Joyce. *Minor Characters*. New York: Penguin, 1999. Print.
Jonas, George. *Vengeance: The True Story of an Israeli Counter-Terrorist Team*. New York: Simon & Schuster, 1984. Print.
Jones, Hettie. *How I Became Hettie Jones*. New York: Grove, 1996. Print.
Jones, LeRoi/Amiri Baraka. *The Autobiography of LeRoi Jones by Amiri Baraka*. New York: Freundlich, 1983. Print.
———. "Black Art." *The LeRoi Jones/Amiri Baraka Reader*. Ed. Amiri Baraka, Imamu Amiri Baraka, and William J. Harris. New York: Basic Books, 2000. 219–220. Print.
———. *Blues People: Negro Music in White America*. New York: Harper Perennial, 1999. Print.
———. "the last days of the American empire (including some instructions for black people)." *Home: Social Essays*. New York: Akashic, 2009. 214–235. Print.
———. "The Slave." *Dutchman and the Slave*. New York: Harper Perennial, 1971. 39–88. Print.
Jones, Lisa. *Bulletproof Diva*. New York: Anchor, 1997. Print.
Jong, Erica. *Fear of Flying*. New York: Signet, 1993. Print.
Kafka, Franz. *Amerika*. New York: Schocken, 1996. Print.
Kallen, Horace. *Cultural Pluralism and the American Idea: A Philosophical Essay*. Philadelphia: U of Pennsylvania P, 1956. Print.
Kaniuk, Yoram. *The Last Jew*. Trans. Barbara Harshav. New York: Grove, 2006. Print.
Kaplan, Brett Ashley. "Anatole Broyard's Human Stain: Performing Postracial Consciousness." *Philip Roth Studies* 1.2 (2005): 125–144. Project Muse. Web.

Kaplan, Steven. "If There Are No Races, How Can the Jews Be a 'Race'?" *Journal of Modern Jewish Studies* 2.1 (2003): 79–96. Taylor & Francis Online. Web.

Kassow, Samuel. *Who Will Write Our History? Emanuel Ringelblum, the Warsaw Ghetto, and the Oyneg Shabes Archive.* Bloomington: Indiana UP, 2007. Print.

Katchor, Ben. *The Jew of New York.* New York: Pantheon, 1998. Print.

———. *Julius Knipl, Real Estate Photographer: The Beauty Supply Shop District.* New York: Pantheon, 2000. Print.

Kazin, Alfred. "Jews." *New Yorker.* 7 March 1994. Web.

Kellman, Steven G. "*The Tenants* in the House of Fiction." *Studies in the Novel* 8.4 (1976): 428–467. Project Muse. Web.

Kennedy, Ruby Jo Reeves. Review of *Intermarriage: Interfaith, Interracial, Interethnic*, by Albert Gordon. *Journal for the Scientific Study of Religion* 4:1 (1964): 135–137. JSTOR. Web.

Kerouac, Jack. *On the Road.* New York: Penguin, 2011.

Kirsch, Adam. "John Updike, the Jew." *Tablet.* 7 June 2012. Web.

Kitaj, R. B. *First Diasporist Manifesto.* London: Thames & Hudson, 1989. Print.

Kolb, Harold H., Jr. "Defining the Canon." *Redefining American Literary History.* Ed. A. LaVonne Brown Ruoff and Jerry W. Ward, Jr. New York: MLA, 1990. 35–51. Print.

Korzenkhov, Alexander. *Zamenhof: The Life, Works, and Ideas of the Author of Esperanto.* Trans. Ian Richmond. New York: Mondial, 2010.

Kosinski, Jerzy. *The Painted Bird.* New York: Grove, 1995. Print.

Kramer, Michael. "My Critics and Mai Nafka Mina: Further Reflections on Jewish Literary Historiography." *Prooftexts* 21 (2001): 231–265. Project Muse. Web.

———. "Race, Literary History, and the 'Jewish' Question." *Prooftexts* 21 (2001): 231–265. Project Muse. Web.

Kushner, Tony. *Angels in America: A Gay Fantasia on National Themes.* New York: Theatre Communications Group, 2003. Print.

Kushner, Tony, and Eric Roth. *Munich.* Daily script. Web.

Kushner, Tony, and Alisa Solomon, eds. *Wrestling with Zion: Progressive American Responses to the Israeli-Palestinian Conflict.* New York: Grove, 2003. Print.

LaCapra, Dominic. *Representing the Holocaust: History, Theory, Trauma.* Ithaca, NY: Cornell UP, 1994. Print.

Lackritz, Andrew. "Identification and Difference: Structures of Privilege in Cultural Criticism." *Who Can Speak? Authority and Critical Identity.* Ed. Judith Roof and Robyn Wiegman. Urbana: U of Illinois P, 1995. 3–22. Print.

Lambert, Joshua. "It All Begins with the Jewish Nose: A Review of Jess Row's *Your Face in Mine.*" *Ha'aretz.* 15 August 2014. Web.

Larsen, Nella. *Passing.* New York: Martino, 2011. Print.

Lee, Felicia. "In A Novelist's World, You Choose Your Race: Jess Row's 'Your Face in Mine' Explores Racial Reassignment." *New York Times.* 11 August 2014. Web.

Lee, Jonathan. "Always on Display: An Interview with Joshua Ferris." *Paris Review.* 19 May 2014. Web.

Levi, Primo. *Survival in Auschwitz.* New York: Touchstone, 1995. Print.

Levinson, Julian. *Exile on Main Street: Jewish American Writers and American Literary Culture.* Bloomington: Indiana UP, 2008. Print.

Liu, Eric. *The Accidental Asian: Notes of a Native Speaker.* New York: Random House, 1998. Print.

Lott, Eric. *Love & Theft: Blackface Minstrelsy and the American Working Class.* Oxford: Oxford UP, 1993. Print.

Loving v. Virginia. Oral arguments. U.S. Supreme Court Media. Oyez.org. Web.

Loving v. Virginia. U.S. Supreme Court. 388 U.S. 1 (1967). Lawnix. Web.

Madsen, Deborah. *American Exceptionalism.* Oxford: U of Mississippi P, 1998. Print.

Magid, Shaul. "In Search of a Critical Voice in the Jewish Diaspora: Homelessness and Home in Edward Said and Shalom Noah Barzofsky's *Netivot Shalom.*" *Jewish Social Studies* 12.3 (2006): 193–227. Project Muse. Web.

Malamud, Bernard. "The Angel Levine." *The Complete Stories.* Ed. Robert Giroux. New York: Farrar, Straus & Giroux, 1997. 157–166. Print.

———. *The Assistant.* New York: Farrar, Straus & Giroux, 1966. Print.

———. "Black Is My Favorite Color." *The Complete Stories.* Ed. Robert Giroux. New York: Farrar, Straus & Giroux, 1997. 331–339. Print.

———. *Dubin's Lives.* New York: Farrar, Straus & Giroux, 1979. Print.

———. "The Jewbird." *The Complete Stories.* Ed. Robert Giroux. New York: Farrar, Straus & Giroux, 1997. 322–330. Print.

———. "The Last Mohican." *The Complete Stories.* Ed. Robert Giroux. New York: Farrar, Straus & Giroux, 1997. 200–220. Print.

———. *The Magic Barrel.* Philadelphia: Jewish Publication Society of America, 1958. Print.

———. *The Tenants.* New York: Macmillan, 2003. Print.

Marcus, Ben. *The Flame Alphabet.* New York: Knopf, 2012. Print.

Max, D. T. "Twilight of the Old Goats." *Salon.* 16 May 1997. Web.

McGrath, Charles. "Zuckerman's Alter Brain." *New York Times.* 7 May 2000. Web.

McGurl, Mark. *The Program Era: Postwar Fiction and the Rise of Creative Writing.* Cambridge, MA: Harvard UP, 2009. Print.

McPherson, James A. "To Blacks and Jews: Hab Rachmones." *Tikkun* 4.5 (1989): 15–18. Web.

———. "Interview with J. M. Spalding." *Inertia* 1 (2002). Web.

Melnick, Jeffrey. *A Right to Sing the Blues: African Americans, Jews, and American Popular Song.* Cambridge, MA: Harvard UP, 2001. Print.

Melville, Herman. *Moby-Dick.* Oxford: Oxford UP, 2008. Print

Mignolo, Walter. "Canon a(nd) Cross-Cultural Boundaries (Or, Whose Canon Are We Talking About?)." *Poetics Today* 12.1 (1991): 1–28. Project Muse. Web.

Morgan, Thomas B. "The Vanishing American Jew." *Look* 28 (1964): 42–46. Web.

Munich. 2005. Film.

Neal, Larry. "The Black Arts Movement." *The Portable Sixties Reader.* Ed. Ann Charters. New York: Penguin, 2003. 446–453. Print.

Newton, Adam Zachary. *Facing Black and Jew.* Cambridge: Cambridge UP, 1999.

Norich, Anita. "On the Yiddish Question." *Mapping Jewish Identities.* Ed. Laurence J. Silberstein. New York: NYU P, 2000. 145–158. Print.

North, Michael. *The Dialect of Modernism: Race, Language, and Twentieth-Century Literature.* Oxford: Oxford UP, 1998. Print.

Novick, Peter. *The Holocaust in American Life.* New York: Mariner, 2000. Print.

Omer-Sherman, Ranen. *Diaspora and Zionism in Jewish American Literature.* Waltham, MA: Brandeis UP, 2002. Print.

Omi, Michael, and Howard Winant. *Racial Formation in the United States: From the 1960s to the 1990s.* New York: Routledge, 1994. Print.

Ozick, Cynthia. "Bech Passing." *Art and Ardor.* New York: Knopf, 1984. 114–129. Print.
———. "Cultural Impersonation." *Art and Ardor.* New York: Knopf, 1984. 113–114. Print.
———. "Envy; Or Yiddish in America." *A Cynthia Ozick Reader.* Ed. Elaine Kauvar. Bloomington: Indiana UP, 1996. 20–63. Print.
———. "Levitation." *Levitation: 5 Fictions.* Syracuse, NY: Syracuse UP, 1995. 3–20. Print.
———. "Literary Blacks and Jews." *Art and Ardor.* New York: Knopf, 1984. 90–112. Print.
———. "A Mercenary." *Bloodshed and Three Novellas.* Syracuse, NY: Syracuse UP, 1995. 13–52. Print.
———. *The Messiah of Stockholm.* New York: Vintage, 1988. Print.
———. "The Rights of History and the Rights of Imagination," *Quarrel and Quandary.* New York: Vintage, 2001. 103–119. Print.
———. *The Shawl.* New York: Vintage, 1990. Print.
———. "Usurpation (Other People's Stories)." *Bloodshed and Three Novellas.* Syracuse, NY: Syracuse UP, 1995. 129–185. Print.
———. "Who Owns Anne Frank?" *Quarrel and Quandary.* New York: Vintage, 2001. 74–102. Print.
Palumbo-Liu, David. *The Ethnic Canon: Histories, Institutions, and Interventions.* Minneapolis: U of Minnesota P, 1995. Print.
Perez, Gilberto. *The Material Ghost: Films and Their Medium.* Baltimore: Johns Hopkins UP, 2000. Print.
Podair, Jerald. *The Strike That Changed New York.* New Haven, CT: Yale UP, 2004. Print.
Podhoretz, Norman. *Ex-Friends.* New York: Simon & Schuster, 2001. Print.
———. "My Negro Problem—and Ours." *Commentary.* February 1963: 93–101. Web.
Posnock, Ross. *Philip Roth's Rude Truth: The Art of Immaturity.* Princeton: Princeton UP, 2006. Print.
———. "Ralph Ellison, Hannah Arendt, and the Meaning of Politics." *Cambridge Companion to Ralph Ellison.* Cambridge: Cambridge UP, 2005. 201–216. Print.
Prell, Riv-Ellen. *Fighting to Become Americans: Assimilation and the Trouble between Jewish Women and Jewish Men.* Boston: Beacon, 2000. Print.
Rice, Herbert William. *Ralph Ellison and the Politics of the Novel.* New York: Lexington, 2003. Print.
Richler, Mordecai. *Solomon Gursky Was Here.* New York: Knopf, 1990. Print.
Rody, Caroline. *The Interethnic Imagination.* Oxford: Oxford UP, 2009. Print.
Rogin, Michael. *Black Face, White Noise: Jewish Immigrants in the Hollywood Melting Pot.* Berkeley: U of California P, 1998. Print.
Roskies, David. *The Jewish Search for a Usable Past.* Bloomington: Indiana UP, 1999. Web.
Roth, Henry. *Call It Sleep.* New York: Picador, 2005. Print.
Roth, Philip. *American Pastoral.* New York: Houghton Mifflin, 1997. Print.
———. *Goodbye, Columbus: And Five Short Stories.* New York: Meridian, 1960. Print.
———. *The Human Stain.* New York: Houghton, 2000. Print.
———. *Operation Shylock: A Confession.* New York: Vintage, 1994. Print.
———. *The Plot against America.* New York: Houghton Mifflin, 2004. Print.
———. *Portnoy's Complaint.* New York: Vintage, 1994. Print.
———. "Writing about Jews." *Commentary* 36:6 (1963): 446–452. Web.
———. "Writing about Jews." *Who We Are: On Being (and not Being) a Jewish American Writer.* Ed. Derek Rubin. New York: Schocken, 2005. 42–63. Print.
Rothberg, Michael. *Multidirectional Memory: Remembering the Holocaust in the Age of Decolonization.* Palo Alto, CA: Stanford UP, 2009. Print.

Rottenberg, Catherine. "Passing: Race, Identification, and Desire." *Criticism* 45 (2003): 435–452. Project Muse. Web.

———. *Performing Americanness: Race, Class, and Gender in Modern African American and Jewish American Literature*. Hanover, NH: UP of New England, 2008. Print.

Row, Jess. *Your Face in Mine*. New York: Riverhead, 2014. Print.

Rubel, Nora L. *Doubting the Devout: The Ultra-Orthodox in the Jewish American Imagination*. New York: Columbia UP, 2010. Print.

Rubinstein, Rachel. *Members of the Tribe: Native America in the Jewish Imagination*. Detroit: Wayne State UP, 2010. Print.

Said, Edward. *The Question of Palestine*. New York: Vintage, 1980. Print.

Salaita, Steven. *The Holy Land in Transit: Colonialism and the Quest for Canaan*. Syracuse, NY: Syracuse UP, 2006. Print.

Sarna, Jonathan. *Jacksonian Jew: The Two Worlds of Mordecai Noah*. New York: Holmes & Meier, 1981. Print.

Saving Private Ryan. 1998. Film.

Schindler's List. 1993. Film.

Schlievert, Chelsea D. "Self-Narratives and Editorial Marks: Inventing Hettie Jones." *Women's Studies* 40.8 (2011): 1092–1115. Taylor & Francis Online. Web.

Schreier, Benjamin. "The Failure of Identity: Toward a New Literary History of Philip Roth's Unrecognizable Jew." *Jewish Social Studies* 17.2 (2011): 101–135. Web.

Schulz, Bruno. *The Street of Crocodiles*. New York: Penguin, 1992. Print.

Schwartz, Lynn Sharon. "The Melting Pot." *The Melting Pot*. New York: Penguin, 1989. 1–35. Print.

Segal, Lore. *Her First American*. New York: New Press, 2004. Print.

———. *Other People's Houses*. New York: New Press, 2004. Print.

———. *Shakespeare's Kitchen: Stories*. New York: New Press, 2007. Print.

Seidman, Naomi. "Fag-Hags and Bu-Jews: Toward a (Jewish) Politics of Vicarious Identity." *Insider/Outsider: American Jews and Multiculturalism*. Ed. David Biale, Michael Galchinsky, and Susannah Heschel. Berkeley: U of California P, 1998. 254–268. Print.

———. *A Marriage Made in Heaven: The Sexual Politics of Hebrew and Yiddish*. Berkeley: U of California P, 1997. Print.

Senna, Danzy. *Caucasia*. New York: Riverhead, 1999. Print.

Shakespeare, William. *King Lear*. London: Bloomsbury Arden, 1997. Print.

———. *The Merchant of Venice*. New York: Simon & Schuster, 2004. Print.

Shandler, Jeffrey. *Adventures in Yiddishland: Postvernacular Language and Culture*. Berkeley: U of California P, 2005. Print.

Shapiro, Susan. "Écriture Judaïque: Where Are the Jews in Western Discourse?" *Displacements: Cultural Identities in Question*. Ed. Angelika Bammer. Bloomington: U of Indiana P, 1994. 182–201. Print.

Shelley, Percy Bysshe. "Queen Mab." *The Complete Poetry of Percy Bysshe*. Ed. Donald H. Reiman, Neil Fraistat, and Nora Crook. Baltimore, MD: Johns Hopkins UP, 2012. 3:53–68. Print.

Shenker, Israel. "After 'Portnoy,' What?" *New York Magazine*. 12 May 1969. 46–47. Web.

———. "For Malamud, It's Story." *New York Times*. 3 October 1971. Web.

Shohat, Ella, and Robert Stam. "*Zelig* and Contemporary Theory: Meditation on the Chameleon Text." *Enclitic* 9 (1985): 176–193. WorldCat. Web.

Shteyngart, Gary. *Super Sad True Love Story*. New York: Random House, 2010. Print.

Siegel, Fred. "The Cult of Multiculturalism." *New Republic*. 18 February 1991. Web.

Silberman, Charles E. *American Jews and Their Lives Today.* New York: Summit, 1986. Print.
Silverman, Lisa. "Beyond Anti-Semitism: A Critical Approach to German Jewish Cultural History." *Nexus: Essays in German Jewish Studies.* Ed. William C. Donahue and Martha B. Helfer. New York: Camden House, 2011. 1:27–45. Print.
Singh, Nikhil Pal. *Black Is a Country: Race and the Unfinished Struggle for Democracy.* Cambridge, MA: Harvard UP, 2004. Print.
Slezkhine, Yuri. *The Jewish Century.* Princeton: Princeton UP, 2004. Print.
Smith, Anthony. *Chosen Peoples: Sacred Sources of National Identity.* Oxford: Oxford UP, 2003. Print.
Smith, Bessie. "Long Old Road." *The Complete Recordings, Volume 4.* 1931. CD.
Sollors, Werner. *Beyond Ethnicity.* Oxford: Oxford UP, 1987. Print.
———. *Neither Black nor White yet Both: Thematic Explorations of Interracial Literature.* Cambridge, MA: Harvard UP, 1999. Print.
———. "Of Mules and Mares in a Land of Difference; or Quadrupeds All?" *American Quarterly* 42.2 (1990): 167–190. Project Muse. Web.
Spevack, Edmund. "Racial Conflict and Multiculturalism: Bernard Malamud's *The Tenants.*" *MELUS* 22.3 (1997): 31–55. JSTOR. Web.
Spiegelman, Art. *The Complete Maus.* New York: Pantheon, 1996.
Spitz, David. "Politics and the Realm of Being." *Dissent* 6.2 (1959): 56–65. Web.
Spivak, Gayatri. "Can the Subaltern Speak?" *Marxism and the Interpretation of Culture.* Ed. Cary Nelson and Lawrence Grossberg. Basingstoke, UK: Macmillan International, 1988. 271–313. Print.
———. "Subaltern Studies: Deconstructing Historiography." *In Other Worlds: Essays in Cultural Politics.* Ed. Ranajit Guha and Gayatri Spivak. London: Routledge, 2012. 270–304. Print.
Stanislawski, Michael. *Zionism and the Fin de Siècle.* Berkeley: U of California P, 2001. Print.
Staub, Michael. *Torn at the Roots: The Crisis of Jewish Liberalism in Postwar America.* New York: Columbia UP, 2002. Print.
Stern, Daniel. "Interview with Bernard Malamud." *Paris Review* 61 (1975). Reprinted in *The Art of Fiction* 52. Web.
Stratton, Jon. "Not Really White—Again: Performing Jewish Difference in Hollywood Films since the 1980s." *Screen* 42.2 (2001): 142–166. Web.
Styron, William. *The Confessions of Nat Turner.* New York: Vintage, 1992. Print.
———. *Sophie's Choice.* New York: Vintage, 1992. Print.
Sundquist, Eric. *Strangers in the Land: Blacks, Jews, Post-Holocaust America.* Cambridge, MA: Belknap, 2005. Print.
Teicholz, Tom. "Interview with Cynthia Ozick." *Paris Review* 102 (1987). Reprinted in *The Art of Fiction* 95. Web.
Theroux, Alexander. "Interview with Ben Katchor." *BOMB* 88 (2004). Web.
Thompson, Deborah. "Keeping Up with the Joneses: The Naming of Racial Identities in the Autobiographical Writings of LeRoi Jones/Amiri Baraka, Hettie Jones, and Lisa Jones." *College Literature* 29.1 (2002): 83–101. JSTOR. Web.
Time. Editorial. 25 June 1965. Academic Search Premier. Web.
Tyler, Carole-Anne. "Passing: Narcissism, Identity, and Difference." *Differences* 6.2–3 (1994): 212–248. Project Muse. Web.
UNESCO. "The Race Question." 1950. Web.

Unger, Arthur. "Ben Wattenberg's 'Walkabout' Look at American Politics." *Christian Science Monitor*. 30 May 1980. Web.
Updike, John. *Bech: A Book*. New York: Knopf, 1970. Print.
Uris, Leon. *Exodus*. Garden City, NY: Doubleday, 1958. Print.
Voltaire. *Complete Works*. Ed. Theodore Besterman. Toronto: U of Toronto P, 1968. Print.
Wagner, Richard. *Judaism in Music and Other Essays*. Lincoln: U of Nebraska P, 1995. Print.
Wallace, David Foster. "Westward the Course of Empire Takes Its Way." *Girl with Curious Hair*. New York: Norton, 1989. Print.
Warren, Robert Penn. *Who Speaks for the Negro?* New York: Random House, 1965. Print.
Weissman, Gary. *Fantasies of Witnessing: Postwar Efforts to Experience the Holocaust*. Ithaca, NY: Cornell UP, 2004. Print.
Wenger, Beth. "Memory As Identity: The Invention of the Lower East Side." *American Jewish History* 85.1 (1997): 3–27. Project Muse. Web.
Wiener, Jon. "Arctic Jews: An Interview with Michael Chabon." *Dissent*. 14 April 2007. Web.
Wiesel, Eli. *Night*. New York: Hill & Wang, 2006. Print.
Winant, Howard. "Behind Blue Eyes: Contemporary White Racial Politics." *Off White: Readings on Race, Power, and Society*, 2nd ed. Ed. Michelle Fine. New York: Routledge, 2004.
Wisse, Ruth. *The Modern Jewish Canon*. New York: Free Press, 2000. Print.
———. "Slap Shtick." *Commentary*. 1 July 2007. Web.
Wordsworth, William. "Song for the Wandering Jew." *Lyrical Ballads*. New York: Penguin, 2006. 2:222. Print.
Zangwill, Israel. "The Melting-Pot." *From the Ghetto to the Melting Pot*. Ed. Edna Nashon. Detroit: Wayne State UP, 2005. Print.
Zierler, Wendy. "My Holocaust Is Not Your Holocaust: 'Facing' Black and Jewish Experience in *The Pawnbroker, Higher Ground,* and *The Nature of Blood*." *Holocaust and Genocide Studies* 18.1 (2004): 46–67. Project Muse. Web.
Zelig. 1983. Film.
Zimmermann, Moshe. "Muscle Jews versus Nervous Jews." *Emancipation through Muscles: Jews and Sports in Europe*. Ed. Michael Brenner and Gideon Reuveni. Lincoln: U of Nebraska P. 15–28. Print.

Index

Aarons, Victoria, 60
acculturation, 3, 7–8, 10, 19, 63, 72, 94
Aczel, Richard, 36–37
Adorno, Theodor, 92
affirmative action programs, 94, 126
Africa, 21, 83; African diaspora, 111; African-ness, 21, 70; and "A Mercenary" (Ozick), 68–77, 157n21; "politically African," 68–74
African Americans, 6, 9, 13, 15–19, 120, 140, 147; and *Amerika* (Kafka), 50; and "Black Boys and Native Sons" (Howe), 17; and black idiom, 23–25, 27–28, 31; and *The Confessions of Nat Turner* (Styron), 9; and *Her First American* (Segal), 52–57; and Holocaust/Holocaust literature, 63–65, 67–71, 77–88; and *How I Became Hettie Jones* (Jones), 49–51; and *The Human Stain* (Roth), 4, 93, 97–106; and interracial romances/marriages, 41, 44–57; as jazz musicians, 50, 155n16; and "the last days of the American empire..." (Jones), 22; and "Looking for Mr. Green" (Bellow), 83; and *Loving v. Virginia*, 41, 44; and "A Mercenary" (Ozick), 68–71, 77–78; and *Mr. Sammler's Planet* (Bellow), 58, 79–88, 157n29; and "My Negro Problem—and Ours" (Podhoretz), 80–81; and "Negroes Are Anti-Semitic Because They're Anti-White" (Baldwin), 18–19; and Ocean Hill–Brownsville school crisis (1968), 19, 39–40, 153n40; and *Other People's Houses* (Segal), 57; and passing, 2, 4, 51, 93, 97–106, 135; and "Reflections on Little Rock" (Arendt), 4, 15–17; and Roth's "American trilogy," 96–97; and slavery, 9, 22, 26–27, 56, 64; and "spooks," 102, 104, 159n18; and *The Spook Who Sat by the Door* (Greenlee), 159n18; and *The Tenants* (Malamud), 21–40, 67; and "The World and the Jug" (Ellison), 17; and *Your Face in Mine* (Row), 142. *See also entries beginning with* black; *names of African Americans*

Alaska, 119, 130–137, 161n35
Alcoff, Linda, 7–8, 10, 37
alienation, 13, 49, 55; and the literary canon, 91, 94–96, 102
Allen, Woody, 1–6
ambivalence, 6–7, 13; and Holocaust/Holocaust literature, 64, 66, 158n10; and *How I Became Hettie Jones* (Jones), 48; and *The Human Stain* (Roth), 105; and the literary canon, 95–96, 105; and *Loving v. Virginia*, 45; and *Munich* (film), 112; and *The Tenants* (Malamud), 25–26, 35; and *To Rise Again at a Decent Hour* (Ferris), 144; and "Writing About Jews" (Roth), 95–96; and *The Yiddish Policemen's Union* (Chabon), 136; and *Zelig* (film), 3, 5
American literature, 4–6, 93, 142–147; and diaspora, 119, 136; and Holocaust/Holocaust literature, 66–67, 82; and *The Human Stain* (Roth), 97–99, 105–106; and interfaith/interracial marriages, 45–46; Jewish American literature, 4, 8–9, 11–13, 46, 60, 66–67, 90, 105–108, 119, 137; and *Mr. Sammler's Planet* (Bellow), 82; and passing, 97–99, 104–106; and *The Tenants* (Malamud), 20–21, 33, 37, 39; and *The Yiddish Policemen's Union* (Chabon), 136. *See also* canon, literary; *titles of literary works*

Americanness, 18, 54, 86, 128–129, 136, 141. *See also* culture, American
American Pastoral (Roth), 96–97, 159n11
Americans for Peace Now, 135
American Studies Association, 109
anarchy/anarchists, 22, 79, 89
Anderson, Benedict, 120–121
"The Angel Levine" (Malamud), 34, 83
Angels in America (Kushner), 119
Annie Hall (film), 2
anthropology/anthropologists, 79, 83, 120, 157n26, 161n35
Antin, Mary, 47, 154n10
anti-Semitism, 6, 10, 143, 162n2; and "The Jewbird" (Malamud), 36; and *The Jewish Century* (Slezkine), 70; and *The Jew of New York* (Katchor), 123, 127; and the literary canon, 95–96; and Ocean Hill–Brownsville school crisis (1968), 39; and *The Plot against America* (Roth), 96; sovereignty/anti-Semitism, 111; and *The Tenants* (Malamud), 21, 31–33; and *To Rise Again at a Decent Hour* (Ferris), 144; and Wagner, 37; and "Writing About Jews" (Roth), 95; and *Zelig* (film), 3, 149n1
anxieties, African American, 22, 30, 44
anxieties, Jewish, 4–6, 8, 13, 150n19; and *American Pastoral* (Roth), 96; "anxiety of appropriation," 13; castration anxiety, 22, 80, 159n20; and diaspora, 112–115, 118, 120, 127, 131; and Holocaust/Holocaust literature, 63, 67, 78, 80; and *How I Became Hettie Jones* (Jones), 50; and *The Human Stain* (Roth), 100, 103; and *Intermarriage* (Gordon), 43, 46; about Jewish identity, 34, 37, 44, 50; and *The Jew of New York* (Katchor), 120, 127; and the literary canon, 91–93, 96, 100, 103; and *The Merchant of Venice* (Shakespeare), 154n8; and *Mr. Sammler's Planet* (Bellow), 78, 80; and *Munich* (film), 112–116; about nationhood, 110; and *The Tenants* (Malamud), 24, 28–30, 33–34, 37; and "Writing About Jews" (Roth), 96; and *The Yiddish Policemen's Union* (Chabon), 120, 131; and *Zelig* (film), 5–6
appropriation, politics of, 9–10, 12–13, 141–142, 147; and *Bech: A Book* (Updike), 72; and *Blues People* (Jones), 155n16; and Holocaust/Holocaust literature, 67, 72–73; and "The Melting Pot" (Schwartz), 59–60; and *The Tenants* (Malamud), 23, 25; and *Your Face in Mine* (Row), 142; and *Zelig* (film), 3

Arab world, 85–88; Dome of the Rock, 134, 136; and *Munich* (film), 110, 114–115; and *Operation Shylock* (Roth), 111; and *The Yiddish Policemen's Union* (Chabon), 134–136. *See also* Palestine/Palestinians; Six Day War; *names of Arab countries*
Ararat (in Katchor's *The Jew of New York*), 119, 123, 128–129, 161n29
Arendt, Hannah, 4, 15–19, 38, 151nn1–2, 151n6, 151n10, 153n39; arrogance of, 15, 17; "Reflections on Little Rock," 15–17, 19, 38, 40, 151n1
Arthur Mervyn (Brown), 46, 154n9
artists, African American, 6, 18; performing artists, 150n12; and *The Tenants* (Malamud), 21–22, 27, 31. *See also* writers, African American
artists, Jewish, 3–4, 14, 22, 37; and diaspora, 109–112, 126, 129; and *The Jew of New York* (Katchor), 126, 129; and "A Mercenary" (Ozick), 76; and *Munich* (film), 109–112; and Ocean Hill–Brownsville school crisis (1968), 40; and *Operation Shylock* (Roth), 111; and *The People* (Malamud), 153n36; and *The Tenants* (Malamud), 21, 37, 153n38; and *Zelig* (film), 3, 5. *See also* writers, Jewish American
Ashkenazi Jews, 111, 140
Asian Americans, 42, 52, 94, 107, 149n7; and *Fear of Flying* (Jong), 45; as "new Jews," 94, 127, 140, 149n7; and *Super Sad True Love Story* (Shteyngart), 146; and *Your Face in Mine* (Row), 143
assimilation, 18; and anti-assimilationists, 4; and *Arthur Mervyn* (Brown), 46; and *Blues People* (Jones), 155n16; and *Her First American* (Segal), 55; and Holocaust/Holocaust literature, 65; and *The Human Stain* (Roth), 98–100; and *Intermarriage* (Gordon), 43; and interracial romances/marriages, 43–44, 46, 55; and "The Jewbird" (Malamud), 36; and *The Jew of New York* (Katchor), 123, 128–129; and "the last days of the American empire . . ." (Jones), 22; and the literary canon, 92, 94, 98–100; and "The Melting Pot" (Schwartz), 60; and *The Melting Pot* (Zangwill), 60, 161n27; and "Negroes Are Anti-Semitic Because They're Anti-White" (Baldwin), 18; and *Your Face in Mine* (Row), 142; and *Zelig* (film), 2–3, 5, 149n1
The Assistant (Malamud), 25, 36, 38
Association for Asian American Studies, 109
athletes, Israeli, 109–110, 112, 116, 159n2, 160n15

INDEX

Atlas, James, 83, 85, 157n21, 158n10, 158n32
authenticity, 10, 12, 18, 144–146, 150n16; and Black Arts movement, 38; and diaspora, 112, 114–115, 125, 127, 129, 134–135, 137, 160n23; and Holocaust/Holocaust literature, 62–64, 66–67, 70–71, 76–78, 81, 156n10, 156n19; and *The Human Stain* (Roth), 100; and Jewish women writers, 48; and *The Jew of New York* (Katchor), 125, 127, 129; and "A Mercenary" (Ozick), 70–71, 76–78, 156n19; and *Munich* (film), 112, 114–115; and "My Negro Problem—and Ours" (Podhoretz), 81; racial authenticity, 21, 71, 81, 100; and *Super Sad True Love Story* (Shteyngart), 146; and *The Tenants* (Malamud), 21, 24, 27, 38, 141; and *To Jerusalem and Back* (Bellow), 86; and *To Rise Again at a Decent Hour* (Ferris), 144–145; and *Witz* (Cohen), 162n4; and *The Yiddish Policemen's Union* (Chabon), 134–135, 137; and *Your Face in Mine* (Row), 142–143; and *Zelig* (film), 149n3
autobiography, 7, 152n18; and Black Arts movement, 38–39, 49–50; of Cayton, 57–58; and *Her First American* (Segal), 57–58, 154n6; and *How I Became Hettie Jones* (Jones), 47; and the literary canon, 94; and *Other People's Houses* (Segal), 57–58; and *The Painted Bird* (Kosinski), 73; slave narrative as, 26; spiritual autobiography, 47; and *The Tenants* (Malamud), 26, 29, 32–33, 39. *See also entries beginning with Autobiography*
Autobiography (Jones), 49–50, 154n14
Autobiography of an Ex-Colored Man (Johnson), 97, 99, 101
autochthony, Jewish, 115–118
Azoulay, Katya Gibel, 51

Bakhtin, Mikhail, 153n30
Baldwin, James, 17–19, 24, 26, 57, 80; "Negroes Are Anti-Semitic Because They're Anti-White," 18–19, 22, 64, 152n12
Baraka, Amiri, 47–49, 51. *See also* Jones, LeRoi
Baron Cohen, Sacha, 3, 149n5
Beat generation, 47–48, 79–80, 154nn11–12
Beauvoir, Simone de, 143
Bech: A Book (Updike), 71–72, 95, 144, 156n19
Bellow, Saul, 1–2, 12–13, 17, 58, 60, 67–69, 71, 77–89, 93–94, 96, 144, 147, 150n19, 151n9, 157n21, 157n24, 158nn31–32; and anthropology, 79, 83, 157n26; *Dangling Man*, 84; and diaspora, 120; *Henderson the Rain King*, 83, 157n26; *Herzog*, 84, 157n26; and Holocaust/Holocaust literature, 12, 58, 67–68, 69, 77–89, 156n15, 157n28, 158n5, 158n8, 158n10; introduction to *The Closing of the American Mind* (Bloom), 82; and the literary canon, 94–95, 107; "Looking for Mr. Green," 83; *Mr. Sammler's Planet*, 12, 58, 67–68, 69, 77–89, 120, 156n15, 157n28, 158n5, 158n8; and neoconservatism, 82–83, 87, 157n21; as *Newsday* correspondent, 85–86; and Nobel Prize for Literature, 157n23, 158n10; as noted Yiddishist, 157n25; and Ozick correspondence, 158n10; "Papuans and Zulus," 157n21; *To Jerusalem and Back*, 78, 82–83, 85–88, 134; *The Very Dark Trees*, 83, 158n32
Berman, Lila Corwin, 42–44
Berman, Paul, 44
Bhahba, Homi, 75–76
Biale, David, 91, 158n3
Bible, 74–75, 117–118, 133; biblical chosenness, 139–140
Bildung tradition, 47, 54; *Bildungsroman*, 98
"Black Art" (Jones), 18–19, 32
Black Arts movement, 6, 13, 18, 47; post-"Black Art" America, 13; and *The Tenants* (Malamud), 21, 29, 38–40
"Black Is My Favorite Color" (Malamud), 34, 83
black-Jewish relations, 13, 17, 19, 149n5, 150n12, 152nn12–13; and "To Blacks and Jews: Hab Rachmones" (McPherson), 22–23; decline of, 26, 51; and *Her First American* (Segal), 55–56; and Holocaust/Holocaust literature, 79–84; and interracial romances/marriages, 45, 51, 55–56; Jew/black as mind/body, 81, 157n27; and *Loving v. Virginia*, 45; and "A Mercenary" (Ozick), 77; and *Mr. Sammler's Planet* (Bellow), 79–86; and "My Negro Problem—and Ours" (Podhoretz), 80–81; and Ocean Hill–Brownsville school crisis (1968), 19, 39; and *The Tenants* (Malamud), 22–30, 34–35, 37–39, 153n33
blackness: and Broyard, 104–105; "colored," 41, 44; and *Her First American* (Segal), 54–55; and Holocaust/Holocaust literature, 69–71, 74–75, 77–86; and *How I Became Hettie Jones* (Jones), 50–51; and *The Human Stain* (Roth), 97–106, 145; and interracial romances/marriages, 41, 44, 50–51, 54; jazz as black-identified, 50; and "A Mercenary" (Ozick), 69–71, 74–75, 77–78; and *Mr. Sammler's Planet* (Bellow), 79–86;

blackness (*continued*)
and "My Negro Problem—and Ours" (Podhoretz), 80–81; "speaking black," 33; and "spooks," 102, 104, 159n18; and *The Tenants* (Malamud), 25–26, 33; and *Your Face in Mine* (Row), 142. *See also* race; *entries beginning with* black
Black Panthers, 161n38
Black Power, 18, 39, 63, 69, 83, 157n24
Black September terrorist organization, 109–110, 112, 114, 159n4
black-white binary, 42, 48, 51, 55, 79, 106; and post-binary era, 99–100. *See also* black-Jewish relations
blood: and diaspora, 112, 115, 118; and *The Human Stain* (Roth), 97, 101–102; and "The Melting Pot" (Schwartz), 58–60; and *Munich* (film), 112, 115; and *Nationalism and History* (Dubnow), 118; and *Oedipus the King* (Sophocles), 101–102
Bloom, Allan, 82–83, 126–127, 157n21; *The Closing of the American Mind*, 82, 160n25
blues songs, 25–27, 152n24
Boas, Franz, 83
Bonnie and Clyde (film), 79–80
Boyarin, Daniel, 122, 160n16; "Diaspora," 117–119
Boyarin, Jonathan, 120, 122, 160n16; "Diaspora," 117–119
Branch, Taylor, 65–66
Brice, Fanny, 149n3
Brodkin, Karen, 4; *How Jews Became White Folks and What That Says about Race in America*, 159n22
Brown, Charles Brockden, 46, 154n9
Broyard, Anatole, 104, 159n21
Budick, Emily Miller, 17, 23–24, 28, 84–86, 151n2, 152n11
Buruma, Ian, 158n4
Butler, Judith, 98, 150n9

canon, literary, 4, 6, 12, 60, 90–108, 144, 150n14; and *Call It Sleep* (Roth), 52; and *The Closing of the American Mind* (Bloom), 83; "ethnic canon," 108; and Holocaust/Holocaust literature, 67, 83, 87; and *The Human Stain* (Roth), 4, 93, 95–108; Jewish canon, 90, 107; and *The Jew of New York* (Katchor), 126–127; and *To Jerusalem and Back* (Bellow), 87; and *The Tenants* (Malamud), 25, 32–33, 38; and *To Rise Again at a Decent Hour* (Ferris), 144; and "Writing About Jews" (Roth), 95–96, 100; and *Zelig* (film), 6. *See also* culture wars
Carver, Raymond, 77; *What We Talk about When We Talk about Love*, 157n22
Casteel, Sarah, 136, 162n1
castration anxiety, 22, 80, 159n20
Catholicism, 51, 64, 88, 156n14
Caughie, Pamela, 103
Cayton, Horace, Jr., 45, 57, 155n26
center/periphery, 100, 111, 119, 159n15
Chabon, Michael, 4, 13, 112, 119–122, 130–138, 147, 161nn36–37, 161n40, 162n3; comic books of, 133; "Guidebook to a Land of Ghosts," 121–122, 132; and Jewish exceptionalism, 135, 139, 141; *New York Times* op-ed, 135, 139–141; *The Yiddish Policemen's Union*, 4, 13, 119–121, 130–138, 141, 161n32, 161nn38–39
chameleonism, racial: and *The Human Stain* (Roth), 98–99; and *Moby-Dick* (Melville), 6; and *Zelig* (film), 1–3, 5–6
Chekhov, Anton, *The Seagull*, 47
Cheyette, Bryan, 13
children: and *Bulletproof Diva* (Jones), 51; and diaspora, 113–115, 132; and Holocaust/Holocaust literature, 68, 70–71, 73–75, 87; and *How I Became Hettie Jones* (Jones), 49–51; and *The Human Stain* (Roth), 97–100, 159n12; and interracial marriages, 44; and "A Mercenary" (Ozick), 68, 70–71, 74–75; and *Munich* (film), 113–116; and "My Negro Problem—and Ours" (Podhoretz), 80–81; and Ocean Hill–Brownsville school crisis (1968), 39; and *The Painted Bird* (Kosinski), 73; and school desegregation, 16; and *To Jerusalem and Back* (Bellow), 87; and *The Yiddish Policemen's Union* (Chabon), 132
chosenness, Jewish, 115, 127–128, 139–140, 160n17
Christians/Christianity, 162n1; and *Bech: A Book* (Updike), 72; and "Diaspora" (Boyarin and Boyarin), 118; and Holocaust/Holocaust literature, 63, 72, 74–75, 77, 155n4; and *The Human Stain* (Roth), 101; and interfaith marriages, 61; and *The Jew of New York* (Katchor), 125, 128; and "Levitation" (Ozick), 156n19; and the literary canon, 95, 101; in Malamud's work, 36; and "A Mercenary" (Ozick), 74–75, 77; Protestants, 40, 95, 143; and *To Rise Again at a Decent Hour* (Ferris), 145; Updike as Protestant, 95; and *Your Face in Mine* (Row), 143; and *Zelig* (film), 2. *See also* Catholicism

INDEX 179

circumcision, 31, 86, 92, 113, 117, 135
class, social, 5; and *Her First American* (Segal), 54; and *How I Became Hettie Jones* (Jones), 47, 49; and *The Human Stain* (Roth), 98–100, 103; and "The Melting Pot" (Schwartz), 60; and "A Mercenary" (Ozick), 70–71, 73–74; middle class, 39, 47, 63, 99–100, 103; and WASPs, 5, 22, 96, 98, 143; and *Your Face in Mine* (Row), 143
Cleaver, Eldridge, 21, 26
Clifford, James, 11, 120, 160n10
Clinton, Bill, 100–101, 105
Cohen, Hettie. *See* Jones, Hettie Cohen
Cohen, Joshua, 162n4
Cohen, Shaye, 155n27
colonialism, 16, 68–71, 73–77, 83
"color-blindness," 11, 54, 58, 82, 102
color line, 4, 39, 46, 48, 52
Columbus, Christopher, 140
Combahee River Collective, 63
Commentary, 15, 95, 126–127, 136, 151n1, 157n21, 158n31
communists, 22, 115–116
The Confessions of Nat Turner (Styron), 9, 61, 67
conservatives, 66, 83, 93–94, 141, 159n16. *See also* neoconservatism
conversion, 42, 59, 61, 154n8
cosmetic surgery, 142–143
cosmopolitanism, 14, 39, 70, 159n17, 162n1; and "First Diasporist Manifesto" (Kitaj), 111; and *The Human Stain* (Roth), 93, 101; and *Munich* (film), 116
Coughlin, Father Charles, 5
counterfeits, 73, 76
counterterrorism, 112–113, 115
Crenshaw, Kimberlé, 155n17
critical race theory, 11, 93
Crouch, Stanley, 19
"Cultural Impersonation" (Ozick), 68, 73
cultural pluralism, 8, 10, 14, 17, 19, 149n8, 157n24; "high cultural pluralism," 8, 10, 93, 107, 143, 150n17; and *The Jew of New York* (Katchor), 128–129; and *Mr. Sammler's Planet* (Bellow), 78; waning of, 17, 19, 78
culture, American, 4, 6–7, 12, 142–143, 146, 150n9, 158n8; American puritan impulse, 104–105; and *Autobiography* (Jones), 50; and diaspora, 121, 129, 132; and *Her First American* (Segal), 52–56, 58; and Holocaust/Holocaust literature, 62–68, 75, 78, 84–85, 156n8; and *The Human Stain* (Roth), 98–99, 104–105, 107; and *Intermarriage* (Gordon), 42–44; and interracial romances/marriages, 42–44, 46, 50,

52–56; and "The Jewbird" (Malamud), 36; and *The Jew of New York* (Katchor), 121, 129; and the literary canon, 93–95, 98–99, 104–105, 107; and "A Mercenary" (Ozick), 67–68, 78; and *Mr. Sammler's Planet* (Bellow), 68, 78, 84–85, 158n8; and "naturals," 58, 98; and white ethnic revivalism, 64–65; and "Writing About Jews" (Roth), 95; and *The Yiddish Policemen's Union* (Chabon), 121, 132; and *Your Face in Mine* (Row), 142–143
culture wars, 12, 90–91, 107, 109, 121, 160n25; and *The Human Stain* (Roth), 4, 93, 141; and *The Tenants* (Malamud), 38. *See also* canon, literary

Dangling Man (Bellow), 84
daughters, Jewish, 59, 84, 88–89
Davis, Philip, 23, 35
de Certeau, Michel, 132–133, 161n34
Deleuze, Gilles, 110
Deresiewicz, William, 137
descent, 10, 105–106
desegregation, school, 4, 15–17, 40, 151n1
The Diary of Anne Frank, 155n4
diaspora, 12–14, 19, 63–64, 109–138, 160nn7–8; and *Adventures in Yiddishland* (Shandler), 121–122, 124; and "Diaspora" (Boyarin and Boyarin), 117–119; *diasporism* as concept, 111–112; as feminine, 113; and "First Diasporist Manifesto" (Kitaj), 111; and "Guidebook to a Land of Ghosts" (Chabon), 121–122; and Israel, 109–117, 119–122, 125–127, 130–131, 135–137; and *The Jew of New York* (Katchor), 13, 119–132; and *Munich* (film), 109–117, 119–120, 134, 137; and *Nationalism and History* (Dubnow), 118; and New York City, 114, 116, 119, 122–130; and *Operation Shylock* (Roth), 111, 119; and supranational geography, 111–112, 118; and *The Tenants* (Malamud), 37; and *The Yiddish Policemen's Union* (Chabon), 4, 13, 119–121, 130–138
diasporic studies, 11
Dickstein, Morris, 7, 40
difference, racial/ethnic, 3–8, 10, 12–14, 17–19, 90, 109, 142–143, 147; and *Call It Sleep* (Roth), 52; and diaspora, 109, 112–113, 117, 120–121, 126–128, and "Diaspora" (Boyarin and Boyarin), 117; and *Her First American* (Segal), 55; and Holocaust/Holocaust literature, 62, 64–67, 78, 82, 85–86, 157n24; and *How I Became Hettie Jones* (Jones), 48–49, 51–52;

difference, racial/ethnic (*continued*)
and *The Human Stain* (Roth), 96, 98–100, 103, 107; and interracial romances/marriages, 44–45, 48–49, 51–52, 55, 60; and the Irish, 64; and "The Jewbird" (Malamud), 36; and Jewish exceptionalism, 141; and *The Jew of New York* (Katchor), 13, 121, 126–128; and the literary canon, 91–92, 94, 96, 98–100, 103, 107; and "The Melting Pot" (Schwartz), 60; and *The Melting Pot* (Zangwill), 58; and "A Mercenary" (Ozick), 78; and *Mr. Sammler's Planet* (Bellow), 82, 85; and *Munich* (film), 109, 112–113; and "Negroes Are Anti-Semitic Because They're Anti-White" (Baldwin), 18; and neoconservatism, 11, 82; and "Reflections on Little Rock" (Arendt), 17; and *The Tenants* (Malamud), 21, 25, 29–31, 34, 36–38; and *To Jerusalem and Back* (Bellow), 86; waning of, 109, 112; and *The Yiddish Policemen's Union* (Chabon), 121; and *Your Face in Mine* (Row), 142–143; and *Zelig* (film), 2–3, 5–6
digital age, 142, 144–147
Diner, Hasia, 62, 129, 161n30; *We Remember with Reverence and Love*, 155n1
disasters, "American," 67, 156n13
Dissent, 15–16, 151n1
Django Unchained (film), 156n13
drag, racial, 4, 13, 72; Jewish drag, 72
Drake, St. Claire, 57
Dreyfus, Alfred, 2
Dubin's Lives (Malamud), 35
Dubnow, Simon, 118
dystopias, racial, 12, 27, 40; and *Mr. Sammler's Planet* (Bellow), 89, 158n8; and *Super Sad True Love Story* (Shteyngart), 146; and *The Tenants* (Malamud), 158n8

Edwards, Jonathan, 47
Egypt, 56, 65, 156n6
Eisner, Will, 129
"Eli, the Fanatic" (Roth), 158n9
Eliot, T. S., "Tradition and the Individual Talent," 32
Ellis Island, 65, 140
Ellison, Ralph, 15, 17–18, 28, 83, 152n11, 153n33; *Invisible Man*, 17, 83, 158n31; *Juneteenth*, 158n31; as "race man," 17–18; "The World and the Jug," 17
Emancipation, 90, 158n1
embodiment, racial/ethnic, 17; and diaspora, 113, 117–118, 122, 124–126, 129, 131, 136–137; disembodiment, 27, 104; embodied voice, 8–10, 27; and *Her First American* (Segal), 54; and *The Human Stain* (Roth), 95, 102, 104, 107, 117; and *The Jew of New York* (Katchor), 13, 122, 124–126, 129; and *Mr. Sammler's Planet* (Bellow), 83, 88–89; and *Munich* (film), 113; and *The Tenants* (Malamud), 27–28, 30, 33, 37–38; and *The Yiddish Policemen's Union* (Chabon), 4, 131, 136–137; and *Zelig* (film), 2, 5
empathic imagination, 16, 25, 37, 53, 147
"emplacement," 137–138
endogamy, 92, 113, 117
Englander, Nathan, 77; *What We Talk about When We Talk about Anne Frank*, 157n22
Enlightenment, 11, 78, 84, 90–92, 110, 158n1, 158n5
"Envy; or, Yiddish in America" (Ozick), 73
"Epstein" (Roth), 158n9
Esperanto, 132
essentialism, 11–12, 151n21, 153n35; essential Jewishness, 88; and *The Human Stain* (Roth), 97–98, 106; and "A Mercenary" (Ozick), 69–71; and *Mr. Sammler's Planet* (Bellow), 88; and "one-drop rule," 97; racial essentialism, 11–12, 69–71, 97–98, 106; strategic essentialism, 35–36; and *The Tenants* (Malamud), 30, 35–36; and *Your Face in Mine* (Row), 143; and *Zelig* (film), 2
ethical issues, 4, 147; and *Amerika* (Kafka), 50; and blackface, 149n4; and "Can the Subaltern Speak?" (Spivak), 7–8, 60; and diaspora, 120, 126, 134–135, 137; ethics of appropriation, 73; ethics of occupation, 87–88; ethics of passing, 103, 106; ethics of power imbalance, 7–8; ethics of recognition, 55; ethics of speaking for and about others, 69; ethics of ventriloquism, 19–20, 27, 50; and *Her First American* (Segal), 55; and Holocaust/Holocaust literature, 66–67, 69–70, 76, 87–88, 156n12; and *The Human Stain* (Roth), 103, 106; and Jewish exceptionalism, 139–140; and *The Jew of New York* (Katchor), 126; and "A Mercenary" (Ozick), 69–70, 76; and moral relativism, 89; and *The Tenants* (Malamud), 27; and *To Jerusalem and Back* (Bellow), 87–88; and *The Yiddish Policemen's Union* (Chabon), 134–135, 137
ethnicity, 5, 10, 149n8, 150n10, 150n16, 150n19, 151n23, 154n7; and *Amerika* (Kafka), 50; and *Call It Sleep* (Roth), 52; and diaspora, 111, 124, 126–129; ethnic "impersonation," 71; ethnic Jewishness,

47, 49, 56, 65; and *Her First American* (Segal), 55–56; and Holocaust/Holocaust literature, 63–66, 71, 74, 79, 87–88, 156n10, 157n24; and *How I Became Hettie Jones* (Jones), 48–50, 154n13; and *The Human Stain* (Roth), 93, 96, 100–101, 103, 105–107; "interethnic imagination," 107; and *Intermarriage* (Gordon), 43; and interracial romances/marriages, 43–50, 55–56, 59–61, 154n13; and *The Jew of New York* (Katchor), 124, 126–129; and the literary canon, 93–96, 100–101, 103, 105–108; and "The Melting Pot" (Schwartz), 59–60; and "A Mercenary" (Ozick), 71, 74; and *Mr. Sammler's Planet* (Bellow), 79; and Ocean Hill–Brownsville school crisis (1968), 19, 39–40; and *Operation Shylock* (Roth), 111; panethnicism, 79; and *The Plot against America* (Roth), 96–97; and *Super Sad True Love Story* (Shteyngart), 146; "symbolic ethnicity," 65, 156n10; and *The Tenants* (Malamud), 22, 31, 153n38; and *To Jerusalem and Back* (Bellow), 87–88; whitening of, 22, 39, 48, 55, 64–66, 95–97, 154n13; and *Your Face in Mine* (Row), 142–143
eugenics/eugenicists, 44–45
Europe/Europeans, 18; and diaspora, 111, 113–116, 120–121, 127, 133; and Enlightenment, 11, 78, 84, 90–92, 110, 158n1, 158n5; European Jewry, 16, 22, 36, 64, 66, 88, 97, 120–121, 130–131, 133, 151n6; European nation-states, 91–92, 158n4; and *Her First American* (Segal), 52–56; and Holocaust/Holocaust literature, 16, 36, 64, 66–67, 69–71, 73, 78, 88, 97, 140; and *The Human Stain* (Roth), 97; and *The Jew of New York* (Katchor), 127; and "A Mercenary" (Ozick), 69–71; "the mind of Europe," 32; and *Mr. Sammler's Planet* (Bellow), 78, 88; and *Munich* (film), 113–116; and Nazi-era racial policies, 53–54, 70–71; and *Operation Shylock* (Roth), 111; and *The Painted Bird* (Kosinski), 73; and *Super Sad True Love Story* (Shteyngart), 146; and *The Yiddish Policemen's Union* (Chabon), 130–131, 133. *See also* German Jews
Everyman, 7, 16–17, 151n9
exceptionalism, American, 7, 14, 64, 140–141
exceptionalism, Jewish, 7, 14, 135, 139–141, 160n8; and *Her First American* (Segal), 56; Holocaust exceptionalism, 77, 156n12; and "Reflections on Little Rock" (Arendt), 4, 16
exile, 14, 160n13; and Arendt, 4; and "Diaspora" (Boyarin and Boyarin), 117, 119;

exilic literary production, 111; feminized exile, 113; and "First Diasporist Manifesto" (Kitaj), 111; and *The Flame Alphabet* (Marcus), 162n5; and *The Jew of New York* (Katchor), 120–121; and "A Mercenary" (Ozick), 77; and *Munich* (film), 113–116; and *Nationalism and History* (Dubnow), 118; and *The Yiddish Policemen's Union* (Chabon), 120–121, 131–132, 134, 136–138, 161n39. *See also* diaspora
Exodus narrative, 56, 117–118, 155n24
exogamy, 46, 154nn7–8

Facebook, 144, 147
family: and *Call It Sleep* (Roth), 52; and diaspora, 110, 112–116, 118, 122, 134–135, 137, 160n6; and "Diaspora" (Boyarin and Boyarin), 118; family planning, 93; and Le Group (in *Munich*), 113–114; and *Her First American* (Segal), 56; and Holocaust/Holocaust literature, 71, 88–89; and *How I Became Hettie Jones* (Jones), 49, 52; and *The Human Stain* (Roth), 97, 99–100, 103, 106; and "The Jewbird" (Malamud), 36; and Jewish women writers, 49, 52, 56, 59; and Katchor's comic strips, 122; and the literary canon, 95, 97, 99–100, 103, 106; and "The Melting Pot" (Schwartz), 59; and "A Mercenary" (Ozick), 71; and *Mr. Sammler's Planet* (Bellow), 88–89; and *Munich* (film), 110, 112–116, 160n11, 160nn14–15; and *The Yiddish Policemen's Union* (Chabon), 134–135, 137; and *Your Face in Mine* (Row), 142; and *Zelig* (film), 2. *See also* children
Fanon, Frantz, 157n27
fascism, 16, 92, 96. *See also* Nazis
Fear of Flying (Jong), 45
femininity, 49, 51, 112–113
feminism, 63, 95; and *The Human Stain* (Roth), 101, 103–104
Ferris, Joshua, 144–146
Fiedler, Leslie, 22, 154nn8–9; *Love and Death in the American Novel*, 46, 154n8
Flanzbaum, Hilene, 64; *The Americanization of the Holocaust*, 156n8
Forward, 122, 160n21
France, 2, 113–114, 149n2
Franco, Dean, 53, 55, 57, 68, 154n6
Frank, Anne, 67, 73, 155n4
Frankfurt school, 92
Franklin, Benjamin, 129
Freedman, Jonathan, 5, 140, 151n5; *Klezmer America*, 149n7, 150n10, 161n28
Freedman, Samuel G., 126; *Jew vs. Jew*, 141

French Revolution, 92, 158n1
frontier, U.S., 54, 132, 136
Furman, Andrew, 94
The Future of the Moon. See *Mr. Sammler's Planet* (Bellow)

Galchinsky, Michael, 91, 158n3
galut, 113–115, 119; geulah/galut, 111
Gates, Henry Louis, "The Passing of Anatole Broyard," 105
Gaza, 109, 156n6; Gaza freedom flotilla, 135, 139
gender identity, 5, 9, 62, 142–143, 150n11, 159n14; and "black man," 152n15; and diaspora, 112–114, 119, 160nn9–10; gender dysphoria, 142; gender reassignment procedures, 142; and *Her First American* (Segal), 53; and *How I Became Hettie Jones* (Jones), 50, 155n17; and Jewish women writers, 41, 46, 50, 53, 60; and the literary canon, 94, 98; and "The Melting Pot" (Schwartz), 60; and *Munich* (film), 112–114; and "My Negro Problem—and Ours" (Podhoretz), 80–81; and *The Tenants* (Malamud), 153n38; and *Your Face in Mine* (Row), 142–143
genealogies, literary/racial, 12, 21–22; and diaspora, 110, 112, 116–119, 134, 160n17; and "Diaspora" (Boyarin and Boyarin), 117–119; and *The Human Stain* (Roth), 97, 101–102, 105; and the literary canon, 93–94, 97, 101–102, 105; and *Munich* (film), 110, 112, 116–117; and *Nationalism and History* (Dubnow), 118; and *Passing* (Larsen), 97; and *The Tenants* (Malamud), 33; and *The Yiddish Policemen's Union* (Chabon), 134
Gênet, Jean, 80
genetics, 10, 59, 97
genocide, 55, 63–64, 67, 78, 140, 161n26. See also Holocaust/Holocaust literature
German Jews, 15–16, 56, 90, 92, 143; and *Munich* (film), 114; and *Wissenschaft des Judentums*, 90, 92, 110, 158n7; and *The Yiddish Policemen's Union* (Chabon), 131
ghettoes, 7, 34, 66, 129, 133; "ghetto stoop," 124
Gilroy, Paul, 11, 155n24
Ginsberg, Allen, 154n11
Glazer, Nathan, 64
Goebbels, Paul Joseph, 76
Goffman, Ethan, 83–84
Gold, Mike, 7
Goodbye, Columbus (Roth), 51, 95–96, 158n9
Gordon, Albert I., 51; *Intermarriage—Interfaith, Interracial, Interethnic*, 42–46, 154n1

Great Depression, 83
Greece, 115, 160n13
Green, Al, 115–116
Greenlee, Sam, 159n18
Griffin, John Howard, 159n13
Guattari, Félix, 110
"Guidebook to a Land of Ghosts" (Chabon), 121–122, 132; illustrations of, 122

Halakhic proscription, 87
Haley, Alex, *Roots*, 65; television adaptation, 65
Hall, Stuart, 11, 119
Harlem, 27–29, 152n15; *Harlem Herald*, 155n25; Harlem Renaissance, 99, 105
Harper's, 121–122, 132
Harrison-Kahan, Lori, 2, 99, 142, 149n4
Hasidim, 86–87, 133–134, 136–137
Hawthorne, Nathaniel, 130
Hebrew language: and "Guidebook to a Land of Ghosts" (Chabon), 122; and *The Jew of New York* (Katchor), 123–124, 127; and *Mr. Sammler's Planet* (Bellow), 88; and *Munich* (film), 114; and *The Tenants* (Malamud), 35; and *Wissenschaft des Judentums*, 92; and *The Yiddish Policemen's Union* (Chabon), 131; and *Zelig* (film), 2
Heilbrunn, Jacob, 150n14
Hemingway, Ernest, 83
Henderson the Rain King (Bellow), 83, 157n26
Herder, Johann von, 110, 160n6
Her First American (Segal), 45–46, 52–59, 154n6, 155nn19–22, 155nn25–26; and "color-blindness," 54, 58; and naming, importance of, 52–53, 55, 58
Hersey, John, 155n4; *The Wall*, 63, 66
Herskovits, Melville, 83
Herzl, Theodor, 113, 132
Herzog (Bellow), 84, 157n26
Heschel, Susannah, 91, 158n3, 158n7
high art, 27, 29–32
hip hop scene, 27, 143
historical romance, 130, 161n31
Hitler, Adolf, 36, 54, 92
Holocaust/Holocaust literature, 8, 11, 13, 16, 19, 44, 61, 62–89, 154n5, 155nn3–4, 158n10; and diaspora, 114–115, 131–132; and era of memorialization, 64; and *Her First American* (Segal), 54–56, 62, 155n23; Holocaust boom, 66–67; Holocaust consciousness, 62–63, 155n1, 156n14; Holocaust exceptionalism, 77; Holocaust as Jewish/American tragedy, 84; Holocaust remembrance, 78;

INDEX

Holocaust survivors, 55, 67–71, 74–75, 80, 83–85, 88–89, 156n12; and "The Jewbird" (Malamud), 36; and "Levitation" (Ozick), 156n19; and "A Mercenary" (Ozick), 13, 67–78, 156n19; and *Mr. Sammler's Planet* (Bellow), 12, 58, 67–68, 69, 77–89, 156n15; and *Munich* (film), 114–115; and "never again," 63; post-Holocaust, 13, 16, 69, 71, 74, 139–140; and "Reflections on Little Rock" (Arendt), 16; and "The Shawl" (Ozick), 68, 88–89; and *Sophie's Choice* (Styron), 9; and *To Jerusalem and Back* (Bellow), 78, 82–83, 85–88; and unspeakability, 67; and *The Yiddish Policemen's Union* (Chabon), 131–132

Holocaust miniseries (1978), 65

home/homelessness: and *Adventures in Yiddishland* (Shandler), 121–122; and *Call It Sleep* (Roth), 52; and diaspora, 13, 63, 110–112, 114–116, 119–123, 126, 128–129, 131, 133, 137–138; and "First Diasporist Manifesto" (Kitaj), 111; and "Guidebook to a Land of Ghosts" (Chabon), 121–122; and *Her First American* (Segal), 52; and Holocaust/Holocaust literature, 63, 79, 81, 86; and homeland, 13, 112, 115, 119–121, 126, 128, 133; and *How I Became Hettie Jones* (Jones), 49, 52; and *The Human Stain* (Roth), 97; and "The Jewbird" (Malamud), 36; and Jewish "home," 43; and Jewish women writers, 49, 52; and *The Jew of New York* (Katchor), 120–121, 123, 126, 128–129; and *Mr. Sammler's Planet* (Bellow), 79, 81; and *Munich* (film), 112, 114–116, 119–120; and *To Jerusalem and Back* (Bellow), 86; and *The Yiddish Policemen's Union* (Chabon), 120–121, 131, 133, 137–138

Homer, 86, 101

hooks, bell, 154n15

Horkheimer, Max, 92

Hotzeplotz. See *The Yiddish Policemen's Union* (Chabon)

The House of the Seven Gables (Hawthorne), 130

Howe, Irving, 17–19, 28, 151n1, 152n11, 160n23; "Black Boys and Native Sons," 17–18; in *Zelig* (film), 1–2, 149n1

How I Became Hettie Jones (Jones), 47–52, 54–60, 141, 154n12, 154nn14–15, 155nn17–18

Howl (Ginsberg), 154n11

humanism, 7, 19; and Bellow, 84, 86–87; and Homer, 86; and *The Human Stain* (Roth), 93, 98, 101–102, 105; and the literary canon, 93, 98, 101–102, 105; and *Munich* (film), 110; and *The Tenants* (Malamud), 29–30, 38

The Human Stain (Roth), 4, 93, 95–108, 117, 125, 127, 141, 145, 159nn15–16, 159nn18–21; and center/periphery, 100, 159n15; and "color-blindness," 102; and orphaned crow, 100–101; and passing, 4, 93, 97–106, 159nn11–12; and "spooks," 102, 104, 159n18

Hungerford, Amy, 75

Hunter, James Davison, 93

hybridity, 80, 103, 132, 138

identifications, 3–8, 10–13, 16–17, 19, 147, 150n11; and Arendt, 16–17; cultural identification, 11; ethnic identification, 16, 19, 119; gender identification, 119; and *Her First American* (Segal), 55; and Holocaust/Holocaust literature, 72, 77–78, 83–88; and Howe, 17; and *The Human Stain* (Roth), 105; identification-via-hashtag, 147; and interracial romances/marriages, 44, 48, 55, 60; and Jewish exceptionalism, 141; and Jewish women writers, 48, 55, 60; and *The Jew of New York* (Katchor), 125; and "Literary Blacks and Jews" (Ozick), 37–38; and the literary canon, 91, 105; and "Looking for Mr. Green" (Bellow), 83; and "The Melting Pot" (Schwartz), 60; and "A Mercenary" (Ozick), 72, 77; and *Mr. Sammler's Planet* (Bellow), 78, 83–86, 88; and *Munich* (film), 110, 115; overidentification, 8; racial identifications, 2, 10–13, 17, 19, 48; religious identification, 10–11; and *Shakespeare's Kitchen* (Segal), 155n20; and *The Tenants* (Malamud), 29–30, 34, 37–38, 86; and *To Jerusalem and Back* (Bellow), 87–88; and *To Rise Again at a Decent Hour* (Ferris), 144; transracial identification, 3, 6, 12, 48, 93, 147. *See also* sympathetic identification; *entries beginning with* identity

identity, African, 68, 75–77

identity, African American: and "To Blacks and Jews: Hab Rachmones" (McPherson), 23; and *Her First American* (Segal), 54, 56; and *How I Became Hettie Jones* (Jones), 50, 155n16; and *The Human Stain* (Roth), 97, 99; and interracial romances/marriages, 44, 50, 54, 56; and jazz as black-identified, 50, 155n16; and "one-drop rule," 97; and *The Tenants* (Malamud), 23, 25, 33

identity, Asian American, 143

identity, Israeli, 84–85, 139

identity, Jewish, 1–4, 6–7, 10–13, 16–20, 91, 141–142, 144–147, 150n9, 150n19;

identity, Jewish (*continued*)
and *Adventures in Yiddishland* (Shandler), 121–122; and *American Pastoral* (Roth), 96; and "To Blacks and Jews: Hab Rachmones" (McPherson), 23; and *The Closing of the American Mind* (Bloom), 82; collective identity, 17, 110, 117–118; and diaspora, 12, 110–113, 116–125, 127–128, 130, 132–137; and "Diaspora" (Boyarin and Boyarin), 117–119; and *Her First American* (Segal), 55–56; and Holocaust/Holocaust literature, 62–63, 65–71, 76–78, 82, 84–89; and *How I Became Hettie Jones* (Jones), 47–51; and *The Human Stain* (Roth), 97–100, 105–106; hyphenated American Jewish identity, 10, 94; instability of, 135; and *Intermarriage* (Gordon), 43–44; and interracial romances/marriages, 41, 43–44, 47–52, 55, 59, 61; and "The Jewbird" (Malamud), 36–37; and Jewish exceptionalism, 135, 139–141; and Jewish women writers, 41, 46–52, 55, 59, 61; and *The Jew of New York* (Katchor), 123–125, 127–128, 130; and the literary canon, 90–91, 94–96, 98–100, 105–106; and "The Melting Pot" (Schwartz), 59–60; and "A Mercenary" (Ozick), 67–71, 76–78; and *The Merchant of Venice* (Shakespeare), 154n8; and *Mr. Sammler's Planet* (Bellow), 68, 82, 84–86, 88–89; and *Munich* (film), 110, 112–113, 116–117; and *Nationalism and History* (Dubnow), 118; and *The Painted Bird* (Kosinski), 73; and *Portnoy's Complaint* (Roth), 10; public vs. private, 15, 17, 105–106, 159n22; and "Reflections on Little Rock" (Arendt), 4, 15–17; and *The Tenants* (Malamud), 31, 33–34, 36–37; and *To Jerusalem and Back* (Bellow), 86–87; and *To Rise Again at a Decent Hour* (Ferris), 144–145; and "Writing About Jews" (Roth), 96; "Yankee Jew," 48–49; and Yiddish, 121; and *The Yiddish Policemen's Union* (Chabon), 4, 132–137, 141; and *Zelig* (film), 1–3, 5–6, 149n2
identity, Native American, 4, 128, 136
identity, online, 144–147
identity politics, 7–8, 13, 142, 153n35; and diaspora, 116–117; and Holocaust/Holocaust literature, 62–63, 66, 68–69, 73, 82, 88; and "A Mercenary" (Ozick), 69, 73; and *Mr. Sammler's Planet* (Bellow), 82, 88; and *Munich* (film), 116–117; and *The Tenants* (Malamud), 34–36. *See also* entries beginning with identity

imagined communities, 120–121, 128–129
immigrants, Jewish, 3–4, 7, 10, 137, 151n5; and *Amerika* (Kafka), 50; Ashkenazi Jewish immigrant narrative, 140; and *Call It Sleep* (Roth), 52; ethnic allegiances of, 156n10; and *Her First American* (Segal), 52–54, 155n21; and *How I Became Hettie Jones* (Jones), 47, 50; and *Intermarriage* (Gordon), 43; and Jewish women writers, 47, 50, 52–54, 60; and "the last days of the American empire . . ." (Jones), 22; and *The Tenants* (Malamud), 20, 38; and *The Yiddish Policemen's Union* (Chabon), 133; and *Zelig* (film), 1–2
imperialism, 119
impersonation, 161n39; and *Bech: A Book* (Updike), 72; "cultural impersonation," 68, 72–73; and *The Human Stain* (Roth), 100, 125; and *The Jew of New York* (Katchor), 125–126; and "A Mercenary" (Ozick), 71–73, 75–78; and *The Yiddish Policemen's Union* (Chabon), 135; and *Zelig* (film), 3, 6
imposters, 69, 73, 77–78
Indian Americans, 45, 58–59, 79
indigeneity, 115, 120–122, 135–136, 140. *See also* Native Americans
individualism, 17; American individualist ideology, 5, 149n6; and *Her First American* (Segal), 53; and *The Human Stain* (Roth), 104, 106; and "Reflections on Little Rock" (Arendt), 17; and *The Tenants* (Malamud), 29
Inglourious Basterds (film), 156n13
intellectuals, African American, 6, 17–18; and "To Blacks and Jews: Hab Rachmones" (McPherson), 23; and *The Human Stain* (Roth), 104–105; and identity politics, 63; and *Other People's Houses* (Segal), 57; and *The Tenants* (Malamud), 23
intellectuals, European, 4, 15–17
intellectuals, Jewish American, 4, 8, 13–19, 144, 147, 150n14; and "To Blacks and Jews: Hab Rachmones" (McPherson), 22–23; and *Her First American* (Segal), 55–56; and Holocaust/Holocaust literature, 68, 73, 82–84, 86; and *The Human Stain* (Roth), 93, 97, 100–102, 105–106; and Jewish exceptionalism, 141; and *The Jew of New York* (Katchor), 126; and the literary canon, 91, 94–95, 97, 100–102, 105–106, 158n3; and *Mr. Sammler's Planet* (Bellow), 78, 82–84, 158n8; and neoconservatism, 82, 157n21; and Ozick, 68, 73; and *The*

Tenants (Malamud), 23, 37–38, 158n8; and *To Jerusalem and Back* (Bellow), 86; and *Zelig* (film), 1–3. *See also* names of Jewish intellectuals
interfaith romances/marriages, 41–46, 61
interiority, 10, 18, 47
intermarriage, Jewish, 4, 42–45, 58, 61, 151n10, 154n5, 154n8. *See also* interfaith marriages; interracial romances/marriages
Internet, 144–147
interracial fantasies, 3–4, 12, 19, 33–34
interracial romances/marriages, 4, 41–61; and Arendt, 151n10; decriminalization of, 33, 63; and *Her First American* (Segal), 45–46, 52–59; and *How I Became Hettie Jones* (Jones), 47–52, 54–59, 141; and *The Human Stain* (Roth), 97; and *Intermarriage* (Gordon), 42–45; and Jewish women writers, 41, 47–61; and *Loving v. Virginia*, 33, 41–46, 48, 51–52, 55–56, 63; and "The Melting Pot" (Schwartz), 45, 58–59; and *The Tenants* (Malamud), 33–34, 44; and "vanishing of the American Jew," 43–45; and *Zelig* (film), 5
Invisible Man (Ellison), 17, 83, 158n31
Iraq War, 156n12
Ireland, Northern, 64
Irish, 49, 64
Israel, 7–8, 10, 12–13, 19; and *Adventures in Yiddishland* (Shandler), 121–122; Arab citizens of, 85–86; attack on Gaza freedom flotilla, 135, 139; boycott/divestment from, 109; and diaspora, 109–117, 119–122, 125–127, 130–131, 135–137, 160n7; fears of second Holocaust in, 78, 85–87, 114–115, 136; and *Her First American* (Segal), 54–56; and Holocaust/Holocaust literature, 63–65, 72, 76, 78, 84–89; and *The Holy Land in Transit* (Salaita), 109, 159n1; Israeli war heroes, 112; and Jewish exceptionalism, 139–141; and *The Jew of New York* (Katchor), 120–121, 125–127; Lost Tribes of, 125–127, 140; and "A Mercenary" (Ozick), 72, 76; and Mossad, 110, 112; and *Mr. Sammler's Planet* (Bellow), 84–87, 89, 120, 158n34; and *Munich* (film), 109–117, 159nn2–4, 160n15; and Munich massacre, 109–110, 112, 116, 159n2, 160n15; and "never again," 63; and *Operation Shylock* (Roth), 111; and Six Day War, 12, 19, 63–65, 78, 85–87, 89, 114, 117, 120, 154n5, 156n6, 158n34; and soil from Holy Land, 127; and *To Jerusalem and Back* (Bellow), 78, 85–88; war of independence, 112–113; and

The Yiddish Policemen's Union (Chabon), 4, 120–121, 130–131, 135–137; Yom Kippur War, 63
Italians, 22, 49, 83
Itzkovitz, Daniel, 19, 77, 98, 149n6, 159n13

Jacobson, Matthew Frye, 64, 156n10
James, Henry, 7, 9, 20, 56
Japan: Japanese American Citizens' League, 42; Japanese terrorists, 76–77
jazz, 50, 155n16
The Jazz Singer (film), 3
Jen, Gish, 94
Jerusalem, 76, 85–86, 127–128, 156n6; Temple in, 134, 136–137
Jeter, Mildred (Mildred Loving), 41–42
"The Jewbird" (Malamud), 36
Jewish literature, 11, 90–92; and diaspora, 110–111, 117. *See also* American literature; canon, literary
Jewishness, 2–5, 15–17, 19, 142–146, 150nn9–11, 162n3; ambivalent valences of, 45; and *American Pastoral* (Roth), 159n11; and *Bech: A Book* (Updike), 71–72; deracialization of, 105–106; and diaspora, 110, 112–115, 117–118, 124–125, 134–136; and "Diaspora" (Boyarin and Boyarin), 117–118; echt-Jewishness, 115; essential Jewishness, 88; ethnic Jewishness, 47, 49, 56, 65; and *The Flame Alphabet* (Marcus), 162n5; and *Her First American* (Segal), 52–56; and Holocaust/Holocaust literature, 63, 65–66, 69, 71–73, 86–89, 158n10; and *How I Became Hettie Jones* (Jones), 47–51, 154n13, 155n17; and *The Human Stain* (Roth), 98–100, 105–106; and *Intermarriage* (Gordon), 42–45; and interracial romances/marriages, 42–56, 59, 61, 154n13; and "The Jewbird" (Malamud), 36; and Jewish exceptionalism, 141; and Jewish women writers, 4, 45–56, 59, 61, 154n13; and *The Jew of New York* (Katchor), 124–125; and the literary canon, 90, 98–100, 105–106, 109; and *Loving v. Virginia*, 42, 45; matrilineal Jewishness, 10, 59, 113, 118, 155n27; and "The Melting Pot" (Schwartz), 59; and "A Mercenary" (Ozick), 69, 71–73; and *The Merchant of Venice* (Shakespeare), 154n8; and *Minor Characters* (Johnson), 47–48; move from American Jew to Jewish American, 86–87; and *Mr. Sammler's Planet* (Bellow), 83, 88–89; and *Munich* (film), 110, 113–115, 117; and *Nationalism and History* (Dubnow), 118; and passing, 2, 51, 99–100, 142–143;

Jewishness (*continued*)
political Jewishness, 72–73, 87; and queerness, 14, 151n24; and "Reflections on Little Rock" (Arendt), 15–17, 151n4; secular Jewishness, 6, 19, 49, 65, 72, 86–87, 112, 150n11; and *Super Sad True Love Story* (Shteyngart), 146; and *The Tenants* (Malamud), 20–21, 24, 29, 31–33, 35; and *To Jerusalem and Back* (Bellow), 86–87; and *To Rise Again at a Decent Hour* (Ferris), 144–145; waning of, 109, 112, 120; and *Witz* (Cohen), 162n4; and *The Yiddish Policemen's Union* (Chabon), 134–136; and *Your Face in Mine* (Row), 142–143; and *Zelig* (film), 2–3, 5, 149n3
Jewish Question, 11, 18, 90, 116–117, 158n4
Jewish Theological Seminary, 42
The Jew of New York (Katchor), 13, 119–132, 160n21, 161n26; and burial soil from Holy Land, 123, 127; failure at center of, 123, 125, 127–128, 131; as graphic novel, 122, 124–126; and New Jerusalem, 122, 127–128; and paper dolls, 123; and play within the novel, 123–124, 127, 129
Jim Crow South, 96
Johnson, James Weldon, 97, 99, 101
Johnson, Joyce, *Minor Characters*, 47–48, 154n12
Jolson, Al, 3–4
Jones, Hettie Cohen, 4, 45–52, 96, 147, 153n34, 154n11; "dark" appearance of, 48–49, 154n14; *How I Became Hettie Jones*, 47–52, 54–60, 141, 154n12, 154nn14–15, 155nn17–18
Jones, LeRoi, 13, 18–19, 154n11; *Autobiography*, 49–50, 154n14; "Black Art," 18–19, 32; *Blues People*, 155n16; and *How I Became Hettie Jones* (Jones), 47–51, 154n14; *The Slave*, 50; and *The Tenants* (Malamud), 21–22, 24, 29, 32, 38, 153n34. *See also* Baraka, Amiri
Jones, Lisa, 51

Kafka, Franz, 7, 50
Kallen, Horace, 128
Kaplan, Brett Ashley, 105
Katchor, Ben, 13, 112; comic strips of, 122, 129, 160n22; as illustrator of "Guidebook to a Land of Ghosts," 122; *The Jew of New York*, 13, 119–132, 160n21, 161n26
Kazin, Alfred, "Jews," 83, 157n21
Kellman, Steven G., 20, 152n22
Kennedy, Ruby Jo Reeves, 154n1
Kerouac, Jack, 47, 154n11
kibbutz, 113–114

Kindertransport, 57
King Lear (Shakespeare), 20–21
Kirsch, Adam, 156n19
Kitaj, R. B., "First Diasporist Manifesto," 111
Kolb, Harold, 94
kosher laws, 49, 56, 87, 117, 135
Kosinski, Jerzy, 68–69, 73, 75; and plagiarizing, 73
Kramer, Michael, 90–91
Kristol, Irving, 157n30
Kushner, Tony, 109–113, 115–117, 119–120

Lackritz, Andrew, 16
Lambert, Joshua, 142
land/landlessness, 120, 136–137, 156n18; and *Adventures in Yiddishland* (Shandler), 121–122; and autochthony, Jewish, 115–118; and diaspora, 110, 112, 115–122, 126, 128–131, 133–134, 136–138, 160n16; and "Diaspora" (Boyarin and Boyarin), 117–118; and homeland, 13, 112, 115, 119–121, 126, 128, 133; and *The Jew of New York* (Katchor), 120–121, 126, 128–129; and *King Lear* (Shakespeare), 21; and the literary canon, 91, 96; and mobile economic practices, 70, 156n18; and *Munich* (film), 115–117, 137; and *The Plot against America* (Roth), 96; and Promised Land, 111–113, 116–117, 122, 130–131, 134, 136–137; and *The Yiddish Policemen's Union* (Chabon), 120–121, 130–131, 133–134, 136–138
landlords, Jewish, 18, 152n12; and *The Tenants* (Malamud), 20, 22–23, 28, 34, 152n15
Landslayt (inhabitants of same geographic region), 132
Landsmanschaften, 133
Larsen, Nella, 97, 99, 101
"Let's Stay Together" (song), 115–116
Levi, Primo, 62, 66, 155n3
Lewinsky, Monica, 105
liberals/liberalism, 15, 17–19, 92; and "Black Art" (Jones), 18, 32; and Holocaust/Holocaust literature, 80, 82–83, 86, 157n24; and interracial marriages, 44; liberal imagination, 39; and *Mr. Sammler's Planet* (Bellow), 82–83; and "My Negro Problem—and Ours" (Podhoretz), 80; and "Negroes Are Anti-Semitic Because They're Anti-White" (Baldwin), 19; and Ocean Hill–Brownsville school crisis (1968), 19, 39–40; and "Reflections on Little Rock" (Arendt), 15, 151n1; and *The Tenants* (Malamud), 29, 32, 34, 39–40; and *To Jerusalem and Back* (Bellow), 86
liminality, 31, 40, 93, 100

INDEX

Lincoln, Abraham, 132
Lindsay, John, 39
"Literary Blacks and Jews" (Ozick), 37–38, 152n11, 153n39
literary history, Jewish, 6, 8–9, 12, 90–93; and *The Human Stain* (Roth), 97, 101, 106–107; and *The Tenants* (Malamud), 22, 26, 38. *See also* canon, literary
Little Rock (Ark.), 4, 15–17, 40, 151n10
Liu, Eric, 127, 140, 149n7
"Long Road" (song), 25–27, 152n24
Lott, Eric, 13
Loving, Richard, 41–42
Loving v. Virginia, 33, 41–46, 48, 51–52, 55–56, 63; pre-*Loving*, 46, 48, 52, 55–56
Lowe, Lisa, 11
Luftschaefte (unproductive business), 113

Madsen, Deborah, 140
magical realism, 22, 39, 136, 156n19
"The Magic Barrel" (Malamud), 36, 38
Magid, Shaul, 111, 160n7
Mailer, Norman, 71–72, 95
Malamud, Ann, 152n25
Malamud, Bernard, 12–13, 17, 19, 20–40, 83, 147; "The Angel Levine," 34, 83; arrogance of, 22; *The Assistant*, 25, 36, 38; "Black Is My Favorite Color," 34, 83; death of, 23; and diaspora, 120; *Dubin's Lives*, 35; and Holocaust/Holocaust literature, 65–68, 71–73, 75; impudence/impotence of, 38; "The Jewbird," 36; "The Last Mohican," 38; and the literary canon, 94, 96, 104, 107; and magical realism, 22, 39; "The Magic Barrel," 36, 38; and McPherson correspondence, 22–25, 28, 58, 68, 72, 153n31; *The People*, 153n36; *The Tenants*, 12–13, 20–40, 44, 46, 53, 56–58, 65, 67–69, 75, 78, 81, 86, 120, 124, 141, 152nn15–16, 152n22, 152n24, 153nn27–29, 153n32–34, 158n8
Malamud, Paul, 21, 152n17
Malcolm X, 21, 26
Marcus, Ben, *The Flame Alphabet*, 162n5
marginalization, 12–13, 19; and diaspora, 122, 127; and "First Diasporist Manifesto" (Kitaj), 111; and Holocaust/Holocaust literature, 64, 83–84, 87–88; and *How I Became Hettie Jones* (Jones), 47; and interracial marriages, 44, 47; and *The Jew of New York* (Katchor), 127; and the literary canon, 94, 107; and *Mr. Sammler's Planet* (Bellow), 83–84; and Ocean Hill–Brownsville school crisis (1968), 19, 39–40; and *The Tenants* (Malamud), 31; and *To Jerusalem and Back* (Bellow), 87–88; of women in Beat generation, 47
Marjorie Morningstar (Wouk), 50–51
marranos, 71–72, 162n5
Marxists/Marxism, 92, 132
masculinity, 80–81; hypermasculinity, 112; and *Munich* (film), 112–113; and *Muskeljudentum*, 113
masquerade, 60, 72, 93
matrilineal descent, Jewish, 10, 59, 113, 118, 155n27
McGurl, Mark, 8–10, 26, 93, 107, 143–144, 150n15, 150n17, 155n2
McPherson, James A., 22–25, 28, 34, 58, 68, 72, 153n31; "To Blacks and Jews: Hab Rachmones," 22–23; "The Gold Coast," 23
Melnick, Jeffrey, 150n12
melting pot ethos, 3, 12, 18, 58, 128, 140
Melville, Herman, 5–6
memoirs: and *Bulletproof Diva* (Jones), 51; and Holocaust/Holocaust literature, 67–68, 75, 155n3; and *How I Became Hettie Jones* (Jones), 45, 47–51, 54; and "A Mercenary" (Ozick), 75; and *Minor Characters* (Johnson), 47–48; and *The Tenants* (Malamud), 33. *See also* autobiography
memory: collective memory, 66, 159n2; and Holocaust/Holocaust literature, 66, 69, 78, 86, 88; and "A Mercenary" (Ozick), 69; and *Mr. Sammler's Planet* (Bellow), 88; multidirectional memory, 155n23; racial memory, 110; and *The Tenants* (Malamud), 35; and *To Jerusalem and Back* (Bellow), 86; vicarious memories of victimization, 69
mental illness/institutions, 53, 55, 84, 88–89
"A Mercenary" (Ozick), 13, 67–78, 81, 156n19
The Merchant of Venice (Shakespeare), 46, 154n8
MFA programs, 9, 150n15
Michaels, Walter Benn, 96, 149n6
Middle East, 87, 122, 156n6. *See also names of Middle East countries*
Midrash, 111
Mignolo, Walter, 93
mimicry, racial, 30–31, 36, 98, 100
minorities, 92, 127–128; model minorities, 3, 7, 127, 140–141, 149n7
minstrelsy, Jewish: and blackface, 4, 17, 28, 48, 50, 149nn4–5; and "Jewface," 2; and "redface," 17, 149n4; and "yellowface," 17; and *Zelig* (film), 2, 149n4
miscegenation, 15, 33, 47, 96; anti-miscegenation statutes, 41–43, 45
misogyny, 22

Moby-Dick (Melville), 5–6
model minorities, 3, 7, 127, 140–141, 149n7
modernism, 3, 8–10, 149n6, 150nn17–18
modernity: and *The Human Stain* (Roth), 98–99, 107; instability of, 37, 91; and interfaith romances/marriages, 61; and *The Jewish Century* (Slezkine), 69–70; and Jewish *converso*, 61; and *The Jew of New York* (Katchor), 127; and the literary canon, 91–92, 95, 98, 107
Morgan, Thomas, 43
Moynihan, Daniel Patrick, 64
Mr. Sammler's Planet (Bellow), 12, 58, 67–68, 69, 77–89, 120, 156n15, 157n28, 158n5, 158n34; and black thief, 58, 79–88, 157n29; *The Future of the Moon* as original title, 89; and Israeli identity, 84–85; as racial dystopia, 89, 158n8; and voyeurism, 78–79, 85
multiculturalism, 6, 90–95, 121, 158n3, 159n16; and *Caucasia* (Senna), 99; and *The Human Stain* (Roth), 97, 99–107; multicultural canon, 107; post-multicultural era, 91; and *The Tenants* (Malamud), 38; and *Wissenschaft des Judentums*, 90, 92, 158n7
Munich (film), 109–117, 119–120, 134, 137, 159nn2–4, 160n11, 160nn14–15
Muskeljudentum, 113
Muslims, 7, 162n1; "Muslim Question," 88, 158n4

narration: first-person narration, 26, 47, 96; first person plural, 96; and *How I Became Hettie Jones* (Jones), 47; and *The Human Stain* (Roth), 106–107; "interracial narrative," 106–107; and *The Jew of New York* (Katchor), 124; and "The Melting Pot" (Schwartz), 60; and "A Mercenary" (Ozick), 70–71, 75; narrative impersonality, 9–10, 32; and omniscient narrator, 133; and point of view, 124; and reliable narrators, 75; and tense switching, 47, 70; third-person narration, 47, 60
nationalisms, racial, 7, 22, 64, 90–92; and diaspora, 110–113, 115–120, 129–130, 132, 137, 160n6; and "Diaspora" (Boyarin and Boyarin), 117–118; and *genius loci*, 110; and Jewish exceptionalism, 139–140; and *The Jew of New York* (Katchor), 120, 129–130; and the literary canon, 94–95; and *Munich* (film), 112–113, 115–117, 119; and *Nationalism and History* (Dubnow), 118; and *Operation Shylock* (Roth), 111; and *Volksgeist*, 110, 160n5; and *The Yiddish Policemen's Union* (Chabon), 120, 132, 137
Native Americans, 4, 12–13, 26, 149n4; and diaspora, 120–121, 123–128, 130–132, 134–136; and Holocaust/Holocaust literature, 63–64, 82; and *The Holy Land in Transit* (Salaita), 109, 159n1; and interfaith/interracial marriages, 41, 46; Inuit community, 83, 136, 141; and *The Jew of New York* (Katchor), 120–121, 123–128, 161n26; Lenape tribe, 127, 161n26; and *Mr. Sammler's Planet* (Bellow), 82; Native Alaskans, 83, 120–121, 130–132, 134–136, 141; and *The People* (Malamud), 153n36; removal of, 64; Tlingit population, 131, 134–136; and Wounded Knee, occupation of, 63; and *The Yiddish Policemen's Union* (Chabon), 120–121, 130–132, 134–136; and *Your Face in Mine* (Row), 143
Nazis, 53–54, 70–71, 88
Neal, Larry, 18
neoconservatism, 11, 126–127, 157n21; and *Mr. Sammler's Planet* (Bellow), 82–83, 87, 157n30; and Ocean Hill–Brownsville school crisis (1968), 39; roots of, 82, 157n30; and *To Jerusalem and Back* (Bellow), 87
neoliberalism, 140
Newark (N.J.): and *American Pastoral* (Roth), 96; and *Autobiography* (Jones), 154n14; and *How I Became Hettie Jones* (Jones), 49; Newark race riots, 12, 19, 39, 63, 96
New Criticism, 8–10; and narrative impersonality, 9–10, 32; and "Reflections on Little Rock" (Arendt), 17; and *The Tenants* (Malamud), 32; and white male-identified high modernism, 10
New Jersey, 48–49, 96–98
New Left, 39, 63, 82, 150n14
New York, upstate, 122–125, 127, 129
New York City: Broadway, 54, 79, 128; Brooklyn, 19, 27, 34–35, 39–40, 49, 114, 116, 119, 152n25; and Broyard, 104–105; and diaspora, 114, 116, 119, 122–130; East Village, 49; Greenwich Village, 47, 50–51; Harlem, 27–29, 152n15; and *Her First American* (Segal), 52–55, 155n22; Hiram's Museum, 125; Houston Street, 49; and *How I Became Hettie Jones* (Jones), 47–51; Israeli embassy, 116; and "The Jewbird" (Malamud), 36; and *The Jew of New York* (Katchor), 122–130; as jungle, 77, 80, 82, 157n28; and Katchor's comic strips, 122; Katz's delicatessen, 49; Lower East Side,

1, 49, 129, 140, 160n23; map of, 125; and "A Mercenary" (Ozick), 69, 77–78; and *Mr. Sammler's Planet* (Bellow), 78–82, 85, 89, 157n28; and *Munich* (film), 114, 116; and "My Negro Problem—and Ours" (Podhoretz), 80; and Ocean Hill–Brownsville school crisis (1968), 19, 39–40; Queens, 47–51; rent control in, 20; and *The Tenants* (Malamud), 20–21, 27–29, 34–35, 37, 152n15, 152n25; Upper West Side, 79; and *Zelig* (film), 1

New York Times, 25, 29, 104, 135, 139–141, 157n21

Noah, Maj. Mordecai, 119, 122–126, 128–129, 161n29

Noble Savage (literary magazine), 157n26

nomadism, 117–118

Nordau, Max, 113, 132

Norich, Anita, 160n19

North, Michael, 150n18

nostalgia, 3, 94, 122, 129, 146, 160n23

Novick, Peter, 62–63, 65, 155n1, 155n4; *The Holocaust in American Life*, 63

Nuremberg Laws, 117

Ocean Hill–Brownsville school crisis (1968), 19, 39–40, 153n40

Oedipus the King (Sophocles), 101–102; oedipal entanglements, 52

Olympic Games (Munich, 1972), 109–110, 112, 116, 159n2, 160n15

Omer-Sherman, Ranen, 117

Omi, Michael, 11, 64, 151n22

Operation Shylock (Roth), 111, 119

oppression, 9, 16, 18; and diaspora, 119; and *Her First American* (Segal), 55; and "A Mercenary" (Ozick), 69; and "Negroes Are Anti-Semitic Because They're Anti-White" (Baldwin), 18; and "Reflections on Little Rock" (Arendt), 16, 38; and *The Tenants* (Malamud), 21, 29, 34

orality, 10, 26–28, 74–75

Orthodox Jews, 86–87, 133–134, 136–137; ultra-Orthodox Jews, 2, 42, 121

otherness, racial, 4, 8, 10, 13–14, 18, 142–144, 146, 150nn10–11, 162n3; "anguish of the other," 37, 67; and *Arthur Mervyn* (Brown), 46; and *Bech: A Book* (Updike), 71–72; and diaspora, 111, 115, 120, 126, 134–135, 138; and *Her First American* (Segal), 54; and Holocaust/Holocaust literature, 71–72, 74, 80, 82–83, 86–88; and *How I Became Hettie Jones* (Jones), 52; and *The Human Stain* (Roth), 100, 107; immigrant otherness, 60; and interracial romances/marriages, 44–46, 52, 54; and "The Jewbird" (Malamud), 36; and Jewish exceptionalism, 141; Jewish otherness, 37, 61, 86; and *The Jew of New York* (Katchor), 125–126; and the literary canon, 92, 100, 107; and "The Melting Pot" (Schwartz), 59; and "A Mercenary" (Ozick), 71, 74; and *Mr. Sammler's Planet* (Bellow), 80, 82–83; and *Munich* (film), 115; and *Operation Shylock* (Roth), 111; and other others, 4, 10, 80; others-within, 92, 149n6; and *The Tenants* (Malamud), 25–26, 35–37, 40, 67; and *To Jerusalem and Back* (Bellow), 86–88; and *The Yiddish Policemen's Union* (Chabon), 134–136, 138; and *Your Face in Mine* (Row), 142–143; and *Zelig* (film), 2–3, 5

outsiders, 6–7; and *Her First American* (Segal), 52–53, 56; and *How I Became Hettie Jones* (Jones), 48–51; and *The Human Stain* (Roth), 99–101; and Jewish women writers, 48–53, 56, 59–61; and *The Jew of New York* (Katchor), 129; and the literary canon, 94, 99–101; and "The Melting Pot" (Schwartz), 59; "outsider Jew," 48–51; and *The Yiddish Policemen's Union* (Chabon), 13, 132

Ozick, Cynthia, 13, 37–38, 93, 95–96, 144, 155n4, 156n19, 157nn20–21, 157n24; *Art and Ardor*, 71; and Bellow correspondence, 158n10; *Bloodshed and Three Novellas*, 68; "Cultural Impersonation," 68, 73; "Envy; or, Yiddish in America," 73; and Holocaust/Holocaust literature, 66–78, 158n10; "Levitation," 156n19; "Literary Blacks and Jews," 37–38, 152n11, 153n39; "A Mercenary," 13, 67–78, 81, 156n19, 157n21; *Quarrel and Quandary*, 73; "The Rights of History and the Rights of Imagination," 73; "The Shawl," 68, 88–89; "Usurpation (Other People's Stories)," 73, 157n20; "Who Owns Anne Frank?," 73

Palestine/Palestinians, 65, 82–83, 86–88; and diaspora, 111, 115–116, 120, 123, 126–128, 131, 135–136; and *The Holy Land in Transit* (Salaita), 109, 159n1; and *The Jew of New York* (Katchor), 120, 123, 126–128; and *Munich* (film), 115–116; Second Intifada, 121; and *The Yiddish Policemen's Union* (Chabon), 120, 131, 135–136, 141

Palumbo-Liu, David, 93; *The Ethnic Canon*, 107–108

"Papuans and Zulus" (Bellow), 157n21

particularism, ethnic/racial, 10, 16–17, 19; and "Black Boys and Native Sons" (Howe), 19; and *Diary of Anne Frank*, 155n4; and Holocaust/Holocaust literature, 65–66, 76, 78, 84, 155n4, 157n24; and *The Human Stain* (Roth), 93, 100; and the literary canon, 91–93, 100; and "A Mercenary" (Ozick), 76; and *Mr. Sammler's Planet* (Bellow), 78, 84; and *Munich* (film), 110, 112; and "Reflections on Little Rock" (Arendt), 16–17, 19; and *The Tenants* (Malamud), 29, 31, 37–39

passing, 4, 93, 97–106, 142–143; and *American Pastoral* (Roth), 96, 159n11; and *Autobiography of an Ex-Colored Man* (Johnson), 97, 99, 101; and *Bech: A Book* (Updike), 71–72; and *Black Like Me* (Griffin), 159n13; and Broyard, 104–105, 159n21; and *Caucasia* (Senna), 99; and *Flight* (White), 99; and gender/sexuality, 159n14; and *How I Became Hettie Jones* (Jones), 51; and *The Human Stain* (Roth), 4, 93, 97–106, 159nn11–12, 159n21; Jewishness likened to, 2, 51, 99, 142, 159n11; "lost to one's people," 51, 99–100; and marranos, 71–72, 162n5; and "The Melting Pot" (Schwartz), 59–60; and *Passing* (Larsen), 97, 99, 101; and *Plum Bun* (Fauset), 99; and *Witz* (Cohen), 162n4; and *The Yiddish Policemen's Union* (Chabon), 135; and *Your Face in Mine* (Row), 142–143; and *Zelig* (film), 2

Passing (Larsen), 97, 99, 101

performance, racial, 4, 13, 143; and Broyard, 105; and diaspora, 117, 127; and "Diaspora" (Boyarin and Boyarin), 117; and *The Human Stain* (Roth), 98, 100, 105–106; and *The Jew of New York* (Katchor), 127; and "A Mercenary" (Ozick), 75; "performativity," 98, 105, 117, 143, 150n9; and *The Tenants* (Malamud), 23, 27; and *Zelig* (film), 2–3

The Plot against America (Roth), 96–97, 130–131

Plum Bun (Fauset), 99

Podair, Jerald, 39–40, 153n40

Podhoretz, Norman, 22, 152n25; "My Negro Problem—and Ours," 80–82

Poe, Edgar Allan, 36

Poland, 9, 49; and Holocaust/Holocaust literature, 9, 66–67, 70–71, 73, 75–76, 85, 88–89, 156n14; and "A Mercenary" (Ozick), 70–71, 75–76; and *Mr. Sammler's Planet* (Bellow), 85, 88–89; and *The Painted Bird* (Kosinski), 73; and *Sophie's Choice* (Styron), 9, 67, 156n14; Warsaw ghetto uprising, 66; workers' movement, 64

politics, 12–14, 18; and "Black Art" (Jones), 18; and diaspora, 118, 120, 125, 127, 129, 137; of failure/of success, 127; and *Her First American* (Segal), 55–56; and Holocaust/Holocaust literature, 65, 68–74, 77–79, 83, 85–87, 157n21; and *The Human Stain* (Roth), 104; and Jewish exceptionalism, 140–141; and *The Jew of New York* (Katchor), 125, 127, 129; and the literary canon, 91, 93, 104, 107–108; and "A Mercenary" (Ozick), 68–74, 77–78; and *Mr. Sammler's Planet* (Bellow), 68, 79, 83, 85; and Ocean Hill–Brownsville school crisis (1968), 19, 39–40; political correctness, 104, 126; political Jewishness, 72–73, 87; "politically African," 68–70, 72–74; "political territorial" stage of nationalism, 118; "politics of race," 55; and *To Jerusalem and Back* (Bellow), 86–87; and *The Yiddish Policemen's Union* (Chabon), 137; and *Zelig* (film), 3

Portnoy's Complaint (Roth), 8–10, 51, 95–96

Posnock, Ross, 103

postcolonialism, 13, 69–71, 74–76

postmodernism, 10, 13, 61, 150n17, 157n20, 159n3, 161n35; and *The Jew of New York* (Katchor), 124; and the literary canon, 94, 158n8; and *Operation Shylock* (Roth), 111; proto-postmodernism, 32; and *The Tenants* (Malamud), 32, 158n8; and *Zelig* (film), 2–3

poststructuralism, 92, 101

Prell, Riv-Ellen, 155nn17–18; *Fighting to Become Americans*, 155n18

primitivism, 21, 38, 74, 77, 80, 83, 88, 152n16, 157n28

privilege, Jewish, 4, 7, 11–12, 151n6; and Holocaust/Holocaust literature, 64, 69; and "A Mercenary" (Ozick), 69; and *The Tenants* (Malamud), 30–31, 34

progressives, 39, 65, 93, 119, 136, 141. *See also* New Left

Promised Land, 111–113, 116–117, 122, 130–131, 134, 136–137

Proust, Marcel, 35, 83

Puerto Ricans, 49, 53

Puritans, 130, 140; puritan ethos, 104–105

queerness, 14, 151n24

race, 5–6, 8–14, 141–142, 144–147, 149n8, 150n10, 150n16; and *American Pastoral*

INDEX   191

(Roth), 96; and *Amerika* (Kafka), 50;
biologically defined race, 11, 126; and
black-white binary, 42, 48, 51, 55, 79; and
Broyard, 104–105; and *The Confessions
of Nat Turner* (Styron), 9, 61, 67; critical
race theorists, 11, 150n16; deracialization of Jews, 105–106; and diaspora, 110,
112–113, 117–120, 124–126, 128, 134–135, 137,
160n17; and "Diaspora" (Boyarin and
Boyarin), 117–119; and *Her First American* (Segal), 52–55, 62; and Holocaust/
Holocaust literature, 44, 62, 64–71, 74,
77–83, 93; and *How I Became Hettie Jones*
(Jones), 47–52, 154n13; and *The Human
Stain* (Roth), 93, 96–107; and *Intermarriage* (Gordon), 42–45; and interracial
romances/marriages, 4, 41–55, 59–61,
154n13; and "The Jewbird" (Malamud),
36; and Jewish exceptionalism, 140–141;
and Jewish women writers, 41, 45–55,
59–61, 154n13; and *The Jew of New York*
(Katchor), 120, 124–126, 128; and the
literary canon, 90–91, 94, 96–108; and
"Looking for Mr. Green" (Bellow), 83;
and "The Melting Pot" (Schwartz), 59–60;
and "A Mercenary" (Ozick), 67–71, 74,
77; and *Moby-Dick* (Melville), 6; and *Mr.
Sammler's Planet* (Bellow), 68, 78–83,
158n8; and *Munich* (film), 110, 112–113,
117; and "My Negro Problem—and Ours"
(Podhoretz), 80–81; and *Nationalism
and History* (Dubnow), 118; and *The Plot
against America* (Roth), 96–97; and postracial age, 142, 146; "The Race Question,"
62; racial formation, 4, 11, 36, 64; racial
phenotype, 135; "racial reassignment
surgery," 142–143; and "Reflections on
Little Rock" (Arendt), 4, 15–16; strategic
reracialization, 25, 34, 66; and *Super Sad
True Love Story* (Shteyngart), 146; and
The Tenants (Malamud), 21, 25, 35–38, 141,
158n8; third racial category, 99, 142; and
To Rise Again at a Decent Hour (Ferris),
144–145; and white ethnic revivalism, 64;
and "Writing About Jews" (Roth), 96; and
The Yiddish Policemen's Union (Chabon),
120, 134–135, 137; and *Your Face in Mine*
(Row), 142–143; and *Zelig* (film), 2–3, 5–6,
150n10
racialization, Jewish, 11–13, 145–146, 150n10;
and diaspora, 13, 109, 112–113, 117–119,
125–126, 128; and "Diaspora" (Boyarin and
Boyarin), 117–119; and *Her First American*
(Segal), 55; and Holocaust/Holocaust
literature, 66–68; and *How I Became
Hettie Jones* (Jones), 47–48, 51; and *The
Human Stain* (Roth), 96, 105–106; and
"The Jewbird" (Malamud), 36; and Jewish
women writers, 45–48, 51, 55, 59; and *The
Jew of New York* (Katchor), 13, 125–126,
128; and "the last days of the American
empire . . ." (Jones), 22; and matrilineal
descent, Jewish, 10, 59, 113, 118, 155n27; and
"The Melting Pot" (Schwartz), 59; and
Minor Characters (Johnson), 47–48; and
Munich (film), 112, 117; and Nuremberg
Laws, 117; and reracialization, 25, 34, 66;
and *The Tenants* (Malamud), 25, 33–39;
and *To Rise Again at a Decent Hour* (Ferris), 145. *See also* race
racialization, Native American, 126
racism: antiracist whites, 48; and autochthony, Jewish, 117–118; and critical race
theory, 93; and diaspora, 117–119; and
Her First American (Segal), 56; and
Holocaust/Holocaust literature, 64, 80,
82–84; and *How I Became Hettie Jones*
(Jones), 48; and *The Human Stain* (Roth),
97, 102–103, 106; and the literary canon,
93–94, 96–97, 102–103, 106; and "Looking
for Mr. Green" (Bellow), 83; and *Loving v.
Virginia*, 44–45; and *Mr. Sammler's Planet*
(Bellow), 80, 82–84; and "My Negro
Problem—and Ours" (Podhoretz), 80;
and Ocean Hill–Brownsville school crisis
(1968), 39; and *The Plot against America*
(Roth), 96; scientific racism, 44–45; and
The Tenants (Malamud), 21, 23. *See also*
anti-Semitism
realism, literary, 17, 94
Record-Changer, 49–50
Reddit, 10, 145
refugees, Arab, 85
refugees, Jewish, 52, 57, 85, 130–132, 136
religion, 10–11; and culture wars, 93; and
How I Became Hettie Jones (Jones),
48–49; and interfaith marriages, 41–46;
and *Intermarriage* (Gordon), 42–44; and
Jewish women writers, 48–49, 61; and *The
Jew of New York* (Katchor), 126; and the
literary canon, 92, 95; and "A Mercenary"
(Ozick), 77; and *Mr. Sammler's Planet*
(Bellow), 88; religious continuity, 42–43;
and Second Great Awakening, 126; and
To Rise Again at a Decent Hour (Ferris),
144–145; and *The Yiddish Policemen's
Union* (Chabon), 134, 136–137; and *Your
Face in Mine* (Row), 142
representations, 5–9, 11–13, 16–19, 146;
and *Arthur Mervyn* (Brown), 46;

representations (*continued*)
and "Black Boys and Native Sons" (Howe), 17–18; and Ellison, 17–18; and *Her First American* (Segal), 56–57; and Holocaust/Holocaust literature, 65–70, 82–84, 88; and *How I Became Hettie Jones* (Jones), 48–49, 51–52; and *The Human Stain* (Roth), 101; and interracial romances/marriages, 46, 48–49, 51–52, 56–57; and *The Jew of New York* (Katchor), 126, 128–129; and the literary canon, 95, 101; and McPherson, 24; and "A Mercenary" (Ozick), 69–70; and *Mr. Sammler's Planet* (Bellow), 82–84; and muteness, 82–84, 87–88; from object to subject, 5, 8–9, 16, 46, 48–49, 51; and Ocean Hill–Brownsville school crisis (1968), 19, 39–40; and "Reflections on Little Rock" (Arendt), 16–17; representative man, 95; self-representation, 16–17, 57; and *Sophie's Choice* (Styron), 67; and *The Tenants* (Malamud), 34, 37–40; and *To Jerusalem and Back* (Bellow), 88; and *To Rise Again at a Decent Hour* (Ferris), 144–145; and "Writing About Jews" (Roth), 95; and *Zelig* (film), 2, 5

return: and diaspora, 111–112, 116, 119, 138; Eternal Return, 138; and Holocaust/Holocaust literature, 66, 86; and *The Jew of New York* (Katchor), 123; and *Munich* (film), 112, 116; and *Operation Shylock* (Roth), 111, 119; and *To Jerusalem and Back* (Bellow), 86; and *The Yiddish Policemen's Union* (Chabon), 138

Richler, Mordecai, 136

"The Rights of History and the Rights of Imagination" (Ozick), 73

Ringelblum, Emmanuel, 66

Rody, Caroline, 47, 107; *The Interethnic Imagination*, 52

Roe v. Wade, 63

Rogin, Michael, 2, 13, 149n4; *Black Face, White Noise*, 4, 150n9

romances, interfaith/interracial: and *Her First American* (Segal), 45, 52–59, 154n6; and Jewish women writers, 41, 45–46, 51–59, 154n46; and "The Melting Pot" (Schwartz), 45, 58–59; and *Other People's Houses* (Segal), 57; and *The Tenants* (Malamud), 33. *See also* interfaith marriages; interracial romances/marriages

Romanticism, 22; and Aeolus' bag, 28, 153n26; and *genius loci*, 110; and Wandering Jew, 37, 153n37

roots/rootlessness, 9; and diaspora, 119, 122, 128–129, 131, 133; and *How I Became Hettie Jones* (Jones), 49; and *The Jew of New York* (Katchor), 122, 128–129; and "A Mercenary" (Ozick), 70, 78; and *Munich* (film), 119; and *The Tenants* (Malamud), 31–32; and *To Rise Again at a Decent Hour* (Ferris), 145; and *Wissenschaft des Judentums*, 92; and *The Yiddish Policemen's Union* (Chabon), 131, 133

Roth, Eric, 109–113, 115–117, 119–120

Roth, Henry, 7, 52, 71

Roth, Philip, 4, 8–12, 46, 52, 60, 71–72, 95–108, 144; *American Pastoral*, 96–97, 159n11; "American trilogy" of, 96–97; and diaspora, 111, 117, 119, 125, 127; "Eli, the Fanatic," 158n9; "Epstein," 158n9; *Goodbye, Columbus*, 51, 95–96, 158n9; *The Human Stain*, 4, 93, 95–108, 117, 125, 127, 141, 145, 159nn11–12, 159nn15–16, 159nn18–21; and the literary canon, 95–108; *Operation Shylock*, 111, 119; *The Plot against America*, 96–97, 130–131; *Portnoy's Complaint*, 8–10, 51, 95–96; *Reading Myself and Others*, 95; "Writing About Jews," 11–12, 95–96, 100

Rothberg, Michael, 77, 155n23

Rottenberg, Catherine, 98

Rousseau, Jean-Jacques, 92

Row, Jess, 142–143, 146, 162n4

Rubel, Nora, 134

Rubinstein, Rachel, 2; *Members of the Tribe*, 136, 149n4

Sacco and Vanzetti case, 22

Said, Edward, *The Question of Palestine*, 88

Salaita, Steven, 109; *The Holy Land in Transit*, 159n1

Salinger, J. D., 71

The Sarah Silverman Show (television series), 149n5

Sarna, Jonathan, 128

Saving Private Ryan (film), 109

Say It in Yiddish, 121–122, 132

Schenk, Max, 43

Schindler's List (film), 116

Schreier, Ben, 146

Schwartz, Lynn Sharon, "The Melting Pot," 45, 58–60

secularism, 6, 19, 49, 65, 91–93; and *Bech: A Book* (Updike), 72; and culture wars, 93; and diaspora, 19, 109, 112, 122, 134; and *How I Became Hettie Jones* (Jones), 49; and *To Jerusalem and Back* (Bellow), 86–87, 134; and *The Yiddish Policemen's Union* (Chabon), 133–134

INDEX 193

Segal, Lore, 4, 13, 45–46, 52–59, 62; *Her First American*, 45–46, 52–59, 154n6, 155nn19–22, 155nn25–26; *Other People's Houses*, 57; *Shakespeare's Kitchen*, 155n20
Seidman, Naomi, 3, 13, 150n11, 160n10
self, 2, 17, 40, 142–143, 146; and *Her First American* (Segal), 57; and *How I Became Hettie Jones* (Jones), 47, 60; and *The Human Stain* (Roth), 96–97, 102; and Jewish women writers, 47, 57, 60; and "The Melting Pot" (Schwartz), 60; and *Minor Characters* (Johnson), 47; and *Mr. Sammler's Planet* (Bellow), 88; and *Operation Shylock* (Roth), 111; polyglot nature of, 146; and self-fashioning, Jewish, 2–3, 8, 12, 109, 121; and *The Tenants* (Malamud), 30–31, 37–38; and *Your Face in Mine* (Row), 142–143. *See also* speaking the self through others; *entries beginning with* identity
Semites, 10, 126
Senna, Danzy, 99
separatism, racial, 17, 31, 40, 153n34; and Holocaust/Holocaust literature, 65, 157n24; and interracial marriages, 45; and *The Jew of New York* (Katchor), 128; and the literary canon, 92; proto-black separatist movement, 17; and *The Yiddish Policemen's Union* (Chabon), 133
sexuality/sexual relationships, 143, 150n11; and *Her First American* (Segal), 52; and *The Human Stain* (Roth), 103–105; and the literary canon, 103–105; and *Mr. Sammler's Planet* (Bellow), 79–83, 157n29; and "My Negro Problem—and Ours" (Podhoretz), 80–81; and Roth's "American trilogy," 96; sexual orientation, 62, 159n14; and *The Tenants* (Malamud), 33–35, 40, 153n33
Shahn, Ben, 160n23
Shakespeare, William, 20–21, 46, 103, 152n16, 154n8, 157n21
Shandler, Jeffrey, *Adventures in Yiddishland: Postvernacular Language and Culture*, 121–122, 124, 129, 132
"The Shawl" (Ozick), 68, 88–89
Shelley, Percy Bysshe, 153n37
Shohat, Ella, 2
Shteyngart, Gary, 146
Silberman, Charles, 65
silence/silencing, 4, 9, 147; and Holocaust/Holocaust literature, 63, 82–84, 87–88; and Jewish women writers, 48; and "The Melting Pot" (Schwartz), 60; and *Mr. Sammler's Planet* (Bellow), 82–84, 87–88; and Native Americans, 26; and *To Jerusalem and Back* (Bellow), 87–88
Silverman, Lisa, 143
Silverman, Sarah, 3, 149n5
Singer, Isaac Bashevis, 71, 73
Singh, Nikhil Pal, 140
Sitka (Alaska), 130–137, 161n35
Six Day War, 12, 19, 63–65, 154n5, 156n6; and diaspora, 114, 117, 120; and *Mr. Sammler's Planet* (Bellow), 78, 85–87, 89, 120, 158n34; and *Munich* (film), 114, 117
skin color, 18; and *Autobiography* (Jones), 154n14; and *Goodbye, Columbus* (Roth), 51, 96; and *Her First American* (Segal), 53–54; and *How I Became Hettie Jones* (Jones), 48–49, 51, 154n14; and *The Human Stain* (Roth), 97; and "The Melting Pot" (Schwartz), 60; and "A Mercenary" (Ozick), 71; and *The Painted Bird* (Kosinski), 73; and *Portnoy's Complaint* (Roth), 96; and Zuckerman, Nathan (Roth's literary alter ego), 96
slaves/slavery: in *The Confessions of Nat Turner* (Styron), 9, 61, 67; and game of dozens, 27; and *Her First American* (Segal), 56; and Holocaust/Holocaust literature, 64; Leroi Jones's views on, 22; plantation slave quarters, 27; and slave narrative, 26
Slezkine, Yuri, 69–70; *The Jewish Century*, 69–70
Smith, Anthony, 140
Smith, Barbara Herrnstein, 94
Smith, Bessie, 25–27, 152n24
socialists, 22, 122
social media, 144–145, 147
sociology/sociologists, 41–45, 47, 57
Sollors, Werner, 16–17, 46; *Beyond Ethnicity*, 105–106, 151n23, 152n18, 154n7, 155n21
Sontag, Susan, 1–2
Sophocles, 101–102
sovereignty, Jewish, 92, 111, 122, 131, 134, 138; semi-sovereign status, 92; sovereignty/anti-Semitism, 111
Spain: expulsion of Jewish population, 140, 162n1; Moslem Spain, 7
speaking for others, 3–5, 7–10, 13, 15–20, 120, 142–143, 146–147; and Arendt, 4, 15–17, 151n10; and *Bech: A Book* (Updike), 71–72; and "Black Art" (Jones), 18; and diaspora, 122, 131; failure of, 20, 28; and *Her First American* (Segal), 56–57, 155n20; and Holocaust/Holocaust literature, 63, 67, 69–72, 75, 78, 82, 88; and *The Human Stain* (Roth), 4, 103–106, 159n21;

speaking for others (*continued*)
and Jewish exceptionalism, 141; and *The Jew of New York* (Katchor), 122; and the literary canon, 4, 95–96, 103–106; and "The Melting Pot" (Schwartz), 60; and "A Mercenary" (Ozick), 69–72, 75, 78; and *Mr. Sammler's Planet* (Bellow), 82; and "Negroes Are Anti-Semitic Because They're Anti-White" (Baldwin), 18–19; and *The People* (Malamud), 153n36; power dynamics of, 8, 13; and *Shakespeare's Kitchen* (Segal), 155n20; as silencing, 4, 9, 147; and *The Tenants* (Malamud), 20–21, 23, 25–28, 33, 37–38, 40, 65, 67; and *To Jerusalem and Back* (Bellow), 88; and "Writing About Jews" (Roth), 95–96; and *The Yiddish Policemen's Union* (Chabon), 131; and *Your Face in Mine* (Row), 142–143; and *Zelig* (film), 3, 5. *See also* ventriloquism, racial

speaking the self through others, 10, 20, 142–144, 146–147; and *How I Became Hettie Jones* (Jones), 60; and *The Human Stain* (Roth), 96, 104; and "The Melting Pot" (Schwartz), 60; and "A Mercenary" (Ozick), 75; and *The Tenants* (Malamud), 37–38, 40; and *Your Face in Mine* (Row), 142–143

Spevack, Edmund, 38
Spiegelman, Art, 124, 129
Spielberg, Steven, 109–113, 115–117, 119–120
Spivak, Gayatri, 12, 153n35; "Can the Subaltern Speak?" 7–8, 60; "Deconstructing Historiography," 35–36
spokesmanship, Jewish, 17–18; and "Black Art" (Jones), 18, 32; and Holocaust/Holocaust literature, 67–70, 74–76; and *The Human Stain* (Roth), 106; and the literary canon, 95–96, 106; and "A Mercenary" (Ozick), 68–70, 74–76; "Paid Mouthpiece" (in "A Mercenary"), 69–70, 74–76; and *The Tenants* (Malamud), 29–32, 37; and "Writing About Jews" (Roth), 95–96. *See also* speaking for others
"spooks," 102, 104, 159n18
Stam, Robert, 2
Stanislawski, Michael, 113
Staub, Michael, 16
stereotypes, 21, 143, 146; and *Her First American* (Segal), 55; and *The Jew of New York* (Katchor), 129; and *Mr. Sammler's Planet* (Bellow), 157n28; and "My Negro Problem—and Ours" (Podhoretz), 81; and Roth's "American trilogy," 96; and

Super Sad True Love Story (Shteyngart), 146; and *The Tenants* (Malamud), 20–21, 31–32; and *To Jerusalem and Back* (Bellow), 86–87; and *The Yiddish Policemen's Union* (Chabon), 136; and *Zelig* (film), 2, 149n1

storytelling, 9, 70–71, 137
Stratton, Jon, 4–5, 150n9
Styron, William: *The Confessions of Nat Turner*, 9, 61, 67; *Sophie's Choice*, 9, 67, 156n14; *William Styron's Nat Turner: Ten Black Writers Respond*, 9
subaltern studies group, 7–8, 12, 60, 153n35
subject positions, 8–9, 16, 145, 154n15; and *Call It Sleep* (Roth), 52; and *Her First American* (Segal), 58; and *How I Became Hettie Jones* (Jones), 48–49, 51; and *The Human Stain* (Roth), 103–106; and Jewish women writers, 46, 48–49, 51, 58; and *To Rise Again at a Decent Hour* (Ferris), 145; and *Zelig* (film), 5. *See also* speaking for others

suburbs, 42, 47, 49
succah, 63, 156n7
suffering, 16–19; black suffering, 18–19, 34, 55; everyman suffering, 17; and *Her First American* (Segal), 55; and "The Jewbird" (Malamud), 36–37; Jewish suffering, 16–19, 29–31, 34, 36, 38, 55, 84, 141, 151n6; and "Literary Blacks and Jews" (Ozick), 37–38; and *Mr. Sammler's Planet* (Bellow), 84; and *Munich* (film), 110; and "Negroes Are Anti-Semitic Because They're Anti-White" (Baldwin), 18–19; and "Reflections on Little Rock" (Arendt), 16–17; and *The Tenants* (Malamud), 29–31, 34, 37; universal suffering, 29–31, 36–38; "white" suffering, 19
Sundquist, Eric, 23, 55, 79, 84, 103, 153n32; *Strangers in the Land*, 156n15, 157n27
supranational geography, 111–112, 118
Supreme Court, U.S., 41–42, 45–46, 63. *See also Loving v. Virginia*; *Roe v. Wade*
sympathetic identification, 16–17, 19; and Bellow's early work, 83, 86; and *Her First American* (Segal), 55; and Holocaust/Holocaust literature, 64; and *The Human Stain* (Roth), 105; identification-via-hashtag, 147; and *Intermarriage* (Gordon), 44; and "The Jewbird" (Malamud), 36; and Malamud's early work, 37–38, 83; and *Mr. Sammler's Planet* (Bellow), 84–88; and *Shakespeare's Kitchen* (Segal), 155n20; and *The Tenants* (Malamud), 29–30, 34, 86

INDEX

synagogues, 77, 88, 127
Syria, 65, 156n6

Talmud, 55, 134
Tarantino, Quentin, 156n13
Tarzan films, 69–71, 74–76
teachers' strikes, 39
The Tenants (Malamud), 12–13, 20–40, 44, 46, 53, 56–58, 65, 67–69, 75, 78, 81, 86, 141, 152nn15–16, 153nn27–29, 153n32–34; and black idiom, 23–25, 27–28, 31; and blues song, 25–27, 152n24; and diaspora, 120; and dybbuk, 33; endings of, 25, 33–34; epigraphs of, 25–26, 152n22; and game of dozens, 24–25, 27–29, 152n21; and high art, 27, 29–33; and Lesser's *The Promised End*, 20–21, 25, 32–34; and the literary canon, 25, 32–33, 38; and novel within a novel, 124; and Ocean Hill–Brownsville school crisis (1968), 19, 39–40, 153n40; as racial dystopia, 158n8; revision of, 23–24; and Spearmint's *Black Writer*, 29–30, 32–33; and tenancy, 20–23, 28–29, 32–34, 37
territoriality, Jewish: deterritorialized, 110; and "Diaspora" (Boyarin and Boyarin), 118–119; and "Guidebook to a Land of Ghosts" (Chabon), 121–122; and Jewish exceptionalism, 140; and *The Jew of New York* (Katchor), 122, 126; and *Munich* (film), 110–111, 113–114, 117; and *Nationalism and History* (Dubnow), 118; "political territorial" stage of nationalism, 118; reterritorialized, 111; and *The Yiddish Policemen's Union* (Chabon), 130–131, 133–134
terrorism/terrorists, 109–110, 112–115, 147, 159n4
Theroux, Alexander, 129, 160n22
Thompson, Deborah, 48, 55, 154nn13–14
Time magazine, 6–7, 22
To Jerusalem and Back (Bellow), 78, 82–83, 85–88, 134
topos/topography, 119–120, 137
To Rise Again at a Decent Hour (Ferris), 144–146
tragedy: and *Her First American* (Segal), 54; and Holocaust/Holocaust literature, 67, 84; and *The Human Stain* (Roth), 97, 102–103, 105–106; and the literary canon, 97, 102–103, 105; and *Mr. Sammler's Planet* (Bellow), 84; and Ocean Hill–Brownsville school crisis (1968), 40; and *The Tenants* (Malamud), 20–21; tragicomic, 102–103; and *Your Face in Mine* (Row), 142
transience, 20, 37, 111, 122, 136–137. *See also* Wandering Jew

translation, 74–75, 101–102
transnational concerns, 78, 147; and *Wissenschaft des Judentums*, 90, 92, 110, 158n7
transracial identification, 3, 6, 12, 48, 93, 147
trauma, 55, 63, 67, 78, 112
tribalism, 146; and diaspora, 112, 118, 160n17; and "A Mercenary" (Ozick), 74; and *Mr. Sammler's Planet* (Bellow), 84; and *Munich* (film), 112; and *Nationalism and History* (Dubnow), 118; and *To Rise Again at a Decent Hour* (Ferris), 145
Trilling, Lionel, 82
Twitter, 144, 147
Tyler, Carole-Anne, 100

United Federation of Teachers, 39
United Nations, 155n25; UNESCO, 62
United Synagogues of America, 42
universalism, 7, 16–19; and "Black Art" (Jones), 18; and "Black Boys and Native Sons" (Howe), 18–19; and civil rights movement, 65; decline of, 17; and *Diary of Anne Frank*, 155n4; and Holocaust/Holocaust literature, 78, 84, 86, 155n4, 157n24; and *The Human Stain* (Roth), 93, 98, 101–102, 105; and the literary canon, 91–93, 95, 98, 101–102, 105; and *Mr. Sammler's Planet* (Bellow), 78, 84; and *Munich* (film), 110; and Ocean Hill–Brownsville school crisis (1968), 40; and "Reflections on Little Rock" (Arendt), 16–17, 19; and *The Tenants* (Malamud), 25, 29–32, 36–38, 78; and *To Jerusalem and Back* (Bellow), 86; universal suffering, 29–31, 36–37; universal voice, 32, 37
university system, 6, 63, 82, 91, 93–94, 150n14; and *The Human Stain* (Roth), 97, 99, 101–104; and the literary canon, 93–94, 97, 99, 101–104; and "politicization of the curriculum," 93
Updike, John, 71–72, 95, 156n19; *Bech: A Book*, 71–72, 95, 144, 156n19
Uris, Leon, *Exodus*, 120
upward mobility, 6, 129
"Usurpation (Other People's Stories)" (Ozick), 73, 157n20
utopias, 38, 82, 100; and *The Jew of New York* (Katchor), 123–125; and Katchor's comic strips, 122; and *The Yiddish Policemen's Union* (Chabon), 131, 138

Van Gogh, Theo, 158n4
ventriloquism, racial, 3–4, 6, 8–10, 12–13, 17, 19, 90, 146–147, 150n18; and *Amerika* (Kafka), 50; and *Bech: A Book* (Updike), 71–72;

ventriloquism, racial (*continued*)
  and diaspora, 120, 135; ethics of, 19–20, 27; and Holocaust/Holocaust literature, 63, 67, 71–72, 82; and *How I Became Hettie Jones* (Jones), 50; and *The Human Stain* (Roth), 4, 96, 104; and Jewish exceptionalism, 141; and Jewish women writers, 41, 46, 50, 61; and the literary canon, 4, 96, 104; and *Mr. Sammler's Planet* (Bellow), 82; and *Record-Changer*, 50; and "Reflections on Little Rock" (Arendt), 16; and *Sophie's Choice* (Styron), 67; and *The Tenants* (Malamud), 25–29, 33, 36–37; ventriloquist's dummy, 28–29; and *The Yiddish Policemen's Union* (Chabon), 135
Verbovers (in Chabon's *The Yiddish Policemen's Union*), 134, 136–137
The Very Dark Trees (Bellow), 83, 158n32
Vienna, Austria, 52–54
Vietnam War, 63, 140
violence, racial: aural/oral violence, 28; and *Her First American* (Segal), 56; and "The Melting Pot" (Schwartz), 58–59; and "A Mercenary" (Ozick), 69, 71; and *Mr. Sammler's Planet* (Bellow), 78, 81–84; and *Munich* (film), 109–110, 113, 115–116, 159nn2–3; and *The Painted Bird* (Kosinski), 73; and "Reflections on Little Rock" (Arendt), 16; slapstick violence, 71; and *The Tenants* (Malamud), 21–22, 28, 35; and terrorism, 109–110, 112–115, 147. See also Holocaust/Holocaust literature
Virginia, 41–45, 48–49
visibility, Jewish, 7; and becoming invisible, 7; and *How I Became Hettie Jones* (Jones), 47–49; and *The Human Stain* (Roth), 100; and *Minor Characters* (Johnson), 47; and *Mr. Sammler's Planet* (Bellow), 78; visibility of race, 78, 100; and *Zelig* (film), 2
voice, literary, 6, 8–10, 12, 143–144, 146, 150nn16–17, 155n2; and black idiom, 23–24, 27–28, 31; and Broyard, 105; and *The Confessions of Nat Turner* (Styron), 9, 61; and *Her First American* (Segal), 58; and Holocaust/Holocaust literature, 62–63, 67–69, 75–76; and *The Human Stain* (Roth), 93, 96, 100, 104–105; independence of, 95; and interracial romances/marriages, 45–46, 48, 58, 60–61, 154n12; Jew as voiceless other, 5; and "The Jewbird" (Malamud), 36–37; and Jewish women writers, 4, 41, 45–46, 48, 58, 60–61, 154n12; and literary canon, 6, 93, 95–96, 100, 104–105, 107; and "A Mercenary" (Ozick), 68–69, 75–76; and

Mr. Sammler's Planet (Bellow), 68; and *Portnoy's Complaint* (Roth), 8–10; and *The Tenants* (Malamud), 21, 23–27, 36–37, 39, 141; and unspeakability, 67; and "vocal presence," 9; voice of survivor, 66–67; and *The Yiddish Policemen's Union* (Chabon), 131; and *Your Face in Mine* (Row), 143. See also speaking for others; speaking the self through others
Volksgeist, 110, 160n5
Voltaire, 110

Wagner, Richard, 37, 110, 153n37, 160n5
Waldman, Ayelet, 135
Wallace, David Foster, 157n20
Wandering Jew, 6; and diaspora, 110–111, 120, 122, 125, 129; and "The Jewbird" (Malamud), 36; and *The Jew of New York* (Katchor), 120, 122, 125, 129; and *The Tenants* (Malamud), 37, 120, 153n37; and *The Yiddish Policemen's Union* (Chabon), 120
Warren, Robert Penn, *Who Speaks for the Negro?*, 26, 152n23
Wattenberg, Ben, 82, 157n30
Watts race riots, 12, 19, 39
Weathermen, 161n38
Wells, H. G., 79, 89
Wenger, Beth, 160n23
West Bank, 135, 156n6
western literature, 20, 37, 101–102. See also American literature; Jewish literature
White, Walter, 99
whiteness, 3–4, 10–12, 18–19; abandonment into whiteness, 51; almost-white, 40; and *American Pastoral* (Roth), 96, 159n11; Anglos, 49; antiracist whites, 48; and Aryan features, 96; and "Black Art" (Jones), 18; "bleached-out Charlie," 28–29; and Broyard, 104–105; complication/contamination of, 46; Gentiles, 65, 95, 162n4; *goyim*, 49, 95; and *Her First American* (Segal), 52–53, 55; and Holocaust/Holocaust literature, 63–66, 69, 74–75, 79–80, 82–84; and *How I Became Hettie Jones* (Jones), 47–51; and *The Human Stain* (Roth), 96–99, 101, 105–106, 159n12; and interracial romances/marriages, 41, 44–53, 55; and Jewish exceptionalism, 140; Jewish whiteness, 24–25, 95–97, 150n10; and Jewish women writers, 46–53, 55; and *The Jew of New York* (Katchor), 127; and the literary canon, 94–99, 101, 105–106; and *Loving v. Virginia*, 41, 44–45; and "A Mercenary" (Ozick), 69, 74–75; and *Moby-Dick*

(Melville), 6; and *Mona in the Promised Land* (Jen), 94; and *Mr. Sammler's Planet* (Bellow), 79–80, 82–84; and "My Negro Problem—and Ours" (Podhoretz), 80–81; and "Negroes Are Anti-Semitic Because They're Anti-White" (Baldwin), 18–19, 22; and neoconservatism, 11, 39, 82; not-whiteness, 52–53; and Ocean Hill–Brownsville school crisis (1968), 19, 39–40; "ofay," 27, 29–30; old white men, 95; and *The Plot against America* (Roth), 96–97; and Roth's "American trilogy," 96–97; and *The Slave* (Jones), 50; slow fade into whiteness, 25; "speaking white," 33; and *The Tenants* (Malamud), 21–22, 24–31, 33–35, 38, 40; and *To Rise Again at a Decent Hour* (Ferris), 144; white artists/art, 21, 29–30; "white bitch," 33; white ethnicity, 22, 39, 48, 55, 64–66, 154n13; white figurative language, 18; white flight, 96; "white folks," 4, 150n10; white hegemony, 64; white male-identified high modernism, 10; whitening of ethnicity, 22, 39, 48, 55, 64–66, 95–97, 154n13; white prick, 30; white privilege, 4, 11–12, 143; white Protestants, 40, 95; "white racial politics," 11, 82; "white" suffering, 19; white supremacy, 140; white women, 50; white writers, 30–31; "whitey," 27; and *Your Face in Mine* (Row), 142–143; and *Zelig* (film), 3, 6. *See also* black-white binary; race

Wiener, Jon, 132–133
Wiesel, Elie, 62, 67–68, 155n3, 156n12
Wikipedia, 159n21
Winant, Howard, 11, 64, 82, 151n22
Winthrop, John, 140
Wisse, Ruth, 36, 136
Wissenschaft des Judentums, 90, 92, 110, 158n7; as proto-multiculturalism, 92, 158n7
witnessing, 78, 80, 82, 85
women, African American, 154n15; and "Black Is My Favorite Color" (Malamud), 34; and *The Tenants* (Malamud), 25–28, 33–34, 44
women, Jewish: abuse of, 84; and *Arthur Mervyn* (Brown), 46; and *How I Became Hettie Jones* (Jones), 47, 50–51, 155nn17–18; and *The Human Stain* (Roth), 97; and interracial romances/marriages, 41, 45–47, 50–51, 58–60; and "The Melting Pot" (Schwartz), 58–60; and *Mr. Sammler's Planet* (Bellow), 84; and *Munich* (film), 112; and *The Tenants* (Malamud), 24, 33–35, 153n34; and *To Jerusalem and Back* (Bellow), 85–87. *See also* women writers, Jewish

women writers, Jewish, 4, 41, 45–61; and *Her First American* (Segal), 45, 52–58, 154n6; and *How I Became Hettie Jones* (Jones), 47–52, 54–60; and the literary canon, 60; and "marrying out," 4, 59; and "The Melting Pot" (Schwartz), 45, 58–60. *See also names of Jewish women writers*
Wordsworth, William, 153n37
Wouk, Herman, 50–51
Wright, Richard, 17, 21, 26, 57, 153n33
writers, African American, 6, 9, 17–18; autobiographical work of, 26; and Bellow, 83; and "Black Art" (Jones), 18; and "To Blacks and Jews: Hab Rachmones" (McPherson), 22–23; and Broyard, 104–105; and *The Confessions of Nat Turner* (Styron), 9; first-person narration of, 26; and *The Human Stain* (Roth), 97, 99, 101, 104–105; and the literary canon, 97, 99, 101, 104–105; and passing, 97, 99, 101, 104–105; and "Reflections on Little Rock" (Arendt), 17; and *The Tenants* (Malamud), 21–39. *See also* black-Jewish relations; *names of African American writers*
writers, Asian American, 107
writers, Jewish American, 3–4, 6–20, 141–147, 150n19; and *American Pastoral* (Roth), 96; and *Amerika* (Kafka), 50; and *Bech: A Book* (Updike), 71–72; and "Black Art" (Jones), 18; and "To Blacks and Jews: Hab Rachmones" (McPherson), 22–23; and diaspora, 111–112, 119–122, 126–128, 131, 133, 135, 137; and Holocaust/Holocaust literature, 62–63, 66–69, 71–73, 78, 80, 85–88, 157n24, 158n10; and *The Human Stain* (Roth), 93, 97, 100, 104–107, 159n21; and Jewish exceptionalism, 139–141; and *The Jew of New York* (Katchor), 122, 126–128; and the literary canon, 4, 6, 12, 25, 90–91, 93–97, 100, 104–107, 158n3; literary imagination of, 12, 19, 46, 50; and "A Mercenary" (Ozick), 69, 71–73, 78; and *Mr. Sammler's Planet* (Bellow), 78, 85–86, 88, 158n8; and *Munich* (film), 111–112; and "My Negro Problem—and Ours" (Podhoretz), 80; and "Negroes Are Anti-Semitic Because They're Anti-White" (Baldwin), 18–19; and Ocean Hill–Brownsville school crisis (1968), 19, 39–40; and *The Plot against America* (Roth), 96–97; and "Reflections on Little Rock" (Arendt), 4, 15–17;

writers, Jewish American (*continued*)
and *The Tenants* (Malamud), 20–35, 37–40, 141, 158n8; and *To Jerusalem and Back* (Bellow), 86–88; and *To Rise Again at a Decent Hour* (Ferris), 144–145; and "Writing About Jews" (Roth), 95–96; and *The Yiddish Policemen's Union* (Chabon), 131, 133, 135, 137; and *Your Face in Mine* (Row), 143; and *Zelig* (film), 3, 5–6. *See also* women writers, Jewish; *names of Jewish writers*

"Writing About Jews" (Roth), 11–12, 95–96, 100

yekke, 114–115
Yezierska, Anzia, 7
Yiddish, 2, 92, 149n3; and *Adventures in Yiddishland* (Shandler), 121–122; as cultural currency, 121; and diaspora, 114, 120–124, 130–133, 135–136, 160nn19–20; first grammar of, 132; and "Guidebook to a Land of Ghosts" (Chabon), 121–122; and *Her First American* (Segal), 56; and *How I Became Hettie Jones* (Jones), 49; and *The Jew of New York* (Katchor), 120, 123–124, 130, 132, 161n32; as *mameloshen* (mother tongue), 121–122, 132; and *Mr. Sammler's Planet* (Bellow), 78, 157n25; and *Munich* (film), 114; and *Say It in Yiddish*, 121–122; and *The Tenants* (Malamud), 152n15; and *To Jerusalem and Back* (Bellow), 87; and *The Yiddish Policemen's Union* (Chabon), 120, 130–133, 135–136

Yiddishland, 119, 121–122, 124, 129
The Yiddish Policemen's Union (Chabon), 4, 13, 119–121, 130–138, 141, 161n32, 161n39; and abortion, 134, 137; and COINTELPRO operatives, 135, 161n38; failure at center of, 131, 138; and Messiah, 131, 134, 136–137; original title for, 130, 133; and reversion to American control, 131, 136; and "Synagogue Riots," 134–135; and Verbover Hasidim, 133–134, 136–137; and Yiddish Policemen's Union, 133, 137
Your Face in Mine (Row), 142–143, 146, 162n4

Zamenhof, L. L., 132
Zangwill, Israel, 128; *The Melting Pot*, 58, 60, 161n27
Zelig (film), 1–6, 149nn1–3
Zimmermann, Moshe, 113
Zionism, 85–86, 88; and diaspora, 109–113, 116, 119–120, 122, 131–132, 134, 136, 160n7; *fin de siècle* Zionism, 113; as master narrative of Jewish identity, 112; and *Munich* (film), 112–113, 116; and *Operation Shylock* (Roth), 111; Second Zionist Congress, 113; World Zionist Organization, 132; and *The Yiddish Policemen's Union* (Chabon), 131–132, 134, 136
Zuckerman, Nathan (Roth's literary alter ego), 96, 99, 102–104; "dark" appearance of, 96; and *The Human Stain* (Roth), 99, 102–104, 159n15

About the Author

JENNIFER GLASER is an assistant professor of English and comparative literature and an affiliate faculty member in women's, gender, and sexuality studies and Judaic studies at the University of Cincinnati. She has published articles and reviews in venues such as *PMLA, MELUS, American Literature, Early American Literature, Literature Compass, SAFUNDI, American Jewish History, ImageText,* the *New York Times,* the *Faster Times,* the *Los Angeles Review of Books,* and an anthology of personal essays from Random House.

www.ingramcontent.com/pod-product-compliance
Ingram Content Group UK Ltd.
Pitfield, Milton Keynes, MK11 3LW, UK
UKHW041430180426
11947UKWH00007B/362